HISTORIC
HOMESTEADS
OF AUSTRALIA
Volume two

HISTORIC

Cassell Australia Limited

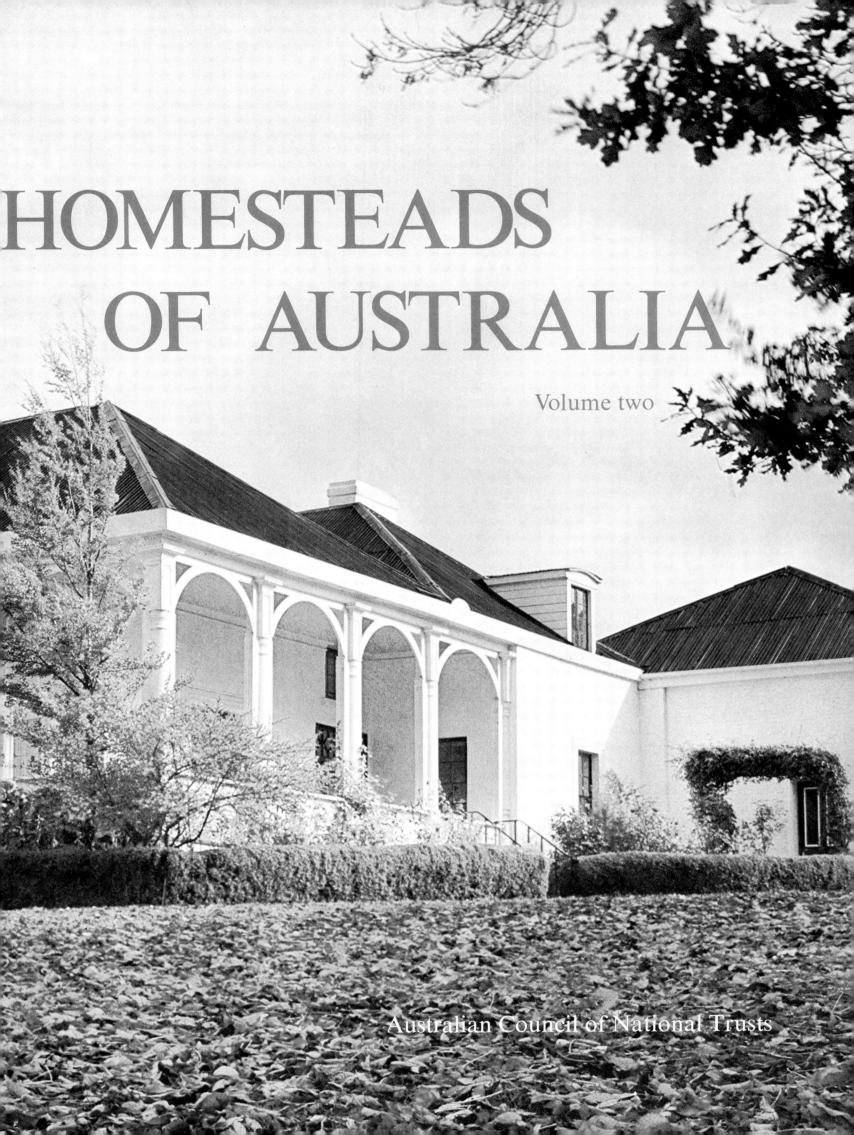

HOMESTEADS OF AUSTRALIA

Volume two

Australian Council of National Trusts

CASSELL AUSTRALIA LIMITED
31 Bridge Road, Stanmore, New South Wales
30 Curzon Street, North Melbourne, Victoria

First published 1976

Edited by Jim Ellis

Designed by Peter Buckmaster

Set in 11/15 Caledonia

Set, printed and bound in Australia by Wilke and Company Limited
37–49 Browns Road, Clayton, Victoria

F.1076

National Library of Australia
Cataloguing in Publication Data
Australian Council of National Trusts.
    Historic homesteads of Australia; Volume two.
    (Historic buildings of Australia; vol. 4.)
    ISBN 0 7269 0004 4.

    1. Country homes—Australia. I. Title.
    (Series).
728.60994

Preface

THE NATIONAL TRUST MOVEMENT is moving from strength to strength in Australia. From its origins in the mid-1940s, the movement is now some 70,000 strong, demonstrating the interest which the community is showing in the aims and activities of the Trust. The Trust is concerned to ensure that our heritage, both natural and man-made, should be preserved and all its members are actively engaged to achieve this objective.

Part of the Trust's role is to arouse more and more public interest in every possible way. It constantly draws attention to problems of conservation through the media in all its forms. It points to things which are happening—which sometimes amount to acts of vandalism—and endeavours to ensure that they do not recur.

It is at least in part because of its education role, that the Australian Council of National Trusts commenced its series of historic publications. They are intended to show how great is our heritage and how much it is necessary that it should not be destroyed. They are also intended to delight the reader—to inform him, both pictorially and verbally, of the beauties which exist in Australia, in the hope that he will be both entertained and inspired. It is our hope that this, the fourth volume in the Series, will achieve both purposes.

The Honourable Mr Justice Sir John Moore,
President, Australian Council of National Trusts

Acknowledgements

THE GREAT STRENGTH of the National Trust movement throughout Australia is the devoted honorary service given to the organization and its work. This honorary service spans all facets of Trust activities but nowhere is it more evident than with this series of books on the nation's great historic buildings.

Hundreds of honorary workers throughout Australia have made this volume, the fourth in the series, possible. In each State a Co-ordinating Committee guided and supervised the work led by the Australian Co-ordinating Committee which I had the honour of chairing. The members of the Australian committee were Mr Peter Buckmaster, Mr James Ellis, Mr Brian Lloyd, Mr Robert Sessions and Mr Peter Staughton. Honorary Advisers helped the Committee at various stages during the preparation of the material and the publication of the volume.

The State Co-ordinating Committees were:—

In New South Wales: Messrs Clive Lucas and John Morris;

In Queensland: Messrs Peter Forrest and Richard Stringer;

In Victoria: Miss Monica Starke and Messrs Brian Lloyd and Peter Staughton;

In Tasmania: Dr G. M. W. Clemons and Mr J. N. D. Harrison;

In South Australia: Mr Stephen H. Gilbert;

In Western Australia: Mrs Valerie Barratt Hill, Mr F. A. Sharr and Mrs F. Stimson.

The names of the author and photographer are recorded in each chapter. In some instances, one photographer did not take all the photographs used in a chapter; when there are joint photographers they are recorded in the heading of the chapter, but when a different photographer took one of the photographs, his name is recorded beside that photograph.

Throughout Australia hundreds of people, institutions, governmental and semi-governmental bodies co-operated and assisted with the work. Historical societies, research workers, historians, archivists and librarians helped and readily gave their knowledge and expertise. Above all the owners of the buildings have generously permitted the Trust's experts to visit their homesteads and have assisted with information. The publishers and printers have devoted more than the usual effort to ensure that the standard of the book is worthy of Australia and its heritage.

At the end of the volume there is a list of acknowledgements but in addition to those specific acknowledgements hundreds of others contributed and assisted. The National Trust movement records its grateful thanks to all those connected with the project.

The net royalties received from all volumes in the series are devoted to the National Trust preservation work throughout Australia. The first three volumes have already contributed over $80,000 to the work of the Trust and have simultaneously recorded part of the nation's heritage and assisted with an ever widening appreciation and realization of the importance of Australia's great historic and architectural heritage.

Rodney Davidson

Rodney Davidson LLB OBE
Australian Co-ordinator, 'Historic Buildings of Australia'

Contents

Contents—continued

The *endpaper illustration* is taken from an 1850s drawing of The Springs, Dubbo, New South Wales.
The *illustration on the title page* is of Quamby, near Hagley in Northern Tasmania.

Introduction

THROUGHOUT THE WESTERN WORLD there has been an upsurge of conservationist thought in recent years, both as this applies to the environment as a whole and to the heritage of traditional buildings in particular. Activists call for a virtual embargo on the galloping physical change and development in our urban areas. Demonstrations abound at the mere mention of possible demolition of a traditional building, be it of genuine historic value or not. Protest follows upon any suggestion of physical change due to the renewal of a district or part of it, such as for the construction of a new through-road.

The reasons for this new concern with the existing environment are manifold; today's deterioration of the urban fabric in industrialized countries is a sad and universally recognized fact. The previously visually coherent and socially functioning patterns of cities have gradually given way to aesthetic disruption and fragmentation of the more serene patterns of the past. There are virtually no effective answers being offered to alleviate this dilemma. With some exceptions, notably in Scandinavian countries, the visual and social decay continues almost unchecked. It is not surprising therefore that past values are being re-examined and, without suggesting that they should be actively emulated in our time, there is something of a re-discovery of aesthetic worth in nineteenth-century and especially Victorian taste.

In the first half of our century (and even beyond) this was quite unheard of; the fashion was to consider it irrelevant. The concern was with 'progress'. This veiled any interest or awareness of value in traditional environmental patterns and building form. Any repercussions in urban problems were moderate by today's standards, owing to the comparatively slow commercial and expansionist tendencies at the time. There was not a great deal of destruction of the nineteenth-century built environment or individual buildings. The taste preoccupations were with the advancement of new building form and technique. The Modern Architecture of Europe and America had finally come to Australia even if in somewhat diluted and mostly misunderstood form. Even so, there was a certain magic about it—it became the fashion, implying a promise of a better physical world.

These new cultural forces—actually little more than a faint echo of developments overseas—were translated into rather poor buildings, evidence of the misunderstandings of the revolutionary ferment that had given rise to a new taste in architecture on the other side of the world. Australia, being the remote outpost of Western culture it is, has always suffered from its geographic disadvantage in that way.

The result of this was an understandable rejection by the public of the increasing volume of new emerging forms, disrupting the aesthetic cohesion and tranquillity of the past. The totality of the new environment, brought about by the lack of effective planning and these early bad modern buildings, resulted in soul-destroying new suburbs and quite horrifying whole new sections of the inner cities.

The fact that this new face of the world was indeed an unlovely thing was the main reason for traditional environments and values gradually becoming fashionable.

Sydney's Paddington for instance, that long neglected area (for a long time considered a slum) with its undulating rows of terrace houses marching up and down the hillsides, suddenly emerged as a fashionable place to live. Even if decayed and often disfigured through insensitive alteration over the years—the area still represented to many a preferable alternative to the gaudy and, at best, visually harsh and incoherent modern housing developments.

This emerging active interest in the past has taken many forms—from a cry to stop demolition of old environments (such as The Glebe and Kings Cross' Victoria Street in Sydney, or Parkville in Melbourne) to the call for renovation and re-adaptation to present needs of buildings such as Sydney's Queen Victoria Building.

Finally, after our disappointing attempts at modernity, we seem to have grown up enough to re-examine and evaluate our environmental heritage, an activity which also finds its parallels in other parts of the world. Just what are the roots of this heritage—where does it come from; what are its counterparts elsewhere; what was the cultural background of those who commissioned, designed and built our early structures?

Obviously the form language has its origins in Europe. Taste there was made by the aristocratic establishment of England which in turn was often influenced by Continental European counterparts. We need only think of the magnificent chateaux of France and the superb elegance of English manor houses (with their own tragic history of destruction in our time) to learn the imagery that forms the basis of eighteenth and nineteenth century taste. When settlement was first made on this continent during England's Georgian period, that taste was directly imported. Equally so and at a similar time, it found its way to England's colonies in other parts of the globe to develop there in a parallel and often fascinatingly different way.

There are, for instance, buildings in Texas (especially St Antonio, Austin and Houston) built in a style and manner almost indistinguishable from Australian counterparts of the time. The preserved French enclave in New Orleans displays a very similar form language to the iron lace-verandahed buildings we have often claimed as uniquely our own (and considerably pre-dates the Australian models).

What all these developments had in common was the transplantation of European taste into areas of a very different climate with entirely different and limited means at the disposal of those who built. What makes these early buildings often so very good, is that they were built by people with personal experience and direct ties to an older developed European culture. They not only brought their taste but also their skills. The essence of their creative act was the sensitive and intelligent translation of these assets into a new visual language.

Their buildings display the unquestioned elements of proportion and massing of the European mode of the time transposed into adaptations that made obvious practical sense in the conditions of the New World. They intuitively gave expression to the strong sunlight, the summer heat, and the altered, simpler way of life to that of the Old World.

It is generally believed that verandahs were actually first encountered in India, where many of the early settlers stopped en route to Australia or even spent some time. Other theories claim that verandahs were really only built as external corridors, attached to buildings whose rooms followed and connected one another without hallways—which is to suggest that verandahs often encircled buildings without consideration of sun-orientation. Be that as it may, this ubiquitous element became the hallmark of the colonial style. The development of the verandah was to result in some most compelling architectural compositions. The colonnaded structures one, two or even more floors in height with characteristically slim (often cast-iron) rhythmically-spaced supports and decorative, beautiful shadow-casting grilles, were developed to a high level of elegance.

The architectural value of these historic buildings varies greatly. There is evidence in the best examples that they were conceived by sensitive and educated people. The dignity and quiet elegance of some examples shows that the results of the new pastoral fortunes were not spent on ostentation so much as on the owners' aspiration for something higher than social pleasure. In examples of less than the peak achievement in architecture, one cannot help but marvel at the hardship and obstacles that must have been overcome by those who, in far flung locations, were at the same time not only proprietor but also architect, builder and supplier of material. It is often evident that the homestead was in fact far more than the home—it constituted a planned settlement where one or more houses were grouped with some most inventive utility buildings to form a unique entity. Of particular interest in these settlements are building types such as the shearing sheds or the ingenious meat houses with their system of refrigeration. Built of double timber walls, they employed the principle of evaporative cooling by keeping hanging hessian sheets between them soaked with water. In contrast to the fine houses built of masonry, many of these early timber buildings are not in good physical condition today. Australian hardwoods do not make the best long term building materials but the way in which frame construction was used is quite remarkable and characteristic of the time's common-sense inventiveness.

No-one would suggest today that we should copy or reproduce the historic buildings in this book for our present use. That would be not only unreasonable and impractical but would also be evidence of a poverty of spirit. The active embracing and reproduction of another era's architectural styles and artistic products and achievements is a culturally backward step. It is a technically and materially questionable pursuit because conditions, both in form language and technology, change so rapidly in our time. However, it is a very different thing to have a deep appreciation of the cultural value inherent in the works of the past. That appreciation may be a passive one which, although it will not make us emulate these works, should make us strong in determination that they must be valued and honoured as irreplaceable objects of our heritage. No effort should be spared to restore and maintain them, so that the cultural continuity they imply will be kept alive for generations to come.

To relate the past to our own time, it is important to appreciate that in the nineteenth century there was not too much divergence of opinion on what constituted good taste. Those of erudition and sensitivity had it, and those without had simple picture book rules to follow which meant that they could not go too far wrong.

In our times we have no simple picture books—the possibilities and demands are too complex and too constantly changing. What will, however, elevate the all too numerous inadequate present efforts into the realm of architecture will be a new sense of historical understanding of continuity. When the best in the new cultural forces of the Western World truly becomes part of us, we may be able in the future to translate these into Australian terms—just as our forebears did, who created our colonial style from the best which they brought from their homeland.

by HARRY SEIDLER
ARCHITECT

Fortunately, the past never completely dies for man. Man may forget it, but he always preserves it within him. For, take him at any epoch, and he is the product, the epitome, of all the earlier epochs.   *Fustel de Coulanges*, The Ancient City

Valleyfield *Tasmania*

Text: G. T. Stilwell   Photographs: Frank Bolt

Valleyfield, situated on the northern bank of the Derwent on the outskirts of New Norfolk, was built as the King's Head Inn, probably in 1822. It has been a private house since 1834. The trellised work of the verandah and the sky lights above the windows date from later in the century.

NEW NORFOLK WAS SO NAMED because many of the Norfolk Island settlers who were evacuated to Van Diemen's Land in the early years of the nineteenth century received grants of land in the district. Valleyfield is composed of several such grants which were amalgamated into a single property by William Abel, the original owner of one of them, who, with his wife and three children arrived at Hobart Town by the *Porpoise* in January 1808.

The present homestead may have been built in 1822. Certainly in that year Abel was granted a licence, which he was to hold until 1826, for the King's Head Inn at New Norfolk. It was definitely constructed by April 1825 when he stated in an application to the Government that he had erected on purchased land a 'large Brick Dwelling, Stable, Barn and 3 outbuildings'. The house is more fully described in this advertisement in the *Colonial Times* of 15 September 1826:

KINGS HEAD, NEW NORFOLK

To be LET, for one year, or a Term not exceeding five years, that well-known and well accustomed Inn the King's Head at New Norfolk. The House, which is of Brick contains 9 Rooms below, and three Lofts; the Out-houses consist of Kitchen, Wash-house, Stable, and Barn; there are also capital Yards, and a well-stocked Garden of 2 Acres, and 40 Acres of land in cultivation. With the above will also be let the Brewing utensils; part of the Furniture, the Fixtures etc. will be allowed to go with the House, at a fair Valuation. Apply to the Proprietor, Mr. WILLIAM ABLE [*sic*], Senior on the Premises.

Abel gave his business as a publican because of an unfortunate accident which had occurred six months previously. The following account of this is taken from the *Hobart Town Gazette* of 8 April 1826.

A lamentable and unfortunate occurrence took place at Mr. Abel's, of the Kings Head Inn, New Norfolk. On the night of Tuesday last, Mr. Able, junior, had returned it appears, unexpectedly at a late hour, and was probably unwilling to disturb the family, was entering by a window. His father, unable to discern who was in the darkness of the night, and receiving no answer to his frequent demands, concluded it was a robber breaking into the house, and as we understand, lifting a pistol and presenting it to the individual, most melancholy to relate, shot him in the breast. The feelings of the father on the occasion are not to be described.

Valleyfield is a typical Australian residence of the 1820s. An unusual feature of its construction was the use of river sand to insulate the ceiling of the ground floor.

Early in 1827 David Watson Bush took over the inn in partnership with George Lowe, who had a shop on the premises. By August of that year Lowe was running the inn as well and, in March 1828, by foreclosing on Abel's mortgage to him, obtained possession of the property. Lowe later ran coaches to Hobart Town. It was he who built the large stone barn which has the monogram 'GL' and the date 1830 carved on the key-stone of the arch. The Quaker Missionaries James Backhouse and G. W. Walker held services in this barn on several occasions in the mid-thirties.

In February 1832 Lowe and his wife Norah sold the King's Head to Captain Richard Armstrong of the East India Company's Bengal Army. Armstrong was then on furlough in Van Diemen's Land and, like so many of his brother officers, decided upon this colony as a place for his retirement which occurred, after a further term of service in India, towards the end of 1834.

After more than 150 years of occupation the homestead at Valleyfield has a settled look rare in this country. The mellowed buildings are surrounded by European trees which have grown well in the alluvial soil. The hop grounds are surrounded by hedges of Lombardy poplars and hawthorns. Like the house this old stone building retains its shingled roof.

Lowe remained in occupation until some time in 1833 but it was not until 19 November 1835 that Armstrong obtained a title to the property, which was renamed Bingfield. The Captain was himself soon in financial difficulties and in 1838 he tried to sell. In the newspaper advertisement the house was then described as being 'lately put in thorough state of repair, containing ten apartments, fitted up in the most comfortable manner'. By 1844, perhaps because of the recent depression, Armstrong was insolvent and the property was sold. He then returned to England where he died at Torquay in Devonshire on 13 September 1857.

The next owners of the estate probably did not live there, and in the early fifties it was acquired by Ebenezer Shoobridge who renamed the property Valleyfield.

Ebenezer Shoobridge was a child when he landed at Hobart Town with his father William in 1822. He came of a long line of farmers and hop-growers in Kent and had considerable colonial experience in these fields, both with his father and on his account, before buying Valleyfield, which was then commonly considered to be 'worked out'.

Commercial hop-growing in the Derwent Valley dates from the mid-forties. Shoobridge saw the potential of these easily irrigated river flats and he and his sons after him worked hard to transform the 240-acre (96-hectare) farm. The old hop kiln probably dates from the mid-fifties; the circular brick kiln was built in 1884. Neither would look out of place in Worcestershire or Kent.

In 1865 Ebenezer Shoobridge was able to buy another and larger property, Bushy Park at Macquarie Plains, to which he moved, leaving his sons William and Robert to run Valleyfield. By the early seventies they had the farm in a high state of production. Sixty-four acres were under cultivation of which twenty-four were orchard and twenty hop ground. This land was irrigated by a ten horse-power engine with water from the nearby Derwent River. The brothers Shoobridge were actively involved in church and community affairs. One of the features of life at Valleyfield in the seventies was the strawberry feast to which people came from near and far. Many even made the journey from Hobart Town by ferry.

Sixty years ago the property was acquired from R. W. G. Shoobridge by the late Mr H. A. Warner whose son, Mr J. H. A. Warner, and his family farm Valleyfield now.

This attractive hop kiln of limewashed brick was built in 1884 by the brothers W. E. and R. W. G. Shoobridge. The tower is 6·4 metres in diameter and 20 metres high.

Quamby *Tasmania*

Text: E. G. Scott   Photographs: Brian J. Lloyd

The northern entrance to Quamby, showing the panelled door with surrounding fan-light.

ONE OF THE MOST important of Tasmania's great country homes is Quamby, near Hagley in Northern Tasmania, now owned by Mr and Mrs John Barnett. Standing on a commanding rise facing the east in a park-like setting, with lawns sloping to the flats below, this noble house dominates the landscape. It is well sheltered from the prevailing westerlies by groves of English trees and hawthorn hedges; whilst its eastern aspect takes in Mount Barrow in the middle distance. In the far distance the bold outlines of Ben Lomond can be seen.

The house, which is said to have been built in the best American Colonial style, has a single storey at the front with a long white stone flagged verandah, and a second storey at the back. Incredible as it may seem, this grand establishment was built by a political exile who had been transported to the colonies for life.

His name was Richard Dry and the story of his rise to wealth and influence is surely a remarkable one. The son of a gentleman farmer, he was born at Wexford in Ireland, and as a young man became involved in the political struggles of the country. Taking part in an armed rebellion at Vinegar Hill in 1798 he was captured by the English and, at his subsequent trial for treason, received the harsh sentence of transportation.

Arriving at Botany Bay in 1800 he was given employment in the Government Stores Department. As a political exile, in contrast to a convict, he appears to have enjoyed almost complete freedom, and during this period he met and later married Anne Maugham Lyons, daughter of a Sydney merchant.

When Colonel Paterson sailed for Tasmania in 1804 to found the northern settlement he took Dry with him and employed him in the Stores Department. Dry proved to be so trustworthy and diligent that he was given his own home on a grant, made to Mrs Dry, of 500 acres (200 hectares), on the outskirts of Launceston.

Here he farmed with such success that when he received a free pardon in 1819 he resigned his government position and applied for extra grants of land, supporting his claim by revealing that he owned 400 head of cattle and 7,000 sheep.

Governor Macquarie noted this fact 'with astonishment', and recommended to Lieutenant Sorell that Dry's application be granted.

As a result Dry became the owner of several tracts of land, the main one being on the Western (now Meander) River, and it was here that Dry, now a wealthy man, decided to build a new home. The old one at Elphin Farm, which he described as a government barrack, being far too small for the growing family.

*The northern aspect, showing the ballroom
(right) and the Italian sandstone fountain
(foreground).*

The site chosen was unsurpassed in the area. Dry commissioned a builder named Wainwright, who recruited a staff of artisans and convict labourers, and building was begun in 1828. The name of the architect is unknown.

So vast and comprehensive was the whole concept that ten years were to elapse before it was completed, although bluestone for the foundations, clay for the bricks, and the necessary timber were all found on the property nearby.

The house was approached by a drive about a kilometre in length, flanked by English trees and shrubs and paved with cobblestones; in its day Quamby Avenue, as it is known locally, was famous throughout the land. It was a delight to all who travelled on it, as it wound around the undulating country before finally emerging on to the broad lawns in which Quamby stands, after passing a garden of well over four hectares, set in a natural amphitheatre, a nut grove and finally a rose garden.

The following description of the house, property and outbuildings, which appeared in a sale catalogue published in 1887, gives the reader an accurate and detailed description of Quamby at that time.

'The homestead is a well built two storey house on stone foundations. Fine raised columnated verandah. Well situated on top of a hill. It consists of 7 sitting rooms, 11 bedrooms, halls, ballroom, conservatory, 3 cellars, linen room, laundry, 2 dairies, wood house, 2 coach houses, coachman's cottage, pantry, detached kitchen, 3 servants rooms, bathroom with two supply tanks, tennis and pleasure grounds.

Managers residence. Compact two storey house, 2 sitting rooms, 4 bedrooms, kitchen and servants room, detached kitchen and loft.

Stabling for 26 horses. Chaff house to hold 40 tons of chaff with grooms and ploughmans quarters.

Barns to hold 20,000 bushels of grain. Blacksmith's shop, store, stone slaughter house, machinery shop all of which are well situated for conveniently working the property and cost an enormous sum of money.

The garden consisting of 11 acres with two storey gardeners cottage is now let to a tenant who supplies the establishment with fruit and vegetables free of cost.'

The Manager's residence, known as the office, with the stables at the rear.

Sadly, Mrs Dry did not live to see the house completed, as she died in Launceston in 1836.

In addition to his original grants, the extent of which are not quite clear, Richard Dry added to his enormous holding by purchasing large portions of neighbouring estates, until eventually, this man who had arrived in Tasmania as a prisoner of the Crown was the proud owner of 30,000 acres (12,000 hectares) of some of the most fertile soil in Tasmania.

In 1843, only five years after the completion of his new home, Richard Dry died in Launceston at the age of seventy-three. Thus he had very few years in which to enjoy the peace and tranquillity he so richly deserved in his country mansion.

His elder son, Richard Junior, born in 1815, who was to make such a name for himself in the public life of Tasmania, inherited the homestead block of 18,000 acres (7,200 hectares), which had as its northern boundary the Meander River.

The front view of house in an autumn setting.

The younger Richard, a brilliant and popular young man who by this time had travelled extensively, assumed the role of the Squire of Quamby as his rightful heritage. His public career had started at the age of twenty-one when he was appointed to the magistracy by Governor Arthur. Then, in 1844, he was appointed to the nominee Legislative Council by Governor Eardley Wilmot. He soon became a leading figure in the Anti-Transportation League and, following a bitter clash with the Governor over the latter's alleged 'unconstitutional conduct', he and five other Councillors walked out of the House in protest, leaving it without a quorum. They became known as the 'patriotic six' and were eventually reinstated by Queen Victoria.

He was elected to the seat of Launceston in the first, partly-elective Legislative Council and, on 30 December 1851, he was unanimously elected as the first speaker of that House. He occupied this position with great distinction until 1854, when ill health forced his resignation from Parliament, a circumstance which caused widespread regret throughout Tasmania.

Five of the twelve bells, showing their intricate system of pulleys, in the section of Quamby leading to the servants' quarters.

The dining-room, with its black Italian marble mantelpiece, deep, cedar skirting boards and original flame mahogany Victorian sideboard. OPPOSITE

The front view of Manager's residence, showing the beautiful Georgian proportions and the unusual design of upper-storey windows.

From 1850 to 1854 he had been a member of the Select Committee appointed to draw up a Constitution for the Colony, and thus it must have been a great disappointment to him when he was unable to nominate for the first responsible Parliament, which was opened on 2 December 1856.

In 1853 Richard Dry married Miss Clara Meredith, daughter of Mr and Mrs George Meredith of Cambria, Swansea, and the couple soon became known for their generous and gracious hospitality.

Unfortunately, the Drys were faced at this period with a severe financial problem due largely, it was said, to Richard's extreme generosity to people in trouble. To avoid bankruptcy he decided to sell the whole of the southern portion of his holding consisting of 6,000 acres (2,400 hectares). This had been sub-divided into farms of a convenient size, and the sale realized £40,000. Thus Quamby was reduced to 12,000 acres (4,800 hectares).

In the late 1850s Richard Dry's health deteriorated still further, and for a time his life was despaired of. On the advice of his doctors he decided to take a trip to England in the hope that a long sea voyage would aid his recovery. Mr and Mrs Dry sailed for England in 1858, and it was with great jubilation that the news was received in Tasmania that, not only had he recovered his health, but that in May 1858 Queen Victoria had conferred on him a knighthood for his part in drawing up the Constitution for Tasmania. He thus became the first Tasmanian-born knight.

Sir Richard and Lady Dry returned to Tasmania on 16 January 1861 and received a tumultuous welcome. Shortly afterwards Sir Richard received a petition from the electors of Launceston requesting him to nominate for the Legislative Council. He agreed only three days prior to the election, but still defeated Sir Adye Douglas for the seat.

Sir Richard's career reached its zenith when, in 1866, at the fall of the Whyte Government, he was requested to form a ministry and became Premier of Tasmania with a cabinet of three.

Quamby was now in its heyday, with 800 people living on the estate as either employees or tenants, and so great was the influence of Sir Richard and Lady Dry on the political and social life of the State that Quamby became known as the 'Government House of the North'.

An important visitor in 1868 was Prince Alfred, Duke of Edinburgh, who was invited to turn the first sod of the Launceston and Western Railway project so dear to Sir Richard's heart.

Due to the strain of office Sir Richard's health again began to fail, but his sudden death due to heart failure on Sunday, 1 August 1869, came as a grievous shock to the whole colony. Messages of sympathy and regret were also received from many parts of the world. His remains were conveyed to Hagley, in a funeral procession lasting four days, and were interred close to St Mary's Church, which he had built and where he had worshipped. The funeral cortège was the largest ever seen in Tasmania. Neither Sir Richard nor his brother the Rev. William Dry left any heirs.

The twenty-metre hallway dividing the main wing of Quamby, and showing the fine ceiling cornices.

The drawing-room, featuring a white Italian marble mantelpiece and surrounding cast-iron grate. The delicacy of the ceiling centrepiece is reflected in the eight-foot high English glass mirror. OPPOSITE

The flagstoned verandah at the front of the house, showing fine pitsawn columns supporting the roof.

Following her husband's death Lady Dry decided to settle in England and Quamby was put on the market. It was purchased by a Victorian grazier, Mr J. J. Phelps, on a walk-in-walk-out basis; almost all the magnificent Dry furniture being left in the house. The new owner never lived at Quamby but appointed as Manager a Mr Nicholas Sadleir, who also owned a station at Darling.

In 1887 Mr Phelps decided to realize on his Tasmanian investment and on 25 April of that year the whole estate, consisting of 39 farms, totalling 12,000 acres (4,800 hectares) was put under the hammer at Launceston.

Almost every farm had a house and outbuildings which had been built by the Drys, father and son, and many of the properties were purchased by the tenants living on them at the time.

The coveted homestead block of 970 acres (390 hectares), including some of the best land in Tasmania, and the house, still containing most of the Dry furniture, was bought by Mr George Gregory for £15/10/- per acre. Mr Gregory was a native of Essex, England, and for some years had been a tenant farmer on the Westwood estate, also a Dry property.

After farming Quamby successfully for twenty-seven years Gregory retired to live in Launceston, and for several years the great house was empty. At his death in 1919 the homestead block, now reduced to some 650 acres (260 hectares) passed to his son Mr W. E. Gregory.

The property remained in the Gregory family until 1955 when the owner at that time, Mr Norman Gregory, sold it to Mr John S. Barnett of Hobart. Also at this time a clearing sale of the Dry furniture was held.

Over the years the century-old house had deteriorated alarmingly. Many of the outbuildings were in a state of ruin, but the new owners set about the task of restoration with such skill, knowledge and dedication that today this fine old house, which has been standing for nearly 140 years, is restored throughout to its former glory.

Douglas Park *Tasmania*

Text: E. V. R. Ratcliff and G. Hawley Stancombe
Photographs: Brian J. Lloyd

LACHLAN MACQUARIE, Governor of New South Wales and Van Diemen's Land, on his first overland journey from Hobart Town to the northern settlements at Port Dalrymple, reached the banks of Relief Creek on 6 December 1811, and renamed the stream Elizabeth after his wife, Elizabeth Henrietta. In 1821, his last year of office, he came again and, on 31 May, chose a site on the north bank of the river for a township which he called 'Campbell-Town in honour of Mrs Macquarie's maiden name'.

Within view of the pleasant Midland town which grew from this beginning, on the sheep-grazed plain to the eastward, stands the fine stone house which Hugh Kean built for Dr Temple Pearson in 1839.

Dr Pearson, a retired surgeon of Douglas in Lanarkshire, Scotland, arrived in Hobart Town with his wife on the ship *Skelton* on 22 December 1822. He brought with him cash and goods to the value of £1,300, and in accordance with the practice then prevailing of making grants of land in proportion to the capital possessed by the aspiring settler, Lieutenant-Governor Sorell granted him 1,000 acres (400 hectares), which he selected on the north bank of the Elizabeth River.

He named his property 'Douglas Park' after his home village on the Douglas Water, and settled there early in 1823. The *Hobart Town Gazette* for 15 February informs us that 'Mr Temple Pearson of Campbell Town, Elizabeth River, is appointed as Chief District Constable for the district of Bathurst, East Side, by the Lieutenant-Governor'. He thus became the first chief constable of the district, and as he also seems to have commenced some practise of medicine soon after his arrival, he was also the first practising doctor in Campbell Town. In 1828, he was appointed District Assistant Surgeon, a Government post which required him to attend all 'Crown servants and prisoners', but he had evidently performed these duties previously without remuneration.

The centre stone of the frieze above the entrance porch is carved in high relief with the rose of England, the thistle of Scotland, and the shamrock of Ireland supporting Dr Pearson's family arms. A shield charged with three heraldic lion faces and a glove is surmounted by a dove bearing a leafy twig, and a scroll with the defaced motto, 'Dum Spiro Spero' (while I live, I hope).

He resigned the posts of District Constable and Pound Keeper in 1825, and seems to have turned largely to farming, for at his death in 1839, he left 16,000 acres (6,400 hectares) to his brother, having added to his lands by the purchase of adjoining smaller holdings. It is uncertain to what extent he practised medicine, for he was undoubtedly addicted to alcohol in his last years. David Melville of Edinburgh, a visitor to the district in 1838, describes in his journal a visit to Dr Pearson's, during which two bottles of wine were consumed by day. Then follows the distressing news of morning seizures, and the doctor 'taken very ill' the following day, having 'been indulging for two or three days and while attending to the bottle had forgot his food and become very exhausted'. Whether this entry, bearing as it does the date, Friday, 28 December, constitutes good evidence of alcoholism is a matter for some argument, Christmas being a 'perilous' time then as now, but we do know that Dr Pearson was dead and buried within a year, and lies in the tiny kirkyard at Kirklands, eight kilometres to the west of the Town.

Hugh Kean (in some references spelt Kane or Kaine), the Irish master stonemason who built Douglas Park, arrived in Van Diemen's Land as an assisted migrant in the *Eliza* on 13 November 1838, with his wife, Mary, and three children, Hubert, Catherine and William. He set up in Campbell Town as a building contractor during a period of great activity in the town, but Douglas Park seems to have been his earliest major work, and must have been begun in 1838.

The present Campbell Town Bridge, a fine structure of three brick segmental arches carried on stone piers, was completed in 1836. Its opening necessitated a new line of main road through the town, which was very disadvantageous to the innkeepers on the old main road, still named Bridge Street despite the loss of its bridge so long ago. Kean arrived in time to build or extend four of the inns on the main road. Three of these structures still remain, and two are still in use as hotels.

His work on the first of them, the Beehive (now the Campbell Town Hotel) began in 1838 and was completed the following year. Martin Cash, the celebrated bushranger who ultimately cheated the gallows and published his memoirs in 1870, worked as a labourer for Kean during 1839.

'I got employment from Mr Kane, who, sometime previous to my arrival, had purchased the goodwill of Hogg's public-house and was then engaged in erecting a new one, fronting on the main road. He was a mason by trade and had just finished the building of a fine house for Dr Pearson about two miles from the township.'

It was after ending his employment with Kean, on completion of the Beehive, that Cash again offended against the Law, was sentenced, absconded, and began the colourful part of his career.

In 1839 Kean erected the Blue Boar, now the badly mutilated Powell's Hotel, and in the following year he completed both the Foxhunters' Return (at present a derelict building by the Bridge, with one of the finest Georgian facades in Australia), and the Rainbow, which stood on the site of the Campbell Town Hospital. Its owner asked Kean to manage it for him, and so Hugh Kean turned innkeeper, purchasing the Foxhunters' Return in 1842 and being its host until his early death in 1848, after which the business was carried on by his widow.

During his ten years at Campbell Town, Mary Kean bore her husband three more children: Agnes, Richard, and Michael. The eldest son, Hubert Kean, was at one time licensee of no less than three of the inns in the Town, and also built the Brewery (now the Masonic Lodge near the Bridge) in 1855. The former Beehive was known as Kean's Hotel until 1891.

Kean's existing buildings show him to have been a first class mason, and a talented architect within the limitations of the well-established Georgian style. His technical ability is evidenced by the excellent condition of most of his known structures today, as well as the splendid geometrical stone stairs in at least four of them. He seems to have chosen his stones with greater care than was often the case in the Colonies, and to have laid them correctly according to their natural set in the quarry, so that very little fretting or flaking is to be seen today.

In designing his formal facades, as at Douglas Park, he gave emphasis to their symmetry by enhancing the centre with his decorative treatment of the entrance and the window above. Carved work, such as the device on the porch at Douglas Park (illustrated), may be naive in design, but is crisp in execution, and it is tempting to imagine that Kean did this work himself. In the realm of 'pattern-book' design, such as the Ionic columns at Douglas Park, he was far from naive, the columns being quite correct in detail and proportion, complete with entasis (bulging of columns to prevent the illusion of concavity), so often omitted in Colonial work. The scholarly nature of Kean's Ionic becomes very apparent when compared with the work of the joiner in the hall doorways, which is simplified and debased in a typically, though delightfully, Colonial manner.

Other buildings attributed to Kean are the former Sherwood Castle Inn at Ross and the nearby Macquarie House, and he may also have built Rose Hill, near Jericho, which has a stone staircase in his manner.

The visitor to Douglas Park today leaves the Main Road through Campbell Town near St Andrew's Presbyterian Church, with its fine stone spire built in 1857, and turns eastward over the eminence occupied by the north end of the Town. The grassy plain drained by the Elizabeth River stretches ahead to the wooded foothills of the Eastern Tiers, the sites of such fine houses as Camelford, Quorn Hall, Riccarton and others, marked by clusters of well-grown European trees. Douglas Park house is immediately apparent at the end of a pine-lined drive, as it lacks the usual screen of trees; perhaps because its original owner died so soon after its completion, leaving it to his brother, John Pearson of Bathgate, Scotland, who remained an absentee proprietor and, in 1846, settled in Portland, Victoria.

The austere dark pines of the drive provide an excellent introduction to the enclosed green square of the front garden, in which a white circular drive brings the visitor to the grey-gold front of the house.

The walls are built mainly of a very hard, gritty siliceous sandstone, with dressings of the finer-grained grey sandstone characteristic of the village of Ross, some eleven kilometres to the south. On the garden front, ashlar work is used, finely pecked on the main wall surfaces, but smoothly finished on quoins, string-course, porch, cornice and parapet, and window surrounds. The side and back walls of the house are of rubble stonework brought to courses, with ashlar quoins and dressings around the openings. The four chimney stacks are of ashlar work.

The superb doorcases of New South Wales cedar in the entrance hall of Douglas Park repeat in simplified form the Greek Ionic order of the stone porch outside.

The main two-storied mass of the house is flanked with low wings set back half the depth of the house. They have ashlar facades and parapets to match the house front, but their other walls are of local blue-grey vesicular basalt.

The roof is almost concealed by the plain stone parapet wall which extends round three sides of the main block. In Tasmanian buildings in late Georgian and Regency styles, parapet walls are exceptional, even in town buildings, simply because of the expense and difficulty of obtaining lead for guttering and flashing at that time. Even the finest of early houses often had no spouting when first built, or else wooden guttering intended more for the collection of roof-water for domestic use; thus adequately overhanging eaves are more usual. But at Douglas Park, and in others of his buildings, Hugh Kean has followed his familiar models at home in Great Britain and Ireland, and has concealed the roof.

At present the roof is covered with the ubiquitous corrugated iron, which replaces the earlier split shingles of wood. This transformation has been almost universal in old Tasmanian houses because the light-weight roof structures, while adequate for the support of a covering of eucalypt shingles, are insufficient to bear a replacement of slates or tiles without extensive reconstruction.

The main part of the house has no attic rooms, which is somewhat unusual in Tasmanian houses of this type, but the wings have garrets for the accommodation of servants.

The four-panelled front door leads directly into the entrance hall with its great stairway and fine cedar doorcases. The flagstones of the floor are now covered with carpet, and the arched window opening at the back now contains an Edwardian glazed door, but otherwise all is as it was, beautifully restored by the present owners. The plaster cornice is an interesting attempt by the forgotten plasterer to produce a chaste Greek Revival design, suitable to the Ionic doorcases, but the ornate plaster rose is the delight of the ceiling.

The geometrical staircase, which became almost a hallmark of Kean's work in the Colony, is a fine example, still in perfect condition. The curved wall of the well above the stair is not continued below it as in some of his other buildings, so that the stone steps must bear the weight of false walling at the corners. In constructing a geometrical stair, the risers, treads, and bearing surfaces of the stones are shaped by the mason before erection, but the finishing of the undersides of the stones is left until after they are in place, to produce the smooth spiral which is such a pleasure to behold today. Unfinished stones can still be seen in the concealment of the cupboard under the stairs at Douglas Park.

The main formal rooms open to each side of the entrance hall, through Grecian doorways with panelled reveals and soffits. The two front rooms have fine plaster cornices; the dining room to the right being decorated with grapes and acanthus leaves, while the drawing-room to the left (now the billiard room) has a Greek anthemion (formalized honeysuckle) pattern. The windows have the very fine glazing bars of the Regency, and internal wooden shutters which fold into the reveals.

On the upper floor, the doorways from the landing have moulded surrounds with turned roundels at the corners to carry the eye from a vertical moulding to a horizontal one. Reveals and soffits are reeded.

One such doorway leads to a remarkable room at the north-east corner of the house, with windows facing northward and eastward. Originally the morning room, it has a superbly-carved white marble mantelpiece decorated with roses and other flowers. The floor, beyond the central space for a carpet square, has polished cedar floorboards, too soft for any but a lady's slippers, and the skirting boards are panelled in cedar. These are both very unusual features.

The door-panels of the first-floor rooms, as elsewhere in the house, have unusually beautiful figuring, as fine as the best mahogany.

The middle front room on the upper floor, placed above the entrance hall, and lit by the relatively ornate central window of the main facade, has the fascinating conceit of a false fireplace, with no provision at all for a chimney. Even in our own time, when the television set so often replaces the hearth, we are not yet used to living in a room without a focus point, and perhaps similar considerations influenced Kean.

At the back of the house, the kitchen courtyard, separated from the nearby farmyard by a substantial stone wall, is a lawn. The kitchen wing is to the east, and the range of servants' dwellings to the west.

Tasmanian colonial building has quite definite regional characteristics, based on the availability of materials, as well as the imported tradition and ability of the builders. In the Midlands, the chief dividing line is between the brick masonry of the north, and the freestone (sandstone) masonry of the south. If a regional boundary can be described, Douglas Park stands very near to it, for Campbell Town is built predominantly of red brick, while Ross, only eleven kilometres to the south, is almost entirely of stone. The stone used at Campbell Town was either brought from near Ross, or was the local basalt, which was only rarely cut for ashlar work, because of its hardness. These facts explain the use of sandstone for the formal parts of Douglas Park, and the basalt rubble used elsewhere.

Because of the early death of Dr Pearson, no old outbuildings remain at Douglas Park. Nothing is known of the original house on his property, which may have been a fairly simple wooden structure. He may even, in view of his other duties, have lived in Campell Town and farmed from afar, for the Land Commissioners in their Journal for 26 June 1827, speak only of Dr Pearson's fine sheep walk, his 'considerable quantity' of fencing,

To the west of the kitchen courtyard is a range of cottage-like servants' quarters constructed, like the kitchen wing opposite, of local vesicular basalt rubble, brought to courses and dressed with ashlar sandstone. Unlike the main house, this wing has garret rooms lit by skylights. The stone transoms over the doors are unusual.

A detail of the stonework on the east wall of the kitchen wing. Pecked ashlar sandstone contrasts with roughly squared bluestone (vesicular basalt) rubble. A storeroom window remains heavily barred.

his 'fine flock of highly improved Sheep', but not of his house. David Melville, however, makes it clear that Pearson was living on his own land at the time of his visit in December 1838, by which time the new house must at least have been begun.

Pearson, although twice married, died without issue, leaving the property to his brother, who almost immediately put it on the market, but without success. Mrs Pearson married James Maclanachan of Ballochmyle, on the Salt Pan Plains near Tunbridge, and Douglas Park was let to George Harrison of Antill Ponds, and later to the Taylors, who held land along the Macquarie River, and whose descendants do so to this day.

By 1860, the property had passed to the estate of the late George Alston of Auchlochlan, Macquarie River, whose widow lived at Howley Lodge, Campbell Town. In 1861, the land, now consisting of 12,000 acres (4,800 hectares), was leased to N. P. Allison of Streanshalh, while, by 1875, the lessee was Dan Archer of Fern Hill, who ultimately purchased the property in 1899, after a period of intervening occupancy by A. R. D. and G. L. P. Finlay.

In 1912, Robert Jones bought the property. He was a descendant of Robert Jones of Pleasant Place on the Jordan River, and his namesake and grandson Mr. R. T. Jones now carries on the estate.

Mr and Mrs Jones are now engaged in truly restoring the house, laboriously removing paint from the magnificent cedar, and founding and tending the garden, which will provide the appropriate setting for the fine stone house which Hugh Kean built for Dr Temple Pearson.

Gidleigh *New South Wales*

Text: Mrs T. L. F. Rutledge   Photographs: Kerry Dundas

A detail of the three-sided bow front of the house.

1975 view of the front of the house facing north. The old front entrance was here, and the drawing-room was the room on the left with three windows set in the three-sided bow front. Now all these rooms are bedrooms. OPPOSITE ABOVE

The house in 1890, showing the short arm of the L-shaped house on the eastern side consisting of the dining-room and kitchen quarters. W. F. Rutledge is seated in the chair with his little son, Thomas. His wife, Mrs Forster Rutledge (the daughter of Jane Styles and R. Morphy) made a beautiful herbaceous border the length of the eastern elevation—now a grass strip, the fate of many of her flower beds. BELOW

GIDLEIGH IS SITUATED near the border of the Australian Capital Territory in the Shire of Yarralumla, the heart of which, the rich limestone plains and high Murrumbidgee valleys, was resumed to form the Territory, leaving the shire with the rugged perimeter. This proximity to a capital city has, in recent years, altered the character of purely rural community and presented the owners of properties adjacent to the border with many unexpected problems.

The land on which the two homesteads were built was an original grant to Phillip Parker King in 1834. P. P. King was born on Norfolk Island in 1791 and was the son of Philip Gidley King, the third Governor of New South Wales. He was named after Governor Phillip, hence the spelling of the first name. Mrs P. G. King was Harriet Lethbridge and came, as did the Kings, from Devon, England, in the neighbourhood of Gidleigh Castle. P. P. King entered the Royal Navy in 1807. He rose to the rank of Rear-Admiral; the first Australian to do so. In recognition of his services surveying the coasts of New South Wales and South America, he was permitted and helped to take up land in the Colony; a privilege not generally allowed to families of governors.

At this time the Home Government was glad to induce naval and military officers to settle in the Colony, their doing so 'giving tone to Colonial Society', and many received important appointments in the Colonial Service. There is little doubt that the Colony did benefit from this policy, whether or not these officers gave the desired tone to society. They were men trained in a very hard school to take responsibility, and well versed in survival techniques. They were born into the Age of Elegance in Britain and knew how a gentleman's house should be. With inadequate tools and skills, they managed to add details of refinement and distinction to the solidly built homes and out-buildings constructed in those very early years.

On his retirement, P. P. King made another successful career for himself in the Colony, and he and his seven sons became well established in New

The view from the front verandah. The wych elms were a lovely legacy left by the Kings with even more splendid ones below the old homestead. The flats on either side of the Turallo Creek were where T. L. F. Rutledge made his first experiments with imported grasses.

The 'Turkey' room was built c. 1907 with money Mrs Forster Rutledge made from raising turkeys: profitable then, as they could forage for themselves and only needed a little grain fed them to keep them tame. When the foxes moved in hard on the heels of the rabbits early in the century, the turkeys proved too expensive and vulnerable to disease to rear in captivity. It is a fine stone-built room. Mrs Rutledge favoured English farmhouse style with dark timbered ceiling and plate rail for blue and white china. The 'primitive picture' painted by the emancipist artist J. Bachler, in 1847, is of her mother Jane Styles and aunt, Mary Futter of Lumley Park, Bungonia. OPPOSITE

South Wales and Victoria. His eldest son, Phillip Gidley King, the younger, described 'a small freehold my father had put together' and named Gidley. He visited his brothers, John and Essington who were then living at Gidley. He did not stay there for any length of time. In 1840 he was droving surplus and unsaleable cattle to Melbourne for his uncle, Hannibal Hawkins Macarthur. He had trouble finding a route not eaten out by other overlanders or poisoned by sheep dying of 'catarrh' (black disease).

The brothers, Essington and Frederic, stayed as managers. In 1840 they were both under twenty years of age, so presumably the early buildings were built under the supervision of overseers using convict labour. Amongst the assigned men at this time was young William Westwood, who made his first escape from Gidley to become the daring bushranger known as 'Jacky Jacky'. As a bushranger he never killed anyone or assaulted a woman. He was continually being recaptured and continually escaping from the high security prisons of Cockatoo Island and Port Arthur. Finally sent to Norfolk Island, he could bear life no longer, and for the first time committed murder, so that he could make his last escape by way of the gallows, at the age of twenty-seven.

Essington and Frederic did not settle down at Gidley. It was said that one of them became engaged to Jane Styles of Reevesdale, Bungonia, but she married Major Richard Morphy. Perhaps this disappointment, on top of bad seasons and losses from that killer, black disease, discouraged them. The little homestead was never finished and still consists of only two rooms. The place was sold to Thomas Rutledge of Carwoola in 1855 and the Kings left the district. They asked that the name of the place be spelt 'Gidleigh' but the wool is still sold with the 'Gidley' brand.

Thomas Rutledge (1818–1904) came from Ballymagirl, County Cavan, to join his brother William (1806–1870) in about 1840. After the discovery of Lake George in 1820, the 'new country' opened up very quickly. To the south of Goulburn the main south road, and later the railway, followed the

The furniture did not originate at Gidleigh. The side-board is an old colonial piece which looks as though it was built for the alcove it is in. The picture above, by a French artist, is of the Italian Maritime Alps. The picture above the mantelpiece is by Conrad Martens, showing the Palmer, later the Riley, Woolloomooloo Farm, built about 1800, in the foreground; St James's Church and Hyde Park Barracks are in the background. The three-piece mahogany table is Georgian and the chairs are sixty-year-old English reproduction Chippendale. The glass cabinet was a doorway until 1935. The thick stone walls are typical throughout this old part of the house.

watershed of the Great Divide via Lake Bathurst, Bungendore and Queanbeyan to outside the Limits of Location: the Monaro and Cooma.

In 1836 and 1837 William Rutledge bought 2,560 acres (1,020 hectares) taken up by Gilbert Henry Smith in 1828 on the Molonglo Plains, and a further 1,260 acres (500 hectares) taken up by Edward John Eyre (the explorer to be). To these he added the Balcombe Farm, whose owner had named it 'The Briars' after his house on St Helena. William, a man of tremendous energy, seized every opportunity that came his way. He eventually settled at Port Fairy in Victoria, leaving his brother Thomas in charge of his interests in New South Wales.

Thomas married his cousin Martha (daughter of Dr Thomas Forster and Eliza, daughter of Gregory Blaxland of Brush Farm). In due course he bought the Carwoola property and built a handsome Georgian house for his bride in the late eighteen-forties—situated twelve miles (nineteen kilometres) from Queanbeyan and Bungendore, on a site where other substantial buildings were already in existence. Throughout his life, Thomas made additions and subtractions to his property which, in 1870, was misleadingly described as 'the Model Farm Par Excellence of N.S.W.', when his territory covered 55,000 acres (22,000 hectares) of purchased land and considerable areas of leasehold beyond.

The cottage verandah, with its home-made brick floor and the shingles under the iron roof.

The 1890 view of the vegetable garden. The sapling just visible at the rear grew into the great oak tree that dominates the courtyard today. ABOVE LEFT

The courtyard was originally the back yard on to which the kitchens opened. There was a verandah (now closed in) similar to the one at the front. Extensive additions were made in 1920, lengthening the kitchen wing with an upper storey for bachelor quarters. A billiards room was built on the south side of the court to join on to the 'Turkey' room with a wooden verandah facing north. It is now the living room. The courtyard once bounded by an ivy hedge has now been opened up to include the large oak tree and, at the end, the King cottage with its formal garden.

The King homestead is built of local stone and rough-cast. The doors are six-panelled and the casement windows typical of the period. The joinery is all cedar.

The earliest building on Gidleigh, built by the Kings as a stable and a stronghold with loopholes. Built of stone and rendered, it has a hipped roof and a large loft. It is now used to provide storage, in rat-proofed rooms, for saddles and similar items.

The paving of the stable floor is made of two-foot hexagonal pieces of hardwood hammered into the ground. There is a similar non-slip paving in the stable of Lanyon, A.C.T.

Gidleigh, closer to Bungendore, was run as an outstation for twenty years until it was made over to Thomas's eldest son, William Forster. W. F. Rutledge registered the Merino Stud, No. 44, in 1882 and in the same year started to build the second homestead, the plans of which were drawn by the distinguished architect, W. W. Wardell. It was said that Thomas Rutledge thought the house was much too large for a bachelor and ordered that the rooms should be made smaller by two feet, so the foundations had to be altered at considerable cost. No one knows now how true this story is or from where the unwanted feet were removed. However, the rooms do seem rather high for their size, but a taller generation appreciates the good clearance in the doorways. Only the drawing-room, now the main bedroom, and the dining-room, have the pretty panelling round the sash windows and deep reveals. The cornices in these rooms and ceiling roses are handsome, and all the rooms have beautiful cedar joinery and hard wood floors.

The house is built of stone, quarried on the place, with a stucco finish now painted pink. It had a double entrance hall leading to a central passage with a side door to the west and a back door opposite the front door. All the rooms have large fireplaces of cedar or marble of good design. Gidleigh was thickly timbered, unlike the plains, and firewood was no problem in the past. Today we are thankful to Thomas that there are not those extra cubic feet of space to heat. The house was originally lit with acetylene gas and lamps; later by an electric generator, not powerful enough to run electrical appliances. After World War Two Gidleigh joined the State grid.

Most of the subsequent additions were made after World War One. These include staff quarters, an upper storey near the entrance for bachelor quarters, and the billiards room that joins on to the 'Turkey' room. The masons were sufficiently skilled to make it unnecessary to use stucco. Further internal alterations were made when Thomas Lloyd Forster Rutledge married.

Gidleigh has been effectively watered by bores and windmills as there is good sub-artesian water on the property and a high water table. This is most necessary, as the creeks cease to run in summer.

T. L. F. Rutledge made a total of 14,000 acres (5,600 hectares) available voluntarily for soldier settlement after both world wars. Since his death the boundaries have contracted considerably, but thanks to his vigorous programme of pasture improvement carried on through the years, the place is able to run the merino sheep (no longer a stud) and an Aberdeen Angus stud. Gidleigh is owned by the Rutledge family under the name of Gidleigh Pty Ltd.

The stone and brick work of the 1920 additions.

The station store. Once, one room was used as a bacon store and there were rat-proof bins big enough to take a truck-load of sugar. A leather room was used to repair harness and make rawhide ropes. T. L. F. Rutledge was skilled in this work, especially plaiting leather. Behind the store was a forge for pointing tools. (The blacksmith's shop was in another farm building where the stables are now.)

The new front door on the south front (c. 1949). The ingenious design is by John Stephen Mansfield. It comes at the end of the long closed-in verandah and fits charmingly into a house in which no part of the additions match any other part. The cottage inspired the proportions of its side lights, six-panelled door and iron grill.

The view west along the splendid flagstone verandah with its eighteen columns; groups of three are at each corner and two pairs are either side of the front door. Finely dressed stone was used for the front of the house and corner quoins; the remainder is constructed of rubble, stuccoed and lined to resemble stone. The family peacocks are very fond of this verandah.

OPPOSITE The verandah with its fine colonnade, returns around each side of the house to the strangers' rooms at the commencement of the wings. These rooms were for late visitors, who did not need to disturb the household. The eastern one is now the kitchen. The parapets above have been extended by the present owner as a reinforcement against earthquake damage. Sadly the rear wings have gone. A previous owner bulldozed them into the cellar and cemented over the entrance and courtyard flagstones. Glenrock still retains the original roof of Welsh slate.

The impressive front door has a generous fanlight, with the radiating lines being continued into the surrounding stone arch. Inside, a cantilevered stair with plain iron rails goes up the left wall of the wide hall. Missing is the entablature, which was decorated with the traditional dentals and hid the verandah roof. The present owners hope to restore this most necessary feature of the classical verandah.

Glenrock New South Wales

Text: Caroline Simpson   Photographs: Kerry Dundas

THE EARLIEST TYPE OF architecture in Australia conforms to the severe classical lines of Georgian designs, and one of the finest examples in this style is Glenrock, at Marulan in New South Wales.

It was built by George Barber, the first settler to this 'new country', which was described on 24 March 1818 by that competent explorer and reporter, Dr Charles Throsby, thus: 'Through a very rotten, stony, poor country, over a small stream of water [Barber's Creek at Tallong] to a beautiful piece of fine forest called Mooroowoolin.'

George Barber was born at Ryde on the Isle of Wight in 1796. He was the son of a sea captain, also named George, and his wife Jane Romaine. While George was still a child, Captain Barber and his ship were lost at sea and a family story tells that Mrs Barber set forth around the world seeking news of her husband and his cargo of grog.

The 1828 census tells us that a Mrs Jane Throsby arrived on the *Coromandel* in 1802. Dr Charles Throsby was also on board as the ship's surgeon, and Mrs Barber became his wife, but where or when is unknown. As families of the ship's company were frequently omitted from the passenger list, and there is no Mrs Barber on *Coromandel*'s list, it may be assumed that they married in England or at sea.

Coromandel was due to call at Rio de Janeiro, but, according to a passenger named George Hall, Dr Throsby decided against this because of the diseases there, and the long voyage was taken with no ports of call.

In 1814 young George Barber arrived in Sydney on board *Broxbornbury* to join his mother and step-father at Glenfield, Minto, where the Throsbys had settled in 1809. On 6 February of the following year he married Isabella Hume at St John's, Parramatta. Witnesses to the marriage were James Meehan, government surveyor, and the bride's parents, Elizabeth and Andrew Hume. The Barbers settled on a 100-acre grant named Elverstock at Appin, in the County of Airds, where Isabella's family were also living.

By 1820 George Barber was finding this property too small for his increasing herds and wrote to Governor Macquarie for land in the County of Argyle. He would have heard about this new country from his brother-in-law, Hamilton Hume, who, by the age of nineteen had made three successful journeys of exploration south as far as the present village of Bungonia.

The Governor obliged by promising 300 acres in Argyle (31 March 1821) and his successor, Governor Brisbane promised 500 acres (5 June 1824) alongside.

In 1826 George and Isabella and five children were settled on their new property named Glenrock. On 10 October that year he wrote to the Colonial Secretary for more land, describing his situation thus: 'I am in possession of 900 acres of land by grant of which 127 acres are cleared. I possess 300 cattle, 1500 sheep and 10 horses. In Airds I have erected a substantial and commodious Dwelling House (£200), a Barn, Kitchen and out-houses (£100). In Argyle I have built an excellent House (£300), a Barn, Men's Huts (£50). I have completed 8 miles of Fence and employed and maintained 7 convict servants.'

This first Glenrock was situated at the gully end of Old Farm Paddock towards Barber's Creek. Later descriptions of this house give it as '40 by 26 feet, mud plastered containing 9 rooms with slab and shingle out-buildings, detached kitchen, stable, dairy, men's huts, school house, barn, tradesmen's shops and piggery'.

Nearby is Greenhill, a treeless hill with a permanent spring on top, ensuring good pasture in dry times. Today one finds on a knoll boulders of granite and sandstone and assorted bricks, all that remains of this homestead. Still blooming are acacias and a pear tree, which have survived the years as well as bushfires, and blue and white iris spread themselves from the flagstone garden paths out into the paddocks.

From old Glenrock one looks eastwards to Long Nose Point across Barber's Creek, which cuts its way through steep gullies to join the Shoalhaven River. It was down one of these gullies that Edward Raworth Barber fell to his death at the age of ten on Boxing Day 1843.

The Great South Road at that time turned left after the Barber's Creek bridge, by the present village of Tallong, and Barber's station was a mile further on. Major Mitchell, writing in 1830 of his proposed New Line of road southwards, now the Hume Highway, said: 'The circuitous direction of the present road, southward from Barber's, which is nearer the Shoalhaven Gullies, crosses some very rocky hills and hollows. The newly marked line avoids these.'

The new road was a relief for the Barber family, as Glenrock was constantly invaded by overnight travellers seeking their fortune in the new country. A memorial to Governor Darling from George Barber in 1829 seeks permission to build an Inn: 'That from the great inconvenience which travellers experience in travelling from Sutton Forest to Goulburn Plains and Inverary for want of accommodation to lodge themselves.' He was supported in this request by other gentlemen of the district: James Atkinson of Oldbury, David Reid of Inverary, and Robert Futter of Lumley—all anxious to rid their houses of the travellers.

During the 1830s George Barber wrote many letters to the Colonial Secretary imploring for the deeds to his grants and applying for land on the Yass Plains, which he had discovered with Hamilton Hume and W. H. Broughton in 1821. After confirmation of the title to his land was finally secured on 4 October 1834, he was probably thinking of a more substantial house for his increasing family of, eventually, fourteen children, and commenced plans for the present Glenrock. About this time he sold some land for town lots in the new village of Marulan (gazetted

Mrs John Morrice lived at Glenrock from 1863 until her death there in 1916 aged ninety-three. She was Jane, a daughter of James Osborne from Yackandandah and Isabella Osborne, a sister of Henry Osborne of Marshall Mount. She remembered seeing Glenrock while it was being built, and recalled that Italian stonemasons were employed—not convict labour. Unfortunately the year of this visit to the Barbers was not recorded and the year of Glenrock's completion remains unknown. Her family recalls that she was never seen with her head uncovered and always wore a lace cap.

These two well-proportioned rooms, once the breakfast-room and dining-room divided by tall panelled folding doors, now make a fine sitting-room. The walls are painted antique gold and the ceiling and cove, twin fireplaces and joinery are all white. Above the near fireplace hangs an eighteenth-century mirror, with figures of Hindu gods on the mantelshelf and, to the left, a painting by Haughton James. Two french windows with panelled reveals open on to the verandah, while at the other end of the room a tall sash window has interior panelled shutters folding into the reveals.

53

From the dining-room, formerly the Morrice sitting-room, one looks through the cedar door into the library. The fine Georgian table is decorated with phoenix from Thailand; around it are Queen Anne style chairs covered in embossed velvet. The fireplace, with its simple cedar surround matching the others in the house, still has its original grate and above, on the mantelshelf, is a Boulle clock. The gentleman's portrait is a Victorian reproduction. The eighteenth-century chandelier is lit by candles, throwing a pleasant light on to the dinner table.

A watercolour of Glenrock, painted in 1935 by E. Warner, shows the classical entablature and the western courtyard wing. This wing contained a dairy, maid's room for two and terminated with the bathroom. In the opposite wing were the pantry, the scullery and the kitchen at the end. On the side elevations are blind windows to balance the real ones, thereby giving the four corner bedrooms more wall space. All over the garden grew that sweet-perfumed rose, the pink Countess Bertha, planted during the last century. The circular beds were full of iris and bright verbenas, with an occasional buddleia to attract the butterflies and birds.

The coach house and stables, with accommodation for four horses, are made of random stone with dressed stone lintels. The loft above was converted to an architect's office by the present owner. Nearby is a similar stone building, once the laundry and yardman's room, which has been converted with additions to a manager's cottage. Both these buildings once had double ladder stairs to their lofts. The disastrous fires of 1964 swept away all other outbuildings, including the woolshed which stood over the railway line by Woolshed Creek. This was a slab building with shingle roof, later covered with iron by George Morrice, and was known as the coolest shed in the district.

11 March 1835), which was situated where Major Mitchell marked a tree to divide the south road to Goulburn and Bungonia.

One wonders where George and Isabella found the design for the new Glenrock. Was it copied from a house they knew in England or did a contemporary architect design it for them?

Tragedy then struck, just as the family settled into their beautiful new house. Returning from Goulburn one evening, George Barber disappeared. He was last seen passing the New Inn at Towrang and his horse was found later by the swollen Wollondilly River at Lockyersleigh. Three months later his body was found by Charles Lockyer further down this river. His father-in-law, Andrew Hume had meanwhile offered rewards of £25 for the recovery of the body and £100 for evidence of foul play, but the *Sydney Morning Herald* reported on 9 September 1844 that he was 'accidently drowned on a dark tempestuous night'.

At the old Marulan cemetery there is an endearing memorial to George Barber inscribed on the vault which Isabella had built for her father after his death at Glenrock in 1849. This vault has undergone recent restoration by their descendants.

Isabella continued at Glenrock with her younger children until her death in 1855. Among marriages of the elder children were Mary Romaine to David Reid Jnr; Ann Elizabeth to Dr Robert Waugh; and Charles Hume Barber to Mary Ann Hume. It was this last-named couple who changed the spelling to Barbour, which some say was the original spelling, but Andrew Hume persuaded his son-in-law to use 'common English' so that that generation remained Barber.

In 1862 Glenrock was for sale—'a building of cut stone on 944 acres adjoining Marulan township—excellent grazing land and a comfortable income from the great number of teams constantly camped there'. It was bought by Mr and Mrs John Morrice of Sutton Forest.

John Morrice, lately a tea planter in Jamaica, had arrived in Sydney in 1834 on board the *James*, a vessel chartered by Dr John Dunmore Lang

for free immigrants. At Pernambuco provisions ran so short that Dr Lang was obliged to borrow some money from John Morrice to replenish supplies. In repayment, Lang gave his grant of 1,000 acres at Sutton Forest to John Morrice.

At All Saint's, Sutton Forest, on 9 November 1838, John married Jane Osborne, and they settled on this land where, during the 1840s, they built Eling Forest; while a brother, William Morrice, built Comfort Hill. In 1863, with the younger children from a family of twelve, they moved to Glenrock.

The railway reached Glenrock in 1867. A new township called Mooroowoolen was planned around the station, then the busy terminus of the southern line, and John Morrice sold town lots for this purpose. Meanwhile Marulan declined and was abandoned, the name being transferred to the village with the railway station.

John Morrice died in 1876 from a heart attack after fighting bushfires. After his widow's death in 1916, their bachelor son, George Joseph Morrice, took over Glenrock.

An energetic man, he enlarged the holding to 8,000 acres (3,200 hectares), re-fenced it and eradicated the rabbits. He would scythe the garden grass himself; grass through which ixias, wild orchids and wood hyacinths flowered in profusion between scythings. (Our present method of mowing does not give bulbs and wild plants such a chance.)

This detail is the top of one of the fluted sandstone columns, beautifully carved from one piece of stone. The sandstone came from the Bundanoon direction, as Glenrock is on granite country, and was hauled the ten or so miles by bullock teams. These columns, along with the windows and chimneys, are carefully balanced about the central doorway; a symmetry typical of Georgian architecture.

A view across the garden to the house, framed with tall elms and pines which managed to survive the 1964 bushfire, has an air of restfulness beside the clean lines of the house. Today a pond and lawns planted with silver birches and willows replace the flower beds for easier management. Originally the front garden was enclosed with a circular top-rail fence, planted inside with a white hawthorn hedge, clipped to fence level. A double picket gate gave access to the front door across the lawn—there was never a carriage loop at Glenrock.

George Morrice lived at Glenrock until his death in 1944 at the age of ninety-six. For his last twenty years his niece, Miss Sylvia Morrice, kept house for him. She recalls that life with uncle, 'a dear and a character', had quite a nineteenth century air about it.

Water was carried from the pump at the well in the courtyard which filled from the roof rainwater. In the wintertime six or so fires would be kept going all day, the wood being supplied by the yardman, who also milked the cow. Every morning the maid whitewashed these fireplaces with pipe clay from Lumley Park. To take a bath, one carried a bucket of hot water drawn from the kitchen tank on the fuel stove across the courtyard to the bathroom. Uncle did, however, allow some modern inventions to intrude: the petrol lamps were replaced with electric lights and his four-wheel buggy was discarded for a Studebaker which he drove immediately, seeing no reason for a lesson nor a licence.

The twenty-eight beneficiaries of George Morrice's estate put Glenrock on the market, and it was bought by the Government to be divided amongst soldier settlers. The house was emptied of its furniture and the contents of a century; the coach house of its carriages and harness; and the barns of the horse-drawn machinery. Fortunately records of the whereabouts of some pieces belonging to both the Morrice and Barber families have been kept by the Misses Morrice.

Little interest was shown locally in this fine house over the next few years when it suffered some unfortunate alterations, including the demolition of the rear wings and the removal of the verandah entablature. Due to the sub-divisions the entrance was moved to the Bundanoon road. (Originally it was on the highway opposite the All Saint's Rectory.) In 1964 Carol and Peter Muller bought Glenrock with 800 hectares, and they have both devoted much time and care to its sympathetic restoration.

The bookshelves and panelling in the library are of maple, stained a cedar colour, and were built by Peter Muller for this room. The hardwood floor of pit-sawn planks here and through to the dining-room are original. Elsewhere the floors were replaced during the 1930s because of dry rot, encouraged it is believed by the linoleum floor coverings of that era. A Balinese painting decorates one wall and beside the sofa stands a nineteenth-century collection of lithographs of Japan's national treasures. This room has a sash window similar to the one in the sitting-room.

Emu Bottom *Victoria*

Text: Elisabeth Grove   *Photographs: Irvine Green*

FOR MOST OF US, Melbourne begins with Batman and Fawkner, those ambitious individualists who, without the blessing of the Government of New South Wales, both laid claim to the rich grazing lands of Port Phillip in 1835. Even so, a number of other pioneers deserve equally to be remembered with the first; among them George Evans, builder and earliest inhabitant of Emu Bottom. Evans's individuality, however, was of the kind to thrust him away from the centre of attention very early in the history of the Port Phillip settlement.

By 1836, primitive Melbourne had not long been formed by the combined, if competitive, efforts of John Batman and John Pascoe Fawkner, both of whom had found Van Diemen's Land too small for their swelling pastoral ambitions. Most accounts of the founding of the city tell of Batman first: 'purchasing' the land for his Port Phillip Association from the incumbent Doutta Galla tribe, leaving a few men stationed at Indented Head; then of Fawkner's party actually deciding on the present site of the city, building the first shelter and tilling the soil. What is often forgotten is that this first settlement did not immediately include Fawkner who, forced by acute sea-sickness, had put ashore and turned back soon after leaving Georgetown. Among those on board his aptly named vessel the *Enterprise*, which sailed up the Yarra on 29 August 1835, was George Evans, who, as a builder, almost certainly had a hand in constructing the first building in Melbourne. As 'Garryowen' reports in his *Chronicles of Early Melbourne* this was a crude hut of 'sods, earth and branches, a kind of structure by which to shelter their provisions and themselves'.

On his own report, it was Evans who first rebuffed Batman's absolute claim to the land on the Yarra. Perturbed at sighting the *Enterprise* in the Bay, a man called Wedge, together with others of Batman's Indented Head camp, arrived at the new settlement claiming prior possession. The test Evans applied to this claim was a canny one: he agreed to relinquish the land only if Wedge could demonstrate by way of marked trees or any other sign that his party had been there previously. When Wedge was unable to fulfil this condition, Evans and his group stayed firmly put, refusing again to leave when Batman himself, a much more impressive opponent, arrived later to establish himself with family, servants, supplies and a wooden house (which, prefabricated, he had brought with him).

By the end of 1835, Batman and Fawkner having reached a workable but unfriendly compromise over the distribution and ownership of land, the young settlement began to attract increasing numbers of prospective squatters and speculators. At this point, the fortunes of the future city and

The idle buggy standing by lends an increased air of desertion to the rough slab cowshed, its long bark roof battened down with an openwork of saplings. This primitive sturdy structure fitting the grounds so well is, in fact, a recent reconstruction of a previous outbuilding.

58

of George Evans diverge. After a short period which from one account may have been spent superintending Fawkner's notoriously uncomfortable public house, the only one in town, Evans set about organizing the transport of his own stock and provisions from Van Diemen's Land, in company with two others of the original party, the brothers Samuel and William Jackson, one an architect, the other a carpenter. Undaunted by losing a large number of their precious sheep in a mishap off Georgetown, they landed at Williamstown on 10 July 1836 and struck out on horseback in search of promising pasture. This they found in abundance some sixteen miles inland among the rolling hills and rich alluvial flats of the country round the creek called Sunburra by the Aborigines. Here, on the banks of the creek which gave Sunbury its name (though some say the town is named after a village on the Thames), the company made its first settlement of wattle-and-daub huts.

Even today, approached by freeway and well-surfaced country road, past those symbols of twentieth-century prosperity, airport and brick-

The ancient gum in the foreground (seen more slenderly elegant in the 1880s photograph on page 60) is a fitting companion to the homestead and its attached stable. Solid, sober, and still fresh from restoration, the homestead's white-painted walls gleam in the sunlight. A sloping verandah shelters the oldest section of the house, once separate from its right-angled later addition; neatly overlapping cedar shingles recently replaced the galvanized iron which had been superimposed on the early hand-cut shingles.

59

Seen from across the creek, the homestead as it was in the 1880s, when its two wings were still detached. Apart from this, the low picket-fence partly obscuring it, and the chimney on the wall of the verandah-less wing, the house was much as it is now. There is still some dispute about the small precariously-propped hut (CENTRE) which may predate the homestead. It is, understandably, no longer there.

OPPOSITE *Sapling poles supporting the verandah of the oldest wing contrast with the bulky post-and-rail fence and the still-growing trees which overshadow the grounds in front and sketch themselves on the sky behind. The later addition of the right wing to the house gave opportunity for larger windows and increased living space.*

The solid elegance of the outbuildings is evident in the sweep of shingled roof from the peak of the stable to the smithy front, and in the pleasing blend of uneven white-washed stone with rough timber slabs. The chimney rising from the centre of the smithy was added recently to enable this vanishing craft to be practised again.

veneered suburbs, the trip to Sunbury is not short. It is not difficult to imagine how very arduous it was then for that first group of settlers who, without benefit of maps or previous training, explored, surveyed and settled so much undomesticated territory. But domesticate it they did, particularly Evans; when their combined flock increased beyond the capacity of the first run, he parted company with the Jacksons and taking his servant-shepherd Evan Evans, moved two-and-a-half miles further upstream. The run he called Emu Bottom, because it was low-lying ground and the haunt of numerous emus. At the time, and given the enormous physical difficulties of this newly discovered area, the stone house he built for himself was a surprisingly solid and ambitious construction, grander by far than the makeshift slab or wattle-and-daub huts usually cast up by busy squatters. Such land-holders would, as their fortunes prospered, then assert permanency and status, aggrandizing their houses as outward and impressive signs of success. Evans, no doubt, also erected temporary huts, but from the manner of its construction his house was very early and meant to last: its two-feet-thick walls of silurian sand-stone were hand-hewn from the encircling hills, the blocks packed together with mud.

To an eye accustomed to the Victorian splendours of Western District homesteads—Italianate decoration, neo-Gothic fantasies, draughty amplitude—Emu Bottom must seem modestly unpretentious. Constructed on a simple L-plan, its two wings thrust at right angles to each other, verandahed on one side, single-storeyed and protected by a scatter of similarly low-slung outbuildings. And on such comparative terms it *is* a humble building. Yet its recognizable Georgian origin and features should be kept in mind, for the first wing is said to date from the late 1830s, when Victoria's reign had scarcely begun: this would put it among the oldest surviving homesteads in the State. With other domestic buildings of the period, Emu Bottom shares a sensibly human scale, a classical solidity and simplicity of line. Typically, twelve-paned, deeply-recessed windows recall the mathematical finesse of the Old World. Perhaps, though, the un-Georgian qualities of the house are even more distinctive: it is without the elegant symmetry, high finish, smooth surfaces and interior flourishes of so much Georgian architecture. More improvised, masculine and rough-hewn, the homestead is intelligently adapted to a new, utterly different environment, at one with the harshness of an untamed landscape and reflecting the rigours of pioneering life. Such details too as the wide verandah shading the east-facing first wing, a feature not altogether usual at the time, and the ample loft of the second wing, a means of storage and insulation, both witness to an inventive architect.

And by all accounts Evans *was* a shrewdly resourceful man: independent, practical and solid, though without the flamboyant ambitions of pioneers like Batman and Fawkner. Mostly, what we know of him derives from the quite detailed history and memories of Sunbury produced in the early years by Isaac Batey, a neighbour and younger contemporary of Evans. From this and other sources we learn that, born in 1785, fifth son of a Plymouth builder, Evans was a boy of fifteen when he participated in the

Carrying the shingles overhead, the sturdy crossed beams of the verandah roof are surprisingly at one with the squares of the twelve-paned window, light and elegant. The thickness of the stone walls appears in the recessed doorway visible on the left; neither door boasts surrounding jamb or decoration, but is set squarely into the heavy walls.

This open-sided lean-to was reconstructed on the model of a smithy at Bacchus Marsh, and furnished with old equipment from it, so that the blacksmith's dying trade could be revived, temporarily at least, when the homestead was open to visitors.

battle led by Nelson in Copenhagen Harbour. There he is reputed to have lost a finger displaying such gallantry as earned Nelson's praise: 'the young man must not be lost sight of'. But Evans does drop from sight; little is known of his career up to 1824 save that he became a builder after completing naval service. His trade, and doubtless the impulse to improve his fortune, drew him to Van Diemen's Land in January 1826 when he joined his brother William's established building firm in Hobart.

Typical of his shrewd practicality, Evans adopted the custom while working for settlers around Launceston of receiving payment not in the usual form of promissory notes but in ewes, which in those days bred even faster than money, thus establishing a substantial flock and his future way of life. So excited was he by Batman's boasting tales of the potential pastoral riches of Port Phillip that, having been refused a place in the Port Phillip Association, he then formed a party with Fawkner and several others to explore the area for grazing. The determination of Evans, Fawkner and party to reach Port Phillip is evident in the story of their confrontation with the Hentys, who at that time had chartered a ship to their whaling station at Portland. Learning of the ship's imminent departure, the Fawkner-Evans party arranged with the Captain to be taken on board and landed at Port Phillip. They had sailed no further than Georgetown when the Hentys objected to the presence of additional passengers and demanded their removal on the grounds of having sole charter of the vessel. But the intruders were equally adamant: having paid for passage they refused to leave. The dispute was resolved only by the intervention of the Georgetown magistrates, who upheld the legality of the Hentys' case and ordered passage-money to be refunded to the off-loaded passengers. Far from dispirited, they managed to cross Bass Strait not long afterwards in the *Enterprise* purchased by Fawkner, the others paying a portion of the cost as passage money.

In Evans's casting himself off from the growing Port Phillip settlement the same kind of determination is manifest, and no less in the kind of dwelling he established at Emu Bottom. Isaac Batey's description of the man tends to corroborate this impression:

> Mr George Evans, though with no claim to be considered handsome, had a fine ruddy face and a pleasant appearance, and was held in respect by all his neighbours. Although his education was scanty he was more of a gentleman than many whom he associated with, and he had a courtesy that was really stately: to show the progressive ideals he entertained, while some were living still in wattle and dab he resided in a comfortable stone house.

Standards of comfort were then, particularly in those circumstances, rather less exacting than our own; it is clear that Evans had little to spend in the early years on luxurious embellishments, let alone such necessities as larders or cellars. Even now, though, his capable craftsmanship remains in the directness of straight stone walls embedded firmly in the earth and in the confident austerity of line which manages at once to blend with and assert dominance over the weathered grassy hills and flats of the landscape.

Evans's desire for permanency and respectability did not stop short with the construction of his sturdy three-roomed house. In 1843, at the age of fifty-eight, he married Ann Holden, a girl of eighteen, who bore him six children. We have, of course, no means of knowing why Evans decided so late in life to marry, but perhaps the same mixture of fore-thought and impulsiveness which brought him to Port Phillip in the first place played some part in bringing about this unlikely match. By this time too, his property was well established, and several years of pioneering beyond the fringes of civilization may have eroded his solitary inde-pendence. Certainly, when Batey knew him, Evans lived in the style of a gentleman: 'he sported a gig and sent divers of his family to be educated in Tasmania, while for the younger members he had a tutor at home'. While life was hard at Emu Bottom, then, it was not without some refinement: simplicity, recreation and neighbourliness prevailed. Indeed, Batey's reminiscences suggest a vigorous masculine camaraderie:

> With the squatters of old, except two very busy times in the course of the year, supposing the station were in full working order, there was nothing to kill time save shooting, fishing or calling upon their neigh-bours. Those visits were made on horseback, except it might be with Jack Page, who would foot it to Jackson's or Evans', and if to the home-stead of the latter he would carry a gun. By his account there were occasions when bronzewing pigeons swarmed at Emu Bottom, because he said one day he bagged 30 of those birds at 31 shots.

The early 1850s saw numerous changes in the homestead and the Sunbury district at large. Emu Bottom was gutted by fire in the early years

63

Behind the house, parallel to the first wing and attached by a low wall of the same stone, the stables echo the homestead in construction and material. Their dimensions, 53 feet by 17 feet, are exactly the same as those in the original wing, a fact which suggests their construction at the same time. The more steeply-pitched roof encloses a grain loft. The wooden lattice-work of the windows was another piece of restoration bringing the building into conformity with early descriptions.

The first room in the oldest wing of the house, furnished as a bedroom. The wooden wash-stand, china basin and ewer, and the simple candlestick on the window-ledge recall the austerity of the pioneers' way of life. The sea-trunk below the window (a souvenir of the long trip from England) takes its place as a useful part of the furnishing.

of the decade, probably during the devastating bushfires of 1851. Traces of damage are still to be seen in the charring of doorways, window frames and fire-place in the first wing. According to Batey the rebuilding of the fire-damaged section was followed rapidly by the addition of the second, at right angles to it, but detached from it, as was frequently the custom in early homestead construction. Consistent in style with the earlier wing but much more ample in dimension, it comprised a large kitchen, storage-loft overhead, a cool-room or larder leading off the kitchen, and a spacious, high-ceilinged parlour. The absence of any verandah lays bare the simple symmetry of the new wing and its sturdy irregular stone face. By this time, the family must have found their original quarters extremely cramped and welcomed these new facilities for cooking and entertaining. Though no precise date can be ascribed to the addition, its greater comfort and elegance reflect a later growth of prosperity, respectability, and family.

However, his time at Emu Bottom was to be shorter than Evans can have anticipated. Like other squatters in the outer pastoral areas of the Port Phillip district, he could not own his run. The Government of New South Wales had decreed that all such unsurveyed land remained Crown property and could be held only on a depasturing licence. Under this arrangement the squatter remained extremely vulnerable, as Evans and his neighbours were to discover, after the Sunbury area was officially surveyed in 1851 and became available for purchase. To their dismay the earliest residents found themselves outbid by the immensely wealthy Tasmanian pastoralist, W. J. T. Clarke. In 1853, Big Clarke, as he was not always affectionately called, acquired a huge area of 31,373 acres (12,550 hectares), by what was known as Clarke's Special Survey. This survey swallowed up, among others, the runs held by Evans and the Jacksons— though original occupants did manage by pre-emptive right to retain a homestead block of 640 acres. Jackson sold his to Clarke and moved to a station near Casterton. Rupertswood, the Clarke family residence, a mansion on a grand scale, was later built on the Jackson site. Evans, on the other hand, perhaps out of obstinacy, held onto his block and continued to work it until the late fifties. No longer young, and finding the run too small to be lucrative, he eventually bought himself a hotel in Melbourne, the Royal Oak in Queen Street, to which he moved with his family. Licensee there from 1861 to 1865, and then retired in the house next door, Evans died a city-dweller, aged ninety-two, in 1876. Batey's tribute to him, though incomplete, is a fitting one:

> . . . to give him his due, he was ahead of his brother pioneers in two main essentials. The first was that he did not fool away money; the second—albeit frugal, he was a kind-hearted hospitable man. That he had a reverent care of his health is proved by the patriarchal age to which he attained . . .

Evans's death did not sever his family's connections with Emu Bottom, for the property had been leased since the removal to Melbourne. After building a fine new hotel next to the Royal Oak, and running it for several years, Mrs Evans and several of her children returned in 1888, or thereabouts, to the homestead, where she died in 1893. During those few years she is said to have effected a number of alterations to the property, among which may have been the gaily decorative but incongruous stencilled and painted ceiling in the first bedroom of the old wing. Though both decorator and date are uncertain, the fact that there was a vogue for this kind of design at the time, and that such stylishness is less likely to have been to George Evans's taste than his wife's, suggest this as a likely period for its execution.

Entered through a short passage-way whose opening appears on the left of the last photograph, this room was furnished as a children's bedroom of the 1840s, before being closed to visitors. The decorative knobs and twirls of the cast-iron bed and cot, with their handworked coverlets and curtaining, the carriage-borne china doll, and the array of toys of the period, all evoke surroundings in which the six children of Evans's old age must have played.

Straining forward in mock stone, the fore-shortened bulging putti *intensify the Italianate air of the elaborately stencilled and painted ceiling of the master bedroom. In faded red, green, and grey, and incongruous as it is, this piece of decoration, whose origins are uncertain, strikes a note of formal gaiety above the irregularity of the stone walls.*

Its windows exactly similar in design to those of the old wing, but more ample, the parlour of the second wing reflects the increased prosperity and domestication of the 1850s. The furniture brought into the house by Mr and Mrs Elliott manages to capture the simple comfort and stylishness of the room—as in the elegant curves of the classic Georgian reading-chair drawn close to the table with its reading-lamp. The portrait to the left is a likeness of George Evans himself, copied from a photograph taken in old age. His gaze is concentrated, unsmiling, but not ungenial, framed by a brush of white beard and vigorous side-whiskers.

66

It was not until after 1916 and the death of Evans's eldest son Robert, that Emu Bottom passed from the family. It was owned briefly by Brigadier-General Clarke, and then purchased in 1920 by Mr H. L. Webb. During his ownership, the homestead, which had always been in a slow process of addition and modification, was quite radically altered. Its old name was discarded in favour of Holly Green, the name of Mr Webb's cattle-stud. Realizing the historical significance of the homestead, however, the Webbs were at pains to preserve and protect it. And though the additional verandahs and extensive render on rough stone surfaces would not seem appropriate today (since the homestead came to resemble a quaintly English country cottage, rather than itself), these measures did serve to protect the fabric of the house. Like all buildings that are really lived in, the homestead had changed considerably since Evans's day: galvanized-iron roofing overlaid the original shingles, connecting rooms filled the gap between the two wings, plaster replaced the early calico-lined ceilings, and new outbuildings were added to the original sprawl. When the property was inherited by the Stringer family in 1964, it continued to work as a farm and, opened to the public, it became well known as an historical museum.

Since the Stringers sold out to Mr and Mrs Hedley Elliott in 1968, the past of Evans's time has been re-asserted. Deciding themselves to open the homestead to the public, the Elliotts first restored it as far as possible to its early condition. Under the direction of architects John and Phyllis Murphy, expert and painstaking restoration was carried out: the additions of the previous hundred years or so were unmade. Plaster rendering was stripped from walls inside and out; red-cedar shingles replaced galvanized-iron roofs; new verandah-posts and boards, reconstructed out-buildings (some imported from elsewhere) to house such activities as shearing and milking—all these and other changes were made. Faithfulness of detail is evident everywhere, from the gathering of furniture and household bits and pieces of the 1840s, to the calico-clad ceilings of the old wing. At its busiest, the refurbished homestead was the setting for a working panorama of pioneer ways of life. But since early 1975, the flow of tourists and schoolchildren has ceased. The Elliotts are living at Emu Bottom and plan, with minimal alteration for modern convenience, to occupy it as a private dwelling and to work the land: thus returning the house to its traditional use.

The private visitor to Emu Bottom nowadays winds through the low falls and rises of the countryside, a terrain half-hidden in a fold behind the township. Evans's homestead stands secure and independent, its history lovingly preserved; whereas grandiose neighbouring Rupertswood, the expression of a Clarke dynasty's success, which once threatened to engulf the pioneer's modest holding, is now a Salesian college, hemmed in by Sunbury and hard-pressed by its rapid twentieth-century sprawl.

Maryland *New South Wales*

Text: James Broadbent   Photographs: Kerry Dundas

'THE PIONEER SQUIRES chose serene summits on which to place their homesteads. They had no climatic rigours to contend with and feared no hostile invasions. Selecting the tallest hills upon estates presented by the Crown, they built with taste and imagination, settling their white-walled houses like snowflakes fallen on cushions of verdure. Tranquillity surrounded them. Thus situated like monarchs on their own hill-tops, at the head of assigned garrisons, they saw the world at their feet, without thought of conquest. Their ramparts were fences to keep off trespassing cattle.'

In *The Cow Pasture Road* Hardy Wilson evoked the mellow atmosphere of homesteads such as Maryland in rambling gardens where 'plumbago blossoms, and the olive casts its flickering shade', which lay to the south-west of Sydney in the County of Cumberland. Sadly, in the half century since Wilson followed the Cow Pasture Road from Parramatta to Camden, many of these houses have fallen to progress: Greystanes, Bungarribee and Leppington, needlessly destroyed; Denham Court and Horsely stripped of the paddocks they were built to survey, their outbuildings made useless, demolished or crumbling in ruin. Those that remain, like Maryland, are under seige in a way Hardy Wilson could not have imagined on his country walks: their tranquillity endangered by expressways and motor race-ways; their fences now ramparts against encroaching suburbia.

Approaching Maryland on a warm summer day one can appreciate Wilson's romantic evocation of long, hipped-roofed, verandahed cottages, gently crowning their hilltops half hidden in shrubberies. Leaving the Northern Road from Camden, the long, dusty drive crosses paddocks, brown with the summer heat, and climbs slowly towards the elegant, white-painted garden gates. A pretty Gothic lodge of golden sandstone with decorative bargeboards and an open porch, stands guard, or drowses, behind low-clipped hedges of plumbago, which edge the drive as it continues within the dappled shade of overhanging olives to the house. Red geraniums glow in the sunlight that falls on the worn stone-flagged floors of the verandahs and reflects on their white, wide-boarded ceilings. Close by on the lawn stands a rain gauge from which readings are recorded daily, as they have been since Maryland's builder, Thomas Barker, first began the practice in 1867.

As the *Australian Dictionary of Biography* records, Thomas Barker was born in Soho, London in 1799, the son of James and Mary Barker. Orphaned at the age of nine, he arrived in Sydney on the *Earl Spencer* in November 1813 with John Dickson, an engineer and manufacturer to whom he was apprenticed.

'Having brought a Considerable Capital with him and being of an Enterprizing Spirit and persevering Industry' Dickson was regarded by Governor Macquarie as 'a very great Acquisition to the Colony'. His 'Considerable Capital' and 'Enterprizing Spirit' were principally employed in the setting up of the steam-engine which he had brought with him from his Southwark manufactory, intending to use it to power sawmills and tanbark mills. For this enterprise he received a town grant in 1815 on Cockle Bay, now Darling Harbour. The mill commenced operation in the same year but seems to have been used only for milling grain.

Dickson expanded his business in 1826 by establishing with John Mackie a brewery and soap and candle works near his flour mill; however, the partnership was dissolved in 1829. During this time he was also amassing a considerable land holding. By 1828 Dickson had 17,000 acres (6,800 hectares) of land. His first rural grant, in 1815, was of 3,000 acres (1,200 hectares) at Bringelly in the County of Cumberland, which he named Nonorrah.

In 1833 he decided to sell his steam-mill and return to England. In 1838 he instructed his agent, Matthew D. Hunter, to sell parts of his real estate in the countries of Cumberland and Argyle. He died in London in 1843.

Maryland is of stone rubble construction, rendered, with sandstone quoins and delightful Gothic chimneys also of sandstone. The three french doors lead from the verandah into the original dining- and drawing-rooms, now two drawing-rooms. Low hedges of plumbago edge the lawn, which is raised above the drive. In late summer the beautiful, deep pink blossom of oxalis clothes the banks, and tall bunya-bunyas stand like sentinels in the garden below.

A large underground sandstone cistern still supplies water to the house. The old hand pump with its functional, elegant handle was, until 1940, the only source of household water.

The northern or entrance front. Columns of turned timber support the verandah, whose white, wide-boarded ceilings reflect the sunlight falling on the worn stone flagging. Neat hedges of plumbago, a feature of Maryland's garden, edge the verandah to either side of the entrance steps.
OPPOSITE

Old olives overhang the rear courtyard, casting delicate shadows on the paving; the bell, once used to summon workmen, is now silent. The rear sections of the house are believed, traditionally, to be part of an earlier dwelling.

Dickson's apprentice, Thomas Barker, exceeded even his master in being of 'Enterprizing Spirit and persevering Industry'. By 1826, in partnership with John Smith, Barker commenced his own milling operations by erecting a large stone windmill on Woolloomooloo Hill. Another mill followed. Surrounded by the fashionable villas of Sydney's élite, including his own lavish Roslyn Hall, the Barker mills became landmarks on the ridge to the east of the city. Within a short time Barker had purchased and enlarged a steam-flour mill near the corner of Sussex and Bathurst Streets and, in 1847, on land adjacent to his flour mill, he began the construction of a tweed mill which he ran from 1852 until 1862.

Thomas Barker survived the financial crash of the eighteen-forties which ruined many of his contemporaries, including his brother James, who had also entered the milling business in partnership with the architect Ambrose Hallen. His business career spanned a remarkable half century of development, from 1820 to 1870. Making a fortune in the early thirties Barker did not become one of those 'overgrown Millers' whom he set out to oppose in 1826, but earned a reputation for his honesty and reliability in business matters and became a respected figure in public affairs, being a member of the Legislative Council from 1853 until 1856 and a member of the Legislative Assembly from 1856 to 1857. His interest in the encouragement of education is of particular note. In 1831 he was elected to the council of the Australian College, in 1848 he became a member of the Denominational School Board. He was a council member of the Sydney College, and also served as a trustee of Sydney Grammar School and the Sydney Mechanics' School of Arts. His gift of one thousand pounds for a scholarship for proficiency in mathematics was the first direct benefaction to the University of Sydney. In recognition of this his portrait was commissioned to hang in the Great Hall.

In 1823 Thomas Barker married Joanna Dickson, niece of John Dickson and daughter of James and Helen Dickson of Bringelly. Presumably it was on John Dickson's farm Nonorrah that Joanna Barker's parents lived. However, by 1834, according to the diary of D. L. Waugh, Barker had become the owner of Nonorrah, as well as nearby Orielton and Mummel on the Goulburn Plains. There is a tradition, unsubstantiated, that Nonorrah was given as a wedding gift to Thomas and Joanna. He had also obtained further land on Woolloomooloo Hill, and in 1833 built Roslyn Hall to the design of Ambrose Hallen. Joanna Barker died in 1851 and in 1857 Barker married Katherine Heath Grey, a daughter of Charles Heath Grey who had come to Sydney as a clerk in Governor King's time.

It is at this time, when Barker ceases to be a prominent figure in public and business affairs, that Maryland's history really begins. Its history is not that of Thomas Barker's success or of any notable events; it is simply that of being cherished and enriched for over a century by the two generations of the two families who have lived contentedly under its roof. In December 1859 Barker, then aged sixty, sold Roslyn Hall with its 'Fretted roofs—Turkey Carpets & Crystal Handles to the doors', and retired with his new bride to his Cow Pasture hilltop. As if to symbolize a new phase in his life he renamed it Maryland, perhaps in honour of his mother, Mary Shuldham, whose family's arms he had wished to adopt.

A small octagonal skylight in the corner of the vestibule ceiling lights the door to the large drawing-room. The delicacy of its glazing pattern and panelled shaft can, however, only be appreciated from directly below.

The mantelpiece in the smaller drawing-room is of grey marble in an unusually chaste design. The mirror above it, in contrasting dull and burnished gilt, belonged to Thomas Barker, as did the cast-iron fire grate.

Well-to-do, although perhaps not as wealthy as in the palmy years before the depression of the eighteen-forties, and generally respected, he lived quietly at Maryland until his death in 1875.

In 1860 his only child, Thomas Charles Barker, was born. He inherited Maryland from his father and lived there throughout his life, extending the gardens but otherwise leaving Maryland unaltered since his father's day. To him we can attribute the extensive planting, the bold clumps of Chinese elms, callitris, service trees and stone pines, which create the impressive park-like landscape seen from the Northern Road.

Thomas Charles Barker married Emily Macarthur Chisholm of nearby Gledswood, but there were no children, and on his death in 1940 Maryland was sold to the late Mr and Mrs N. A. Thomson, whose daughters Elizabeth and Annette continue to preserve those qualities which Hardy Wilson found so appealing in Cow Pasture houses, while maintaining Maryland's reputation as a fine grazing property.

When the present house at Maryland was built is uncertain. The only record of building activity on the property apparently to survive is contained in a letter to Thomas Barker in the Barker papers, now in the University of Sydney Archives. Headed 'Camden, 8 Decr. 1849', it is written by a Clements Lestir, who was perhaps Barker's agent or manager.

'I have had a Bricklayer over to Nonorah to estimate the cost of repairs required to be done, & he says that it will require between 2 & 3000 Bricks & about 3 weeks labor—he charges 25/- a week—

'In calculating the expense of the new Roofing, I think we made an error —instead of their being 110 squares I think it will be but 30 viz.

Kitchen	8 squares
Shed	2¼ ,,
Roof of House	11¼ ,,
Back ,,	8½ ,,

	30 @ 11/-	16.10.0
Curbing etc at Verandah		1. 0.0
		17.10.0 '

This letter also indicates that Nonorrah was, at this time, rented.

The farm must have supported some form of dwelling since at least the early eighteen-twenties, and it is possible that the house referred to in this letter may date from that time, if one considers thirty years to be the useful life of a shingled roof before replacement is necessary. The areas of shingling required indicate a small verandahed house, with a detached kitchen and small shed. Whether it was of full brick construction is unclear, for the bricks may have been only for chimneys or paving. It is possible that Nonorrah, like its immediate neighbours Birling and Denbigh, both of which were built before 1820, was of framed construction, bricked nogged and weatherboarded. If the house referred to in Lestir's letter was on this same hilltop it must have been demolished to be replaced by the present house, although the rear sections of the present house are traditionally believed to be part of an earlier dwelling.

Occupying the very summit of its hill, Maryland presents to the visitor

two fronts united by a generous L-shaped flagged verandah with turned wooden columns. The verandah roof abuts the walls of the house just below the eaves line of the main roof, forming two tiers of roofing in the manner of later colonial homesteads, rather than being an extension of the main roof as in early colonial bungalows. Having two fronts also sets it apart from the majority of verandahed homesteads, whose plans are simply and symmetrically evolved around a central door and hallway.

The entrance doorway at Maryland is set asymmetrically along the northern front. To its left is a single french door leading from the reception rooms which occupy the eastern front, and to its right are three further pairs of doors leading from the principal bedrooms. Thus within, the vestibule effectively separates the main reception rooms from the bedrooms, which in turn are linked by a central corridor leading to the right from the rear of the vestibule. Further bedrooms are along the southern side of this corridor.

As in many earlier colonial homesteads the cool wide vestibule is floored with sandstone squares set diagonally. The long corridor is also completely flagged—a less common feature. The quality of this flooring is exceptional. Its flawless creamy whiteness, another indication of the care which Maryland has always received from its owners, being a subtle foil to a fine collection of old Persian rugs. A rose marble side table, supported on twin columns of grey marble was originally built into the left-hand wall. Removed many years ago, it now serves as a garden table. Hanging beside the entrance door Thomas Charles Barker's 'fisherman's barometer', made by Negretti & Zambra of Holborn Hill, 'Instrument Makers to Her Majesty', still registers changes in weather. The vestibule is large enough to be used as a summer sitting-room, being furnished with a walnut loo table and several comfortable chairs. A small octagonal skylight in the far left-hand corner of the ceiling lights the door to the large drawing-room.

The reception rooms along the eastern front, originally the dining- and drawing-rooms, now serve as two drawing-rooms. In their architectural detailing they repeat the distinction between the two fronts evidenced in the planning of the house. The french doors to the right of the entrance door leading into the verandah from the bedrooms follow an earlier pattern of small panes of glass with margin bars. They are fully glazed to the floor, without kick panels. The french doors to the left of the entrance door, however, have deep panels below and are glazed with single, large panes. Similarly, the door reveals in the bedrooms are of two vertical

boards with a beaded joint, whereas they are panelled in the eastern rooms to match the internal doors, which are four-panelled throughout. The entrance door, flanked by sidelights, again with margin bars, is six-panelled. The wooden mantelpieces in the bedrooms follow the early colonial pattern of moulded jambs and lintel with square bosses and paterae at the corners. In the drawing-rooms, however, each is a chaste design in grey and black marble without paterae or carving. The detailing throughout is simple and robust, rather than delicate. The rooms are large and well proportioned, and there are always views through the french doors and the shade of the verandah to the garden and the countryside beyond. House, garden and landscape are inseparable. This, more than any other quality, distinguishes Maryland.

A grassed terrace, bordered by low, neatly-clipped hedges of plumbago, and open to the sun, lies before the eastern verandah. From here one can look out across the drive, to the luxuriant tangled garden falling away to shining olives and dark oaks below, and beyond these stretch the fertile pastures of the Cumberland Plains.

'There are blue periwinkles in the shadow of olives over by the fences, and oleanders reaching from the olives for sight of the sun; and at their feet the long grasses where purple flags and oxalis bloom.'

Such were the hilltops which Hardy Wilson discovered fifty years ago.

The stable, like the other outbuildings nearer the house—the winery and the barn—is solidly constructed of coursed rubble with stone lintels, sills and quoins. There is a loft above and a groom's room to the left. The building was extended at the rear with a skilling at an early date, forming the distinctive roofline which in English vernacular architecture is sometimes called a 'cat slide'.

Dyraaba New South Wales

Text: Maurice Ryan   *Photographs: Richard Stringer*

THERE IS A SILENCE about Dyraaba Homestead that arrests and impresses. It is a silence born of another age, as if the buildings were listening to voices from the past or even remembering with respect the generations of Barnes who lie buried in the private cemetery nearby. Perhaps it is no more than that characteristic quiet of the Australian bush; but whatever it is, this quaint old relic, almost perfectly preserved, takes us back to the second half of the nineteenth century when frontier horizons merged with pioneering settlements.

A palatial brick or stone mansion is less likely to feel the blows of demolition or the ravages of nature than a timber home. But because it is neither palatial nor brick Dyraaba is different. The Barnes family, people with a sense of history, have preserved, at a good deal of expense, labour and a resistance to needless change this timber homestead, the oldest part of which dates back to the mid-1840s. It is different because it is timber and its architect and builders were probably no more than bush carpenters whose main qualifications were a strong arm and an appreciation of good timber. These facts alone make Dyraaba one of the gems of our historic homesteads; it is more truly representative of the Australian scene than castle, tower and balcony of some of the grander estates in our short history.

Looking from the rear of the main building to the service centre of the station—the kitchen block with the servants' quarters, store rooms and bake house, divided by a passageway that leads to the walk-in meat safe and dairy. Note the covered walkway on the left.

Dyraaba Station, situated about twenty-five kilometres from Casino in northern New South Wales, is and has always been cattle country. It is the last of the great squatting runs on the Richmond River. Once the centre of a vast cattle empire of almost 80,000 hectares (200,000 acres) it is now reduced in size to the homestead property of about 2,000 hectares.

Initially a squatting run, it was taken up by Commander Hamilton and William Pagan in 1841. In a frontier reshuffling of properties Dyraaba passed into the hands of A. F. Bundock before 1847. Bundock took Henry Barnes into partnership in 1854 with a R. G. Massie who was shortly replaced by Thomas Hawkins Smith. Henry Barnes who had been the overseer at Cassino occupied the Dyraaba run; A. F. Bundock took over Gordon Brook on the Clarence; and T. H. Smith resided at Kyogle Station. It was an impressive linking of stations which later absorbed other large properties such as Tabulam.

In the late 1860s Barnes and Smith bought out Bundock's share of the company. They took in Smith's brother, Henry Flesher Smith, who occupied Lyndhurst Station on the Einnesleigh River, Queensland for the company.

Henry Barnes, the son of a yeoman farmer, was born on 6 February 1818 at Low Blaithwaite, Cumberland, England. In an old sea chest, still in perfect condition and brought by Barnes to Australia as practically his sole possession, there is a character reference dated 20 April 1840, about the time he set sail for Australia. He worked for two years as superintendent at Tremayne before coming to the Richmond River in 1843 as overseer for Clark Irving at Casino.

While the rest of the nation was riding to prosperity on the sheep's back the stations on the high rainfall, lush pastured North Coast were concentrating on beef cattle as a source of income. Their herds, and in particular

Backed by large bunya pines and an aged jacaranda, the low-verandahed main building looks out across a wide sweep of lawn to the timber-clad hills to the north.

The buildings of Dyraaba form an inner courtyard. On the left is the original building built by A. F. Bundock in the 1840s. To the right is the kitchen, while in the centre are the walkway and the rear of main building. Sherwood brick tiles pave all the walks.

the stud at Dyraaba, were to play a significant role in the expansion of the beef industry in eastern Australia. Prosperity came at first from the boiling down of cattle for tallow. Later, as the demand for herd cattle increased, the tallow industry was largely discontinued. Several tallow pots at Dyraaba are mute reminders of a once lucrative even if wasteful industry.

From 1854 until the dissolution of the Barnes–Smith partnership some quarter of a century later in 1879, the success of Henry Barnes is in no small way the story of the beef industry in the eastern States. Barnes and Smith imported some of the finest cattle ever to come from England. These stud cattle along with purchases from the best offering in Australia and New Zealand formed the nucleus of the Dyraaba stud. The other major stations on the river—Wooroowoolgen, Cassino and Runnymede, also imported costly pedigreed stock, which they crossed with the Dyraaba stud. As a result the area produced some of the best blood lines in the colony. Stations in New South Wales and Queensland purchased breeding stock from Dyraaba and the other stations.

Under the verandah of the main building typical pioneer construction is revealed—sturdy beams and closely-spaced rafters to accommodate the bloodwood shingles now backed by galvanized iron. At its lowest point the roof height is less than two metres.

In addition to the above breeds of Shorthorn and Hereford, Henry Barnes also kept a small stud of Ayrshires and Jerseys. Bulls from these herds played an important part in the establishment of dairy herds in the district. Later Barnes also included a Devon stud. And not content with cattle the master of Dyraaba also bred fine horses—thoroughbreds, Clydesdales and ponies. As with his cattle the horses carried the Dyraaba Shield Brand—the hallmark of quality. Many Dyraaba bred horses bearing the shield brand won some of Australia's richest turf events.

The main building at Dyraaba, a low-slung timber construction presenting a wide view from the front, consisted of dining-room with pantry, sitting room, office, main bedroom and sundry other small rooms to accommodate the troupe of young Barnes. Its actual date of construction is not known but presumably it was built somewhere around 1857 when Henry Barnes married. Newspaper reports from the 1870s, describing the neatness of its setting, but also criticizing the low verandahs, fix its date somewhere before that time.

The rose garden and shrubbery are to the west of the courtyard complex, forming a buffer between the buildings and the exercise yards to the left.

Originally the house was built on large girders laid flat in the ground. These ground plates were mortised to accommodate the thick ironbark slabs, which were also mortised into the top plates. A similar method of construction used in the kitchen block was typical of the times. The external walls were then faced with cedar weather-boards, whilst the internal lining was either tin or boards covered with wall-paper. When the building was repaired in 1955 the log foundations were starting to rot. To effect repairs the house was jacked up and the logs replaced by concrete. On some of the dividing walls the slabs were removed and replaced by modern construction, lined with asbestos sheeting and then papered. All of these repairs were effected with a view to retaining the original as far as possible and the mending which has taken place cannot be detected.

An open fireplace and fuel store have conspired with time to conceal the stringy bark ceiling, which adds the right charm to the great slabs which make up the walks. On the right the baking ovens are visible through the door.

Now the living-room in the main building, this was once the dining-room, complete with pantry. It opened on to the front verandah. A door near the bottom right-hand corner of the photograph led to the passageway to the rear of house and connected with the covered walkway.

English pitched roof and colonial verandah meet in architectural simplicity at Dyraaba. The whole view is outward-looking to the lawns, gardens, walks, flats and hills. Life here was to be lived out of doors. Thus doors open on to the front verandah which was obviously designed to keep the sun off the walls and provide shade and protection in this hot, humid, sub-tropical area where summer showers often beat incessantly on tin roof and chimney top.

Like most of its contemporaries Dyraaba was originally covered by a shingle roof. The splendid specimens showing under the present cover of iron on the verandah are bloodwood. This was the most popular shingling timber in these parts because of its good splitting qualities. At a conservative estimate there would be 25,000 shingles on the main building. Just who the shingler was is not known, but he certainly knew his craft. In 1967 all the iron that covered the shingle roof was removed and replaced with new iron. This work was carried out by a local builder, Mr Eric Jordan.

The second major building, the kitchen is of more recent vintage than the main building. It was built by Charlie Matterson in the early 1880s. Matterson was the station carpenter for many years. It follows the same construction of the main building, but the walls of the kitchen proper are not lined. They show to perfection the method of the builder. Here under this high-peaked, smoke stained, stringy-bark lined ceiling one is transported to the past. Even though it is still used periodically by Mrs L. A. MacDonald, one of the owners, modern influences are minimal —no more than an electric light and a power point. Looking across the country, and from the verandah of the kitchen to the first slab house, one would scarcely be surprised if a bushranger materialized.

The foundations of the building are wooden stumps. In 1961 Mr Eric Jordan replaced those on the eastern side with concrete blocks. Earlier in 1953 Wallis Bros of Casino carried out renovations to the southern wall enclosing the dairy, reconstructing it of weatherboard.

One of the unique features of this building is the air vent in the storeroom. This is constructed in a small roof gable with slanted timber slats providing a fixed ventilator. The atmosphere of history picked up in the kitchen is intensified in the half light filtering through the vents on to the rustic objects in the storeroom—butter churns, crockery, fountains, kettles, pots and pans and station bric-a-brac.

Two sturdy chimneys catch the eye in this building: one in the kitchen servicing the open log fire and fuel stove, and the other in the baker's oven. Thoughtfully, the latter is separated from the kitchen proper to provide an escape from the heat generated on baking days.

The oldest cottage on the station—initially built by A. F. Bundock— contains three rooms and a verandah. It is built flat on the ground on heavy bearers and is now showing signs of its age. Slab walled, with a shingle roof now under iron, it contains an interesting and well-preserved calico ceiling. It houses today mainly old photos of the station and the odd possession of numerous generations of Barnes who have passed this way. But despite a sag here and there or a crumbling piece of timber, the old cottage has withstood the passage of a century and a quarter without any obvious major alterations, other than the iron roof.

The first building on Dyraaba Run. It was built in the 1840s. Its rugged slab walls of ironbark and bloodwood have withstood the passage of time. It is lined with shingles, now under iron. The three rooms which it enclosed were used as sleeping quarters for relatives of the family.

Dyraaba has been in the possession of the Barnes family now since 1854. Although changes and demolitions have occurred, successive owners down the years have respected the trust placed in their hands. The present owners in partnership, Mrs L. A. MacDonald and Mr W. N. Barnes (children of Walter Clarence Barnes, son of Henry Barnes Senior), have spent a lot of money to ensure that this gem of Australian history is not lost to posterity. The present manager, Michael W. Barnes, son of Mr W. N. Barnes, and his wife Jennifer, bear that same respect for the past that has led to the preservation of Dyraaba.

Henry Barnes married Grace Isabella Hindmarsh in August 1857; the marriage produced eleven children, one of whom, William, died at the age of six. These sturdy offspring were taught by a private governess in a building known as the school room. This building was demolished in 1954 to make way for a modern cottage to house the manager of the station.

Old photographs of the building show that it matched the main building in construction. It had a verandah on the western side, enclosed by a picturesque white picket fence, presumably to keep the charges enclosed. There were two main rooms of about equal size with three smaller rooms, one of which opened off the northern end of the verandah and was over the cellar. Presumably the governess lived in one of the rooms.

Dyraaba was cattle country. It required stout stock yards to hold the herds on mustering days. This Moreton Bay fig has flexed its muscles against man-made impediments to its growth.

Considerable demolition and rebuilding of other station buildings has occurred over the years. The station hands' cottages which graced the lower slopes below the main house have gone from the scene. Numerous stock buildings such as the old stables, barns, sheds, killing shed, stallion stalls, and fowl houses have been replaced by later structures. Most of them were still standing until 1950, after which date considerable remodelling and renovations were effected.

One building long since gone from its little knoll was the pigeon house. Perched high on stilt legs, the loft catered for the flocks of pigeons kept by Mr Walter Barnes for pigeon shoots, until the shooting of live birds was made illegal.

The gardens of Dyraaba, like many features of the buildings, show the extent of the compromise between transplanted British traditions and colonial necessity. Garden beds border footpaths between buildings;

The main bedroom, with its period furniture, has been tastefully preserved against fugitive fashions. The centre feature is the mirror above the mantelpiece of the marbled fireplace.

shrubs and trees screen views of station buildings, or cover fences and walls. Exotic and native species grow side by side. As the climate did not favour typical English trees, native trees were used not only for their aesthetic appeal but for functional reasons such as providing shade.

Perhaps the best description of the garden comes from the pen of a grandson of Henry Barnes, the late Sir Michael Bruxner, who wrote in his book, *The Shield Brand*:

> In its heyday Dyraaba was a rambling home with a big garden, full of all kinds of trees and plants culled from everywhere. There is the scent of the frangipanni, bringing with it the sense of tropical laziness. The old fashioned sweetness of multi-coloured Quisqualis seems to whisper of age. A native jasmine tree, when in bloom, almost overpowers one with its heavy perfume. There are great pines and Bunya trees, Moreton Bay figs, whose roots run right to a nearby creek and around whose sturdy limbs are twined all manner of flowering cacti. Silky oakes with their gorgeous blooms are everywhere, and the crowning glory is a giant jacaranda whose wide spreading branches reach out over the old house like some guardian.

83

Clay brick square tiles, bearing the name Sherwood, were used to pave the walks and the verandah of the first cottage. Along the walks filigree glazed tiles with a circular top are used to border the paths. They probably date from the turn of the century.

There are countless treasures of an historical nature in and around the Dyraaba homestead—legacies of another age. Within the house one comes across a polished leather box complete with black top hat; while in Henry Barnes's office the first thing to meet the eye is the sturdy old sea chest that he brought to Australia. Inside it is his reference of character signed by yeomen, clergymen, gentlemen, a farmer, seed dealer, grocer and a miller. Newspaper clippings tell of such events as a family wedding in Ceylon, or a prize won by Dyraaba stock in an agricultural show. The walls are adorned with photos and paintings of prize stock and champion racehorses, competing with family portraits and others of station people. A simple breast-plate bearing the name King Morgan reminds us of these devoted members of the Aboriginal tribe which occupied the Dyraaba run. A photo album shows us more of the natives in ceremonial battle dress, or climbing a tree using a rope around their middles. Photos of out-stations, or of other stations in the cattle empire, hang in hand-carved frames. Medallions for prizes at the Royal Easter Show remind us of the great part Dyraaba played in the pastoral industry.

Twin chimneys from the kitchen and bakery reveal an unusual stonework foundation. The walkway to the right connects with the dining-room in the main building. Part of a roof can be seen at the left. This is the only new building: the home of the present manager—Michael Barnes, descendant of Henry Barnes. It occupies the position of the former schoolhouse and cellar.

The stockyards, barn and abundance of shade trees are symbols of a pastoral industry. This barn is of more recent vintage than the house.

The rear of the kitchen block reveals gable-structured air vents in the roof, and slab walls mortised into ironbark bearers. The paling fence is a reminder of the plentiful supply of timber in this region.

A stroll in the garden brings one to the great bunya pines, as old as the house itself. Beneath one of them, in an old stump protected by a capping, is the nest of a native bee—a small black stingless insect—which seems to have always been there. Nearby is the well-trodden circle of the horse-works, where years ago the patient creatures turned the wheel that ground the corn. Beside it the family well—the once permanent source of water to all homes in the bush.

Out past the meat shed to the barn, with its sulkies and carts and drays, the memory is flooded with visions of trotters and huge Clydesdales. A side saddle reminds us that the Barnes womenfolk were also expert riders. Beneath a lean-to shed we come across the bullock wagon. If ever there was a symbol of the frontier it is the wagon. Another shed houses the boiling down pots—big iron vessels which held four or five large beasts quartered. All this equipment is long since stilled—but the visual remains remind us of straining muscles and foam-flecked flanks: the symbols of energy when Dyraaba was young.

McCrae Cottage *Victoria*

Text: Lynne Strahan   *Photographs: Brian J. Lloyd*

The Regency prettiness of twenty-one-year-old Georgiana McCrae's miniature self-portrait contrasts with the Victorian severity of later pictures of her.

OPPOSITE *The verandah, with totem-like posts and fire-coloured brick floor. This vernacular hallmark of Australian houses is rarely mentioned as a haven by Georgiana in her journal, which gives the impression that the peninsula, indeed Victoria as a whole, was subject to continual and incorrigible meteorological turmoil. 'The boasted climate is a myth', she wrote acidly in December 1842, 'and requires a constitution of india-rubber elasticity to sustain it.'*

McCrae Cottage before restoration. In 1961, after more than a century in other hands, the homestead returned to the McCrae family who began the long haul towards restoration. The original acreage had shrunk to an ordinary house block, and a conundrum of unsympathetic alterations and additions had destroyed the house's pioneering starkness, without adding anything convincing in the way of sophisticated improvement. The National Trust subsequently completed the cottage's restoration to 1840s veracity by reference to Georgiana's many drawings and descriptions.

HUGH McCRAE WATCHED HIS FATHER's fly-stitched back oscillate ahead of him through the foreshore scrub, listened to the sand ouch away from sand shoes, and felt the sea suck creamily round the stilted bathing boxes. When the party was strictly masculine they hurled themselves into the sea without their striped togs. Even so, the remnants of modesty persisted among the men until modesty's matter was swallowed by the sea: 'My father and Mrs Annikar's husband were governed by canons of behaviour higher than our own; so that they felt themselves compelled to adopt Venus de Medeci attitudes while they discussed Grahan Berry, or the prices of wool and wheat.'

By the mid-eighteen-eighties, when this flute among Australian poets attended childhood beach parties, the Mornington Peninsula had become Melbourne's watering-place. Hugh McCrae went with family and friends to the nearer beaches, entrained in liver-coloured dog boxes which were as stifling as 'Nebuchadnezzar's oven'. Further from Melbourne, at Dromana, McCrae and Sorrento, the coastal bush was sparsely dotted with low-slung weatherboard houses which dozed in perpetually humming tangles of pine, wattle, ti-tree and agapanthus. Most of these houses were cut, with little variations, from a stock pattern: three-sided verandah, a warren of small rooms which spilt straight into the sitting-room, a skinny kitchen along the length of the back, a hutch of a bathroom, and, discreetly isolated in the hissing branches, a cramped peak-roofed lavatory. On the sand in summer, moulded into striped deck-chairs which gave phrenological distinction to their bottoms, and shielded by the gauzy or steely shadows of sunshade or beach umbrella, beach-baskers gazed at the meeting point of milk-of-magnesia sea and quinine sky. Half-immersed in silvery or lime-coloured sea, children dabbled in trembling rock gardens and exclaimed over the cloudy, ambulant bells of jellyfish.

According to Georgiana's plan of the house, McCrae Cottage is twenty-four feet from front to back. In summer the six-foot wide passageway is a pipe length of hushed gloom which explodes at either end into a humming glare. Pictures on the wall include Georgiana's sketch of Gordon Castle, her one-time home, stretched across the landscape in a series of battlemented excrescences which are fronted by the formality of clipped hedge and fountain.

This skillion room at the end of the verandah was added in 1849. Recent restoration was largely a process of renewal which returned the house to its authentic simplicity. Original door jambs, slabs, banksia doors, messmate flooring and nail-pitted rafters were uncovered. Galvanized iron was stripped off, and obtrusive bay windows discarded.

Forty years earlier, on 9 June 1845, when Hugh McCrae's grandmother, Georgiana, landed near the present McCrae lighthouse, the place seemed rancorous: 'When we came to the landing-place, we cooeed to the boys who ran through the scrub to meet us . . . By the time we got to the hut the moon had set, and the breeze freshened into a gale which raged all night. I had no bedstead, only a mattress on the mud floor, and found it impossible to lie still.'

'Situated on a terrace of sandy soil about two hundred yards up from the beach', with 'a view of Shortlands Bluff lighthouse, the two points . . . Nepean and Lonsdale . . . and, in clear weather, Cape Otway', Georgiana's latest Australian home was as yet only a collection of 'huts'. Eighteen days after her arrival she recorded that 'The paths between the huts have become a mass of mire and there is nothing for us to do but stay inside . . . I am most unhappy . . . The last six months . . . has worn me out'. The next day, Georgiana's spirit, which was tough as well as tremulous, began to reassert itself. She saw a rainbow like Saturn's rings round the granite hump behind the site, and was initiated by her eldest son into the exigencies of the cross-cut saw, accomplishing 'some three inches'.

Within a fortnight a routine of awesome activity was established: bulb-planting, weighing of rations, preparation of grease-lamps, supervision of lessons, upholstery, dress-making and endless needlework. They ran out of beef and wax. Geese ate the crocus, white ants demolished the brown sugar, and dogs devoured soap and candles. Clothes were ousted from tin trunks to make way for flour. Mr McCrae was bushed, slept under a native cherry, and had a cold breakfast. Georgiana was flattened by a flying door during a storm and received a head wound so ugly that the servant was too shocked to dress it. The four McCrae boys swam, though with erratic buoyancy, fished for breakfast flathead or stingray, made friends with the local Aborigines, and chanted their Greek in the window-less hut which was dubbed the 'University of Arthur's Seat'.

Georgiana Huntly McCrae, a daughter of the fifth Duke of Gordon, was born in 1804, and educated with much style and many changes in London, by a series of genteel English ladies and aristocratic, dangerously Roman Catholic French exiles, such as Madame Cognac who 'when she wasn't muttering over the events of the September massacre, gave piano lessons', and Monsieur Bonnivet of the 'thirteen chins' who chewed garlic and made ivory ships. Her artistic talent was also fostered variously and vibrantly: Louis Mauléon, who was adept in the rendition of 'cupids or fountains, mixed up with fleur-de-lis and fauns without end', and who expired by jumping into an empty swimming pool in the Mauritius; John Varley whom she remembered 'crouched over his astrological book, eating bread from his pocket'; M. D. Serres who was pictorially immortalized 'in Oriental negligée'; and John Glover, of whom there is no surprising reminiscence in Georgiana's appreciative hand. Thriving on the skills and eccentricities of her tutors, she won medals as a miniaturist and portrait painter. She then lived as a cultivated member of the nobility at Gordon Castle and briefly in Edinburgh, painting some fifty portraits in three years, before marrying Andrew McCrae, a lawyer. After the March 1830 wedding in crenellated Gordon Castle, bonfires of celebration were lit

nearby. Georgiana had, as she recorded inscrutably in her diary much later against the date, left her easel and changed her name.

After several years practising in Westminster, Andrew McCrae fastened on a move to Australia. He arrived in Sydney in March 1839; but Georgiana, ill after the birth of her fourth child, embarked on the *Argyle* nineteen months later. She landed at 'shingled and clap-boarded' Williamstown in March 1841, before proceeding up the Yarra in the rain, her plaid spread wide to shield her children from the wet. Her first Australian home was wooden Argyle Cottage in Little Lonsdale Street West, 'raised on stumps' and with wooden front steps 'like those of a bathing machine'.

Mayfield, her next house, built from local stone on a nine-acre allotment on the Yarra at Kew at a cost of £3,000, and separated from the city by some of 'the worst country in the world', was ready for occupation in February 1842. She lived there for the next three years, fulfilling domestic obligations whose intensity bordered on slavery: laying down carpets and remaking chair covers; stitching tartan suits and confirmation caps; tailoring and dress-making; planting vine and rose cuttings; removing snakes from the nursery and tying muslin snoods to shield ripening peaches; church-going and entertaining as if her life were not her own; riding, nursing, piano-playing; bearing children with triennial stoicism. In the chambered privacy of her journal she observed, 'Tout passe, tout casse, tout lasse'.

McCrae's financial affairs slowly declined, and his legal partnership was acrimoniously dissolved. For a while it seemed that the family might go 'home' to Scotland where the past was charted and the future malleable; but McCrae, whose personality is walled in a secret garden of reticence, resolved to take out a pastoral run on Jamieson's survey of the Nepean peninsula, and exile was confirmed. He visited the place in 1843, and shortly took up pre-emptive right to 259 hectares of Arthur's Seat and a larger grazing area. As the financial clouds burst in a hail of pressing bills, Georgiana admitted in solitude that she was 'stunned by the prospect before me . . . Reduced to my last shilling and the baker's bill unpaid'. Still resisting the addition of another dark glass of Australian bush to her alienation, she appealed to the Duchess of Gordon for an advance on her promised inheritance to purchase Mayfield, and considered keeping herself and her children by portrait-painting. After some prevarication, the 'reputed Christian woman' belatedly wrote a curt refusal from Scotland;

Elements of defiant subsistence and instinctive pattern-making co-exist in the detached kitchen: beams lashed together with leather, exposed shingles, tables and dresser scrubbed to a smudged white, bellows and water-barrels, scrappy toasting-forks, Pearson pottery and blue-patterned white crockery, glass rolling-pins and jelly-moulds, barley-sugar slats of turned wood. The family's peninsula diet was a combination of luck and invention, scarcity and super-abundance. Beef, flour and sugar were precious and prone to spoil. Contrarily, as if by way of compensation, one of Georgiana's earliest peninsula meals was of 'three courses of veal'. Wild duck and kangaroo tended to walk unaffectedly into the gun muzzle. The boys developed a tolerance for stingray breakfasts; while Mr McCrae liked retiring to the seashore with a friend, often catching enough flathead to feed a platoon.

OPPOSITE *On her plan Georgiana named the thin room off the main bedroom 'My Sanctum', a description which suggests a slightly stern need for privacy and self-communion. The homestead's sense of identification with an individual is intensified in this closet of a room which holds many personal items among the accepted orbit of femininity: Georgiana's wedding-present, her watercolour of Gordon Castle, her portrait of her father, her pencil sketch of her eldest son, her portable easel.*

and the family steered her masterfully away from 'making money that way'. It was a long time and way from the days in Scotland when she could write cheerfully beside a list of her portraits 'painted for "fame"—and money'.

Like a hermit crab insinuated from yet another shell, Georgiana submitted to the move with vigour and without self-pity. She began drawing 'a plan for the house at Arthur's Seat', a dwelling which was eventually to have two fair-sized rooms in front, two middle-sized and two small rooms behind, a central passage, detached kitchen, front verandah with skillion rooms at either end, and a sliver of a room stolen from the main bedroom and named by Georgiana 'my sanctum'. Not entirely reconciled, she packed seeds for Arthur's Seat, while planting seeds at Mayfield and wondering 'for whom will they bear fruit?' Although the advance party of McCrae, the boys and their tutor, arrived at Arthur's Seat in August 1844 and immediately began building, the argument about acceptable ways of making one's living and using one's talent continued into 1845. Before departing in June for her peninsula purgatory, Georgiana sketched her two Melbourne homes, 'anticipating the time when all may pass away'.

Georgiana's music book contained pieces by Purcell and Byrd, lieder of Beethoven and Schubert, German folk songs and Scottish ballads. In England, a budding musical genius visited her mother to play 'a concerto of his own composition', and, when things went wrong, he disappointedly tore the music to shreds. At McCrae Cottage, Aborigines sat attentively on the verandah to listen while Georgiana's border ballads skirled through the casemented windows.

The shingled roof looks like terraced paddy fields. Georgiana's son, William, wrote from Arthur's Seat in March 1845 with the news that the roof of the new house was 'nearly shingled' and the 'chimnies on the Rumford plan' complete. When Georgiana arrived on a wild night three months later, the situation beneath roof and chimnies was less satisfactory. 'Neither Mr. McCrae nor Mr. McLure', she wrote, 'seem to have thought about hearths, each fireplace being hearthless, with great risk, in a wind, of our house burning down . . .'

Her destination had a mixed reputation. First commentators had formed conflicting opinions on its viability for cultivation and pasture. The land itself ranged moodily from swamp and mangrove to fern gully and forest. In 1802 Lieutenant Murray of the *Lady Nelson*, euphoric perhaps on a diet of swans, claimed for the terrain 'inexpressible elegance', and found wheat which made more mundane plantings sound like tare-riddled corn. Ten weeks later, Flinders saw kangaroos, emus, parakeets, duck, black swans, and a vast titillation of oysters which had simply surged in on the surf offering themselves for consumption. Varied and profuse animal and bird life supported small groups of the Bunerong tribe. The surveyor Grimes, however, crossing the peninsula between Rosebud and Bushranger Bay, found the topography treacherous and the soil unpromising; while Lieutenant Collins, given the incalculable task of scaring off the French, clung desperately with his soldiers and convicts to the grainy verges near Sorrento. He pleaded with Governor King to be reprieved from this 'unpromising and unproductive country'. After four months of failure and futility the colony removed to Hobart.

Since those earlier visitations, the bulk of the land had been left to the great grey kangaroo, the coastal fringe to the odd wood-cutter or lime-burner at Tootgarook, and the sea to the occasional sealer or fisherman. The possibility of more permanent settlement was refloated in the late eighteen-thirties and a few optimistic pastoralists began to trickle in.

Andrew McCrae's 12,800 acre (5,100 hectare) run was bounded on the north by Jamieson's survey, and followed the coastline of the bay for more than six kilometres. A water-hole near Bald Hill was shared with the owners of the Mount Martha run. The nearest neighbours were the Meyricks at Boninyong, Captain Reid at Checkinkurk near Mount Martha, and various operators of the Cape Schanck run. Travellers, many of whom appeared at McCrae Cottage sure of sleep and sustenance, announced themselves by blowing bugles through the bush, equivalent in Hugh McCrae's estimation to the cacophonous alarms of 'the municipal geese of Rome'. The foothills were awash with manna gums and the foreshore was liquescent with drooping she-oaks. The bay scalloped into bright circular wafers studded with the lime-burners' boats.

In just over a year the McCraes' living quarters evolved from the random collection of gap-toothed huts into a house of gum tree slabs roofed with shingles, described by Georgiana with a dab of irony 'as comfortable establishment as one could reasonably wish', sparsely furnished, with rectilinear panels of landscape bridging the slabs. In 1848 hail still sped like buckshot through gaps next the "saddleboard", beating a tattoo on our cups and plates'. But in time the main rooms were papered, ceiled with calico or canvas, and filled with those personal possessions which act as plugs against the threat of dissociation. A verandah was added in 1847 and flanked with skillion rooms in 1849 and 1850. A garden and fences staved off the bush.

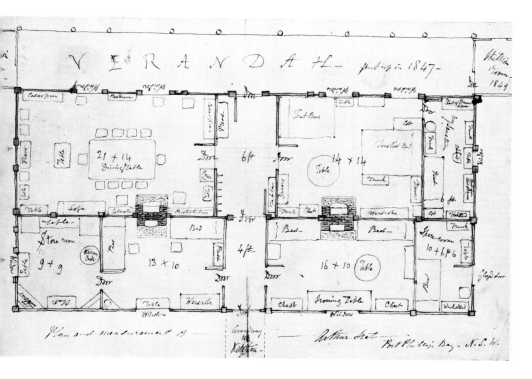

When Georgiana first heard that the family could not afford to continue living in 'Mayfield', the commodious house on the Yarra which she had lived in for three years, she looked longingly towards Scotland. She also considered becoming a professional portrait painter, but that solution was not socially acceptable to her near family. Arthur's Seat, on the pristine southern swing of Port Phillip Bay, was to be her place. Despite misgivings, she immediately began 'a plan for the house at Arthur's Seat'.

The McCraes lived at Arthur's Seat for six years. Georgiana, in whom response seemed always to have overcome temptations to gloom and inaction, tackled the new life with humour and vivacity. The domestic hive, Latin-learning and possum-snaring children, and plentifully itinerant colonial notables, absorbed most of her energies; but she still stole time to sketch, and left behind friendly tenuous images of bay and bush: a cobble of gumtops touching the shore, the odd rowing boat like a beached cuttlefish, sailing ships stuck in a calm, a flag-topped tree presiding irrelevantly over the wilderness, the bay curved like a broken orb, she-oaks dragging heads of hair, the casemented slab homestead, as it grew, from all sides. She also, though more parsimoniously as time went on, continued her diary.

Relentlessly, however, change dogged her. In October 1851, when a young Aboriginal friend of her sons died, she knew that another dislocation was upon her. Leaving the camp of mourning Aborigines, she retreated to the house. In her diary she wrote: 'Johnnie had been a companion to my boys and they felt the loss of him more than I can tell; yet a deeper sorrow has fastened at my heart, since the time has now arrived when I must say good-bye to my mountain home, the house I have built and lived in, the trees I have planted, the garden I have formed.' A move to Gippsland had been decided on.

Much later, when Andrew McCrae became police magistrate at Kilmore, Georgiana stayed in Melbourne. Hugh McCrae visited her the night before she died in 1890 and wrote in *My Father's Best Friend*: 'When my grandmother put her arms about me I felt uncomfortable in her embrace because it was Death's strength that held me. Her mouth, pressed against my own, seemed to be trying to take my life away . . . The old lady pressed into my hand something hard, (a guinea) wrapped in tissue-paper. "Get a book," she said, "to remember me by." '

The kitchen and bread oven were rebuilt by studying Georgiana's many thread-fine drawings of the homestead's close environs. McCrae Cottage was frequently the stopping place for travellers, who seemed undeterred by the peninsula's mostly trackless forest and grassland. They arrived by dray, by horse, by ship, and sometimes on foot. One day 'Mr. La Trobe and Mr. Dana, arriving at five minutes to 7 a.m.', were greeted by Georgiana whose 'apron [was] full of coffee-berries'. Another day 'a man seeming to come from nowhere, asked . . . for accommodation for the night. This was Mr. Meyrick, who explained that his bullocks had been prevented from getting round the "Nose", on account of the tide coming in.' Beyond the bread oven is a mulberry tree, a gnarled survivor of Georgiana's original garden.

Wollogorang New South Wales

Text: *James Broadbent*   Photographs: *Kerry Dundas*

The fenestration of the main facade OPPOSITE *is particularly attractive, being emphasized by the removal of the verandah some forty years ago. There is a surprisingly large proportion of window area to wall area, most noticeable when all the shutters are open. The entrance door with sidelights and transom light is grand and welcoming, and the first floor windows are unusually generous in size, being double casement rather than double-hung sashes. They are glazed in the same delicate pattern as the french doors below, with narrow margin bars. With its row of closely-spaced shuttered casements, with shuttered doors below, its severely rectilinear entrance doorway, and the flagged floor of the verandah now a sunny terrace before it, the main facade of the house appears almost French in character.*

The pedimented 'wings' screening low verandah-rooms to either side, and the separately-roofed passage linking the first floor rooms of the main block with those of the eastern wing, to the left, are clearly shown in this photograph of Wollogorang taken during the Chisholms' ownership, probably circa 1870. The roofs retain their shingles and the sandstone quoins appear to be unpainted. The decorative wooden trellised verandah, with its bold fretworked arches, was removed about forty years ago when another storey was added to the right-hand wing.

WOLLOGORANG IS A PRETENTIOUS, eccentric and thoroughly charming house. It is a house whose complexities of building history and contradictions in building style, scale and form are puzzling and enjoyable. Rachel Roxburgh, who has already written extensively about this homestead in *Early Colonial Houses of New South Wales*, and to whom the present author is greatly indebted, observed that 'Wollogorang, like Topsy, just "grow'd"'. This is one aspect of the house, but Wollogorang is not simply an unsophisticated, vernacular homestead.

The house was built by Henry Edenborough, a retired sea captain who settled at Breadalbane Plains in 1840. The name Wollogorang, however, appears as early as 1828, in Major Thomas Mitchell's diary, when the surveyor camped for the night by the lagoon at the edge of which the house was later built.

In the Census of 1841 Edenborough is listed as living at Wollogorang with a wife, four ticket-of-leave men, five shepherds, eight gardeners and stockmen, and four domestic servants. The size of the household was increased in 1842 and in 1843 by the birth of two sons. By 1859 Edenborough had decided to sell Wollogorang and return to England.

Little is known of Henry Edenborough, and nothing of his wife, not even her name. He was keen on horse-racing, his most notable horse being Artful Dodger; he was a district magistrate; and, apparently, he was noted for his hospitality. Miss Roxburgh quotes a *Goulburn Herald* report of 17 February 1849 on the visit of Governor FitzRoy to Wollogorang, where he 'partook of luncheon' and was 'much gratified at the off-handed and unpretending hospitality of Mr Edenborough, for which the gentlemen of the district know him to be so remarkable'.

Several years ago this sundial was discovered at Collector Police Station and returned to Wollogorang. It is inscribed 'H Y Edenborough, Wallagarong [sic], ARGYLE. Latitude 34° 49' S'. On the back is the curious date 1820. How it came to the police station, when it was taken from Wollogorang, or indeed if it was ever set up at Wollogorang is unknown.

Approaching Wollogorang from the rear, as one does now, one discovers a large, old, rambling farmhouse, a conglomerate of building styles around three sides of a large courtyard. Only the fine glazing pattern of the casement windows on the first floor hints at another aspect of the house. The skilling roof reaches from a low verandah with simple, chamfered wooden posts which links the two wings, to the sills of the casements. The break in the roofline of the wing to the right divides the older, blank walled section, and the turn-of-the-century first-floor billiard-room, lit by three large, four-paned double hung windows on either side. The deciduous branches of an old robinia cast delicate shadows over the courtyard.

In January 1854 Edenborough made a sale offer of his estate to John William Chisholm. This is contained in a most interesting letter, now in the possession of Miss Miriam Chisholm, which Nesta Griffiths first quoted in her *Southern Homes of New South Wales*.

My dear Chisholm,

Since I saw you, the subject of how far it would be to my interest to part with my property here has occupied a good deal of my consideration, more particularly as to whether I should dispose of my house and land at all! And in the next place, as to how I could best meet your views with regard to time, for, as I told you, I feel indisposed to sell for another twelve months, the general impression (when I was in Sydney) being that all description of property will be much enhanced in value by that time, more *particularly stock* and soon *land*, for a railway must bye and bye be projected to Goulburn when landed properties will be doubled and trebled in value, so that these advantages, as well as an increased number of sheep, and another clip of wool, will be lost to me by selling now.

It just comes to this, that if I *do* sell now, the only alternative I have is to make up my mind to leave the Colony at *Once*, instead of next March twelvemonth, for I would not attempt to do so in July, and as to live in Sydney, that would be out of the Question.

I have therefore come to the determination of submitting to you the lowest figure I should feel disposed to accept for my property, and which (when you have thoroughly examined the whole) you will not, I am sure, think out of the way, and I have thought it better to write to you today, previous to my coming over to you on Monday, that you may have time to give the matter your consideration before I come.

Say—Land at 20/-. House, with improvements, £5,750. Sheep at 10/-. Cattle at 60/-. Working bullocks, Horses, drays, carts, harness, Farm implements, stores, wheat, hay, etc. etc. at valuation, or I will sell at public auction, and Furniture on the same terms. Day of delivery 1st March. . . .

And now, having made you the above offer, I do assure you I have done so conscientiously, believing that each price named there is a fair one. The house will bear the closest inspection both for its durability and comfortable arrangement; it would cost a very large sum of money to build one anything like it now.

There is no doubt that my property is of more value to you than to any other person, for the truth is that it completes yours, and makes the whole a valuable estate, and the advantage of being able to walk out of one house into another, ready furnished in every respect, is worth a consideration, but of course you will weigh all these matters, and it now remains with you to say yes or no! . . .

If Monday be fine, I will come over and bring Mrs Edenborough to see Mrs Chisholm in the meantime.

Believe me, my dear Chisholm,
Very sincerely yours,
HENRY EDENBOROUGH

John William Chisholm accepted Edenborough's offer, although the terms are unknown, and the Chisholm family owned Wollogorang for the next fifty years, during which the 'JWC' Shorthorn cattle became well known in both the Sydney and Melbourne markets. In June 1912 Dalgety & Co. in association with De Lauret & Co of Goulburn advertised the subdivision of Wollogorang's '18,500 acres [7,400 hectares] of magnificent grazing, fattening, dairy, agricultural and fruit-growing lands' which had been 'acquired by the Vendors, Messrs Watson Bros, quite recently'. The

property was to be auctioned in lots ranging from 207 to 2,485 acres. Leopold Tamerlane Watson retained the homestead block, and the Watson family has now held Wollogorang for longer than either Edenborough or the Chisholms.

In the Census of 1841 Wollogorang is listed as being of timber construction. Miss Roxburgh has suggested this may have been an error on the part of the recording clerk. However, as the Edenboroughs had been at Wollogorang only since the previous year, it seems unlikely that any substantial dwelling had been erected by then. But when, and in what order could the various parts of Wollogorang have been constructed? Like Miss Roxburgh, the present writer can only make assumptions and, while doing so, try to convey how appealing Wollogorang's complexities and contradictions are.

The eastern wing, shown to the left in the nineteenth century photograph of the house, and to the right in the photograph of the rear courtyard, comprises two rooms below and two above, with a central flue and the stair being within the larger rooms. The main room below is a sitting-room with a good cedar mantelpiece, while the low rooms above, which extend into the roof space, serve as bedrooms. It has been suggested that this wing may be the oldest part of the house, but it is unlikely that it is the first construction at Wollogorang, for all its windows face east and, with the exception of one door into the courtyard, its western side is entirely blank. This is to be expected in a structure built as a wing, but not in an independent dwelling. In addition, the obvious siting of a house is that of the present house: towards the lagoon to the north, not eastwards. Furthermore, there is the record of a timber house in 1841. It is possible that the original timber dwelling faced the lagoon, but was soon

'The homestead is a substantial two-story [sic] building of 20 rooms . . . and every modern convenience, while there are all the necessary outbuildings, fruit, vegetable and flower gardens, a noble avenue of English trees, and ornamental lake. Adjacent are extensive stables embracing 20 loose boxes and many stalls, while in a convenient position is a splendid woolshed fitted with 16 stands of shearing machinery'. So Wollogorang was described in its auction sale notice in 1912. It is essentially the same today. The arrangement of a large mid-nineteenth century station is excellently shown in this aerial photograph. Before the house is the great carriage circle, surrounded by stone pines and shrubbery, with the concentric rings of the flower garden at its centre. The entrance drive (top left) passes through an avenue of elms from the lodge (not shown in the photograph) and joins the carriage circle at a right angle to the axis of the house. At the extreme left can be seen the orchard and vegetable garden, now no longer maintained, separated from the main garden by a further curving hedge of boxthorn. The courtyard behind the house is just visible and, behind this, stone-rubble outbuildings now converted into workshops. In the distance (centre top), can be seen the farm-yard with manager's cottage, men's quarters and shearing shed forming four sides of a square, with the stable at its centre.

extended by the construction of this double-storey wing to the east; and if this wing was built in line with the northern front of an earlier house, it is also possible to explain the unusual planning and form of the present main block, and the peculiar linking of the two blocks at first floor level.

The main section of Wollogorang is basically a two-storied, single pile range, with a skilling behind—that is, a house whose main structure is only one room deep, augmented by another range with a lean-to roof behind. This form is clearly seen in the photograph of the courtyard. Such an arrangement is common in very early colonial houses, the first Government House, Sydney being the earliest, most notable example, and in vernacular cottages and farmhouses, but not in houses of this date with the architectural pretensions Wollogorang exhibits. The ground floor is strictly single pile, being one room thick, with only a transverse corridor separating the reception rooms from the skilling rooms. However, on the first floor, light lathe and plaster walls partition the range into front bedrooms and rear dressing-rooms. Significantly the stair is placed in the front vestibule instead of the back, where it is usually situated in double-pile houses, and in many single-pile ones also.

It is the writer's conjecture that when Henry Edenborough decided to build a 'grand' house, Wollogorang consisted of a small timber cottage the approximate size of the present skilling, and exactly in that position, with a slightly later, slightly more sophisticated two-storied addition beside it. In order to rebuild on the same site and live in the old house meanwhile, the two-storey, single-pile front, and probably its pavilion-like flanking 'wings' were built first—thus necessitating the stair in the vestibule, and the emphatic transverse corridor. On completion of this the old timber house could then have been removed and replaced by the present skilling (whose detailing corresponds with that of the main block).

As shown in the early photograph, the upper rooms of the eastern wing are linked to those of the main block by an ungainly lobby, expressed externally. This is necessary because the end of the wing lines with the rear wall of the corridor, (that is, the back of the main range). The awkward planning and appearance of the junction could have been eliminated if the wing was built later than the house, for it could simply have been set three or four feet forward to line with the inner wall of the corridor, enabling a direct link between the two blocks. Similarly, if the wing is earlier, and no other building existed on the site of the skilling, the main block could have been set back three or four feet to accomplish the same thing. Thus it appears that both the positioning of the wing, and the positioning of the main block could have been determined by the timber cottage recorded in the 1841 Census.

All this is speculation, but Wollogorang is the type of house, with its diversity of forms and contradictions in scale and sophistication, which invites such speculation.

These building operations must have occurred between the Census of 1841 and Edenborough's sale offer of 1854, and presumably several years before the latter date, for Edenborough informed Chisholm that it 'would cost a very large sum of money to build a house anything like it now'.

Wollogorang was altered little until the turn of the century, when the

The raking light of the late afternoon sun emphasizes the pleasing texture of the white-washed stone rubble walls of the outbuildings. The stable, with loft above, is set in the middle of the formally-planned quadrangular farmyard.

eastern wing was extended to the rear by the addition of a first-floor billiard-room generously lit by three large, four-paned double-hung windows on each of its longer walls. About thirty years later the pediment to the right of the main block, that is, the end of the western wing, was removed and the wing extended with a second storey, thus destroying the symmetry of the facade. The very decorative wooden trellised verandah, with elaborate fret-worked arches, shown in the nineteenth century photograph, was removed at the same time.

Approaching Wollogorang from the rear, as one does now, one discovers a large, old, rambling farmhouse, a conglomerate of building styles around three sides of a large courtyard. Only the fine glazing pattern of the casement windows on the first floor hints at another aspect of the house. The skilling roof reaches from a low verandah with simple chamfered wooden posts which links the two wings, to the sills of these windows, unshuttered on this side, which nestle, cottage-like, beneath the main roof of the house. A minimum of wall is exposed on this side of the main block, and this large sweeping roof creates an intimate scale in the courtyard, which is, in fact, quite deceiving, for Wollogorang's main front is far from 'cottagey'.

Edenborough's front facade is engaging and pretentious. Its composition is that of a central block with flanking, pedimented wings or pavilions, an arrangement found, for example, at the Macarthurs' Camden Park, and less grandly at James Laidley's long-demolished Rosebank on Woolloomooloo Hill. At Wollogorang the pediments (only one remains) are no more than wings of a stage set, as the old photograph shows. They are no more than delightful screens rising through the verandah roof to give an air of grandeur to the house, while the 'pavilion' rooms behind were originally small low ceilinged verandah rooms! So bastardized are the pediments themselves, that they are merely allusions to such features. Adding to this bombast, heavy stone quoins define the central block as well as the screens. A classical purist would shudder at the junction of the quoins with the vestigal 'entablature' and 'cornices' of the pediment, but to our catholic eye such irregularities add immensely to the charm of Wollogorang. Likewise, if one closely regards the main facade itself, one can see how oddly the doors are placed, when one would expect complete symmetry.

The room to the right of the front door is slightly larger, by only a few inches, than that on the left, and consequently the french doors to the left are more widely spaced than those on the right, and the front door is slightly off-centre. On the first floor, however, the window spacing is quite regular. The effect is just noticeable enough to appear perverse and, as the difference in size between the two rooms is, in fact quite negligible, and as an impressive facade was desired, one wonders why. It is another of Wollogorang's contradictions. Perhaps such proportions were unavoidable if this range was built in front of, and corresponding to, an earlier building, and Wollogorang's builders perhaps thought that under the shade of the original verandah such irregularities would not be noticed.

The fenestration of the main facade is particularly attractive, being emphasized by the removal of the verandah forty years ago. There is a

The vestibule walls at Wollogorang are lined in imitation of ashlar and were once marbled—a not uncommon decoration for such rooms in colonial houses. The scale of the doorway with sidelight, and transom light with alternate square and lozenge-shaped panes is impressive, although its placement in the wall is somewhat eccentric. The high quality of the joinery is consistent throughout the house, and although the newel post of the staircase, and perhaps its delightfully-carved balusters are replacements dating to the turn of the century, they are equally worthy, seventy years later, of our admiration. Not only in the vestibule but throughout the house, the floors of wide hardwood boards have never been subjected to the destructive, levelling discs of the sanding machine; their exceptional mellow glow is simply the result of being waxed and polished lovingly and consistently over many years.

Enclosing one side of the square farm-yard, the shearing shed is constructed of round bush timber and weatherboards, unlike the other buildings which are of stone-rubble construction.

surprisingly large proportion of window area to wall area. This is most noticeable when all the shutters are open. The entrance door with its side-lights and transom light, with alternate square and lozenge-shaped panes is grand and welcoming, and the first-floor windows are unusually generous in size. As at Camden Park, they are double casement sashes, rather than double-hung, and are glazed in the same delicate pattern as the french doors below, with narrow margin bars. With its row of closely spaced shuttered casement windows, with shuttered doors below, its large, severely rectilinear entrance doorway, and the flagged floor of the verandah now a sunny terrace before it, the main facade of the house appears almost French in character.

Internally the same contradictions in scale and effect are evident. Because of the necessity of the stair being in the vestibule, the room is not as spacious as one would expect. To left and right are the drawing- and dining-room doors, four-panelled rather than six, and of polished cedar which, like all the internal joinery at Wollogorang is beautifully constructed and in excellent condition. The drawing-room has a mantelpiece of white marble in a restrained Gothic design with a shallow arched opening flanked by pilasters capped with delicate mouldings of continuous pendants. In the dining-room the stone or composition mantelpiece has square corner bosses with jambs incised with a Greek key motif. Its smooth, black-painted finish is probably original.

In contrast to the grander reception rooms, are the cottage-scaled skilling rooms. Dividing these two ranges is a transverse corridor running the full length of the house and linking the two wings. At each end and in its centre are three most attractive segmented, semi-circular fanlights, and on the wall beside the second door to the dining-room there is a small cedar folding table with an attractive hinged bracket, once used for serving.

At the head of the stairs is a large lobby, larger in fact than the vestibule below it, and to either side along the front are bedrooms, with dressing-rooms or secondary bedrooms partitioned off behind. The large casement windows have panelled reveals of polished cedar which, in the right-hand room continue to the floor with panelling below the sill. The mantelpieces, following the standard early nineteenth century pattern of moulded jambs and lintel joined with square bosses set with paterae, are also of polished cedar. At Wollogorang there is little painted joinery internally. It is from these light-filled bedrooms with the deep, polished sills of their wide casements set low to the floor, and particularly from the first floor lobby, that one can fully appreciate the siting of the house and the planning of the garden at Wollogorang.

The house faces north across the extensive Wollogorang Lagoon and the Breadalbane Plains ringed with distant hills. No foliage softens the edges of the lagoon save acres of reeds which shelter its wildlife. No wooded hills enfold the scene, softening the landscape. It is impressive, not intimate, and in winter can be harsh. Wisely, Edenborough did not site his house picturesquely on a rise to catch the bitter winds off the snow, but on flat ground beside the lagoon, sheltering it within a ring of planting.

Before the house he described a great circle, and at right angles to this he brought his entrance drive along an avenue of elms from a Gothic entrance lodge. The entire pleasure garden was an impressive carriage circle, with flower beds at its centre. Resistant to droughts, and thriving in the cold winter winds, enormous stone pines ring the drive, with beneath them dark shrubberies of laurestinus and sweetbay or laurel grown far beyond their familiar size. Natives of the Mediterranean—the sacred pine of Mithraism, and the laurel of ancient Greece—they have found, perhaps, in the summer heat and the winds off the snow, antipodean equivalents of the sirocco and the mistral and, by accident or design (at Wollogorang who can tell?), form a most evocative garden. Within this ring are concentric beds of flowers—primroses and forget-me-nots, snowdrops, hyacinths and daffodils. The circular drive, no longer used, is now a grassed walk, and the flower beds were re-arranged many years ago, but the original concept remains.

Wollogorang has evolved as a house of exceptional charm and character. (It is not surprising that it should be accredited with a ghost, and that the ghost should be friendly.) The house is not aloof as it might have been if its architectural detailing was consistent and scholarly, nor is it as un-sophisticated as it would have been without its facade and pedimented 'wings'. It is a large house, but built on an intimate scale—the verandah along the courtyard is almost at head height, and the low casements in the upper floor make it pleasant to sit and enjoy the sheltered garden below. Henry Edenborough intended to build a grand house when he built Wollogorang. Fortunately, he failed.

The unusual stable occupies the centre of the farmyard. On either side of the central longitudinal wall, like the cross stroke of the letter 'H', are open stalls. These are enclosed at each end with harness rooms.

101

Lowlands *Western Australia*

Text and plans: Ian Molyneux

Photographs: Barry Hall, Ian Molyneux, and Wesley Stacey

AFTER A FOUR-MONTH VOYAGE from Gravesend, beset by mutiny and delays, the *Gilmore* arrived at the infant Swan River Colony on 15 December 1829, and entered Cockburn Sound on 31 December. On board a duel took place between her part owner, Thomas Peel Esq., and Captain Geary.

Peel and the Colony's first Governor, Captain James Stirling, RN, had been the main instigators of the settlement. Stirling had been given priority, by the British Colonial Office, to choose 100,000 acres (40,000 hectares) and had been instructed to reserve a claim of 250,000 acres (100,000 hectares) for Peel until 1 November 1829. When Peel failed to arrive by the due date the choice land on the banks of the Swan and Canning Rivers was allocated to the 650 settlers who had arrived earlier. Subsequently Peel took up 250,000 acres extending from Cockburn Sound to the Murray River.

In about 1840 Peel commenced farming in the vicinity of the present Lowlands homestead. The Serpentine Farm, as it was then known, was begun at about the time of regularization of his title, and was an outpost from his headquarters at Mandurah. It was a stronghold from which the northern end of the estate could be administered. The homestead contains the sole remaining dwelling of those built by Peel and his son.

This self-contained group of buildings is approached from the farm entrance gate, through virgin woodland, along tracks meandering with the Serpentine River. The buildings are fleetingly glimpsed through trees, and suddenly the tracks converge at a high timber bridge which spans the

The house complex, viewed from the south, clearly shows the stages of its growth. At right is Thomas Peel Jnr's pug cottage of 1845, connected (centre) to his second more expansive house of 1858. Behind are the roofs of the brick additions of A. R. and H. L. Richardson. The earlier hovering, hipped roofs reflect the first settlers' need for shelter from the bush. The later more strident roofs are the contributions of confident bushmen.

The north elevation of the house was built in three stages. The central gable rises over the sitting-room of circa 1888, and at right a more elaborate gable oversails the bay window of the living-room added in 1900. At left is the kitchen wing built in 1925. The verandahs are the main means of access about the house.

All roofs at the homestead carry their original shingles under later corrugated iron sheeting, except the bull-nosed verandahed sections which were originally roofed in iron.

river and leads into the long home paddock. A magnificent jacaranda, planted in 1884 and believed to be the second of its type planted in the State, terminates the vista from the bridge. Like a village about a green the homestead complex is grouped about the paddock and comprises the house, a barn, a stable with men's quarters, and a workman's cottage. The total orchestration of the approach generates a sense of isolation and arrival which is extremely apt to the timepiece nature of the homestead.

This vitality and dynamism of planning, albeit intuitive or accidental, recurs in the siting of the stable and house complexes. The two buildings terminate the end of the home paddock, forming a welcoming forecourt. With the woodland and river to the south-east they also bound an orchard and billabong, creating an arcadian environment; insulating the homestead from the raw bush environment which so intimidated the early British settlers. The buildings gain an architectural harmony from this vitality of grouping which is 'townscape' design of a high order.

The architectural quality of the individual buildings, like that of most Australian vernacular buildings, is of a low key. They are quiet, self-effacing, simple solutions to functional needs. They do not contribute to the mainstream of development of Western architecture. The house in particular, however, gains tremendous significance as a comprehensive illustration of stages in evolution of the house in Western Australia.

Peel's motive in promoting the Swan River Colony was land hunger.

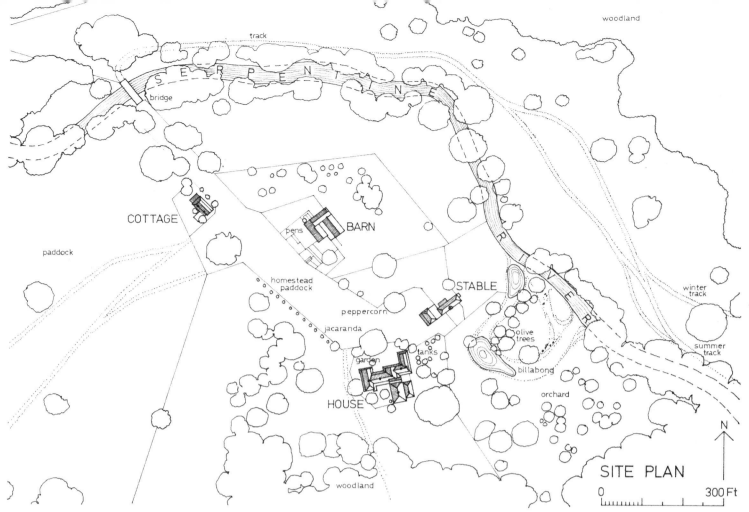

SITE PLAN

0 ⎣⎣⎣⎣⎣⎣⎣⎣⎣⎣ 300 Ft

The site plan of the homestead shows the meandering approach track leading to the bridge and the homestead paddock. The placing of the buildings about the paddock produces a picturesque 'townscape'. A road from the Canning to Pinjarra once forded the Serpentine River and passed the west front of the house.

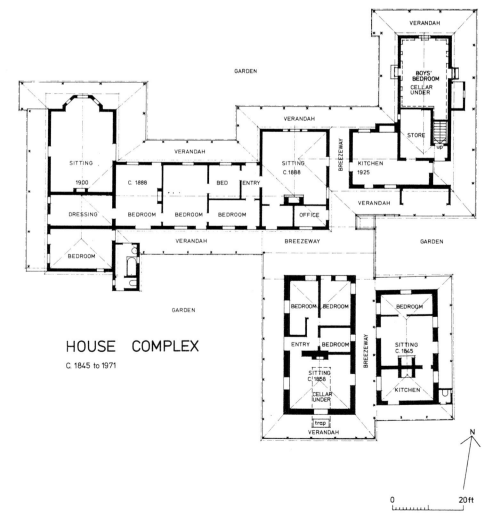

HOUSE COMPLEX

C. 1845 to 1971

0 ⎣⎣⎣⎣⎣⎣⎣ 20ft

The plan of the house shows the thick-walled pug cottages which Peel built in 1845 and 1858. They are connected to each other and to A. R. Richardson's brick additions, of circa 1888 and 1900, by breezeways and verandahs. The kitchen block of H. L. Richardson was similarly connected when added in 1925. The house has developed as a casually related series of pavilions. The verandahs have been increased in width and usefulness with each addition.

The prevalent contemporary attitude in England was that land was a means to, and badge of, rank and personal distinction. For Peel, a land grant promised a wealthy retirement in Britain. By his attitudes he typifies the first generation of European settlers in Western Australia.

Thomas Peel was born in 1793, probably at Peelfold, the family estate near Oswaldtwistle in Lancashire. He married in 1823 and moved (probably as manager) to Carnousie, an estate in Banffshire in Northern Scotland. Here, no doubt, he developed the conviction that he had the necessary experience to manage large estates. From November 1828 until his departure for the Colony he was strenuously engaged, as was Stirling, in promoting its establishment through the Colonial Office.

Even before his departure his plans began to fall into disarray. He had probably gambled away his inheritance and his pregnant wife remained in England. Stores failed to arrive at the Colony, and of the sixty head of cattle he purchased from the *Norfolk* (from Sydney) most were dead four days after the ship sailed from Fremantle. Flooding forced the abandonment of an attempt at farming at the Murray River. One of his ships, the *Rockingham*, ran aground on its arrival. Peel's sleeping partners in Sydney refused to honour his promissory notes. His indentured labourers claimed discharge, and there were deaths from dysentery and scurvy among his people. A second duel resulted in the loss or partial loss of Peel's right hand.

From this time he withdrew to live in two stone hovels at Mandurah; an embittered and cynical man. In April 1834 his wife, two daughters, son Thomas, and mother-in-law arrived. His wife, appalled by the conditions she met, returned to England in 1840. Peel was to have followed her. The remainder of his life, however, was occupied with developing and selling parts of his grant, and repaying debts. He died at Mandurah on 21 December 1865, after eating too many ripe figs; not entirely a pauper but certainly not the country squire he had once dreamt of being.

Thus, not only by his attitudes, but in his tragic failure, Peel is representative of many of the first generation of settlers. He had planned a town at Cockburn Sound, on the pattern of an English town surrounded by estates, and drawing labour from it. The almost feudal basis of the plans indicates the basis of his failure. The Western Australian coastal sand plains were not to be taken by grandiose planning or military expeditions. Where the first colonists were not defeated by their ignorance of the strange conditions, the timeless, ever grey-green land unnerved them and upset their European dependence upon a measured existence.

Consequently the attitudes most prevalently expressed in the early dwellings of such colonists were homesickness, and an extreme desire for shelter and withdrawal from the hostile environment. These attitudes are expressed in those parts of the Lowlands homestead remaining from Peel's time and built by his son Tom.

When Peel commenced farming at the Serpentine in 1840 he was no doubt influenced by what promised to be good wheatland on high ground in the vicinity. He had sold 10,000 acres (4,000 hectares) at the Murray River, and Pinjarra was a quietly growing settlement there. Roads from Pinjarra and Mandurah to the Canning River merged and forded the north

The living-room, built by A. R. Richardson in 1900, is an ornate Victorian room, and yet is accessible only from open verandahs. The reliance upon this means of circulation, without internal passages, illustrates this bushman's total ease with the natural environment.

The northern verandahed elevation of the house meanders and enfolds the garden spaces, in direct contrast to the thick pug walls of the earlier cottages, which, for the first settlers, were barricades against a hostile environment.

105

The workman's cottage was built by A. R. Richardson in about 1888 in the style of the main house additions of that year. The cottage once had a wattle and daub addition which has now been removed.

and south reaches of the Serpentine. This was a strategic place in his vast estate. Near the ford a pug hut was built. Here Peel stayed when visiting the farm, often staying up late and gambling with whoever was willing.

The barn, the earliest surviving building, dates from about 1840. Then, as also applied in later farm settlements, a weatherproof store had priority over housing for the protection of precious tools, stores, and animals. Workmen slept in the loft, and one, David Petty, fell to his death one night in 1861, when he missed his footing on the ladder in the dark. The barn is simply constructed of timber. The original roof shingles remain, now covered with corrugated iron.

Thomas Peel Jnr was born in 1825, the year his parents moved to North Scotland. When his mother returned to England in 1840 he remained in the Colony with his father. In 1843 he went to live at the Serpentine Farm, probably as manager, and in that year his father subdivided an area of 5,000 acres (2,000 hectares) and gave it to him.

Predictably, considering the father's attitudes to land, the allotment was an exact square, excised without regard to the subtleties of landscape. There was, however, nothing arbitrary in the juxtaposition of boundaries and the resources of the land. Young Tom's farm incorporated the Serpentine Farm establishment and was neatly bisected from north to south by the Canning-Pinjarrah road, and from east to west by the Serpentine. Peel Snr thus maintained his family's hold on this vantage point.

Tom Peel built the pug sections of the existing house in 1845 and 1858, closer to the society of the road, where it forded the river, than the original hovel. He was beginning to achieve a moderate level of prosperity when, in 1858, with typical Peel misfortune, fire destroyed his 100 acres of wheat crop. Left without resources to pay his creditors he was forced to auction the contents of his house, his stock and finally the farm itself.

Tom retired with what he had recouped from fifteen years' labour to another part of his father's estate. He settled on a hurst, or sandhill, overlooking a melancholy swamp, and built a limestone house which he cynically named 'Peelhurst' in a mockery of his father's birthplace and aspirations. He died on 20 April 1892, aged sixty-seven.

On 23 November 1859, by order of the Insolvents' Court, the Serpentine Farm was auctioned and knocked down for £3,000 to John Wellard, a wealthy merchant of Fremantle, who brought to the property the confidence and experience of a self-made man who had come to grips with nature at sea and in the bush. He was a successful business entrepreneur, and had broken with the 'Motherland', having lost contact with his family. Homesickness was probably not one of his problems.

Of Wellard's contributions to the house nothing remains. The stylisms of his additions were probably inherited by later additions, but the most important influence was that there was to be no more building in pug.

Wellard also brought to the Serpentine Farm a large household of family and servants including Jimmy Bristow, a 'ticket-of-leave' man. Bristow was a bricklayer by trade and a kleptomaniacal pick-pocket by inclination. The farm diaries regularly report that he had left in a huff, only to return two or three days later. Bristow made the bricks for and built the stable, and probably designed it. He remained at the farm until his death in about

The western facade of Tom Peel's second cottage has an expansive welcoming verandah and entry door with fanlight. Moss roses planted by his sister Dora still flank the approach path. This entry faced the nearby Canning-Pinjarra road, and no doubt Peel was attracted by the society of the road when he moved to the site from the first hovel at the Serpentine Farm.

1917. The stable and men's quarters is a superbly powerful and confidently designed building. Its strength arises from the plasticity of its forms and direct, no-nonsense composition, all of which is matched by its placement in the composition of the homestead group. It is a clear reflection of change of ownership from the first 'generation' of demoralized settlers to the second 'generation' of experienced bushmen. The roof was originally shingled. In 1870 the building was badly damaged by fire, started by two small boys smoking in the hay loft.

In 1874 Wellard's youngest daughter Ellen married Alexander Robert Richardson. Richardson was born in Islington, London, in 1847 and grew up in Portland, Victoria. After working in his father's newspaper office for about a year he rejected an indoor life and in about 1863 he rode 120 miles (190 kilometres) to his uncle's farm on the Skipton Plains to gain experience in station life and management.

On 5 March 1865 a party consisting of Richardson, two cousins and two friends sailed from Portland Bay with 1,600 ewes, horses, equipment and twelve months' supplies, bound for the north-west settlement of Padbury and Wellard. The party was greeted en route at Fremantle by Wellard, and in about July they established Pyramid Station, some thirty miles from the site where Roebourne now stands. At the ripe old age of twenty-one years Richardson became manager of Pyramid, where he stayed, after marrying Wellard's daughter, until 1876. In that year Wellard sold the Serpentine Farm to his son Piercy and Richardson. A few months later Richardson bought his brother-in-law's share. Wellard 'retired' to an active life at nearby Whitby Falls where he died in 1885.

Richardson represents a third 'generation' of settlers and left his mark accordingly on the sections of the house he built. Wellard had served an apprenticeship in the bush, but Richardson had immersed himself in it, and absorbed it almost with his mother's milk. He had Peel's land hunger and yet had the advantage of the native-born, in that he did not yearn for every landscape to be a green English park.

The ultimate development of the verandah is this outdoor room formed by the breezeway connecting the pug cottages with the brick additions.

The western verandah of Peel's second cottage viewed through a glazed door. The organic form of the house gives rise to many such picturesque views and vistas.

Richardson renamed the farm 'Lowlands' after the lowlands of his Scottish ancestors' homeland, betraying the concept inherited from Peel's generation of the feudal estate. Under Wellard the property was indifferently farmed. Richardson turned from wheat-growing to pastoralism, fenced and partially irrigated the property, and in 1896 it was carrying 80 horses, 250 head of cattle, and 3,000 sheep. In 1886 he purchased 2,000 acres (800 hectares), giving the farm a northern boundary which followed the timber railway, providing access to the port of Rockingham.

In 1887 Richardson was elected to the old Legislative Council, and in 1894 (the first year of organized opposition in the Western Australian Parliament) he became Minister for Lands. He retired to Perth in 1922.

In that year Lowlands was sold to A. R. Richardson's sons Hubert Lennox and Rupert, and was divided between them into the present Lowlands and Riverlea. The brothers sold 3,000 acres (1,200 hectares) to the Government, and Lennox took Lowlands, which remains intact with the original buildings. Riverlea has since been divided again into two farms. At the time of the sale of Lowlands a large area of Peel's grant was being drained, as part of the Government's group soldier settlement scheme, for expansion of the State's primary industry. A major diversion drain now forms the farm's western boundary, while the south and east boundaries are the original limits of Thomas Peel's gift to his son.

Lennox Richardson was born in December 1888 in the part of the house that his father had completed earlier that year. At his death in December 1964 he had lived at Lowlands all his life (except for an absence of about seven years) and longer than any other person. In 1919, he married Miss M. A. Clifton, a great-granddaughter of Marshall Waller Clifton, Thomas Peel's old friend and superintendent of the Australind Settlement about 80 kilometres south of Mandurah.

Lennox, too, had pioneering experience in managing one of his father's properties in the Murchison, and his father's adjustment to the bush environment is maintained in the last sections of the house. To him must be given credit for the present state of preservation of the farm. He held it together during the depression of the thirties and during World War II. Major repairs were made to the stables in 1953 and Mrs Richardson has renovated the house since 1970.

Since Tom Peel the house has been occupied by four generations of the Wellard–Richardson family, and its construction spans eight decades. It mirrors three 'generations' of the European settler and his descendants in their acclimatization to the Australian environment. In its development, the enclosure and limitation of spaces gives way to a conscious appreciation of the infinite qualities of space. The appreciation of this discovery of rational science is one of the definitive qualities of modern architecture. Lowlands is an extremely important illustration of development of an appropriate relaxation of life style and exploitation of outdoor spaces.

The house was commenced in 1845 when Tom Peel built a three-room pug cottage overlooking the Serpentine River and its billabong. Only the central sitting room had a ceiling. The flanking kitchen and bedroom have ceilings formed by the roof shingles. The thick low walls are pierced by small openings which reinforce the sense of enclosure from within. The

The sitting-room of the first cottage. Views of the orchard and river are heavily framed by the thick pug walls.

roof spreads over a narrow verandah and hugs the ground so closely as to convey a sense of shelter and retreat from the elements.

When Tom's mother and sister Julia died of consumption in London, his second sister Dora returned to the colony, arriving in 1858. The second house was commenced in this year, presumably to provide expanded and more proper accommodation for the lady of the household. It was similar in character to the first stage, and close to it, so that the verandahs overlapped forming a breezeway. The verandah, however, was wider, with a timber floor giving access to a cellar. The workmanship was better, with large windows, and an elaborate entrance door with fanlight facing the approach from the nearby Pinjarra road. The roof gracefully bells out over the verandah. The sense of primitive retreat, so obvious in the first house, was beginning to take on a softer edge.

The barn is the earliest surviving building. Carts laden high with hay were once driven through the central doors on each side. The door in the gable opens out from a large hay loft.

Fences and pens of split timber surround the barn. Iron-clad bush-pole additions have increased it to five times its original area.

Of some significance is the fact that a passageway was introduced giving access to each room without passage through adjacent rooms. To the north of the two pug cottages Wellard built a brick kitchen and other rooms.

In 1888 and 1900 A. R. Richardson made his additions to the house in brick. The roof of the first was shingled and the second was sheeted with corrugated iron, which was then extended over all the previous shingled areas. Contemporary with the first addition, the workman's cottage was built near the river. In it can be seen the same manner of design, mellow red bricks and light, decorative detailing, with verandahs on the sides exposed to the sun.

In both Richardson's additions the sitting-rooms are emphasized with steep gables on the north elevation. This departure from the ground-hugging, hipped roofs of Peel's cottages might have weakened the sense of shelter, except for the retention of the verandahs. However, while the additions do in fact preserve the sense of shelter, they do so in a less extreme manner. The windows in particular are designed to allow views of the gardens and paddocks outside, and the lightness and greater width and height of the verandah make the sense of retreat less pronounced.

Richardson's acclimatization to the bush environment is reflected in a second characteristic of Australian houses which his additions add to the complex, and that is a marked degree of relaxation or freedom. This is despite some small preoccupation with decoration, which in fact contributes to the lightness of detail. Separation of the verandah roofs into a continuous string ties the house together and emphasizes its horizontal sprawling character, its looseness contributing to the air of relaxation. The house, under A. R. Richardson, took on the same confidence which Wellard had imprinted on the stable complex.

In the purely practical aspects of planning A. R. Richardson's additions reveal his total acceptance of an outdoor life. Whereas Peel's cottages showed a developing tendency, with improving affluence, to provide internal circulation passages, the brick additions of 1888 include a small passage; then, in 1900, this form of access is totally abandoned in favour of the external verandah, on to which all the rooms open. The most grandiose of the rooms, the living-room of 1900, is accessible only from the verandah. All the verandahs exhibit a progressive widening, until they become open living areas.

In later years a thorough appreciation of the domestic usefulness of the verandah had developed. What had initially been introduced as a shield against the oppressive summer sun, also had wet weather functions, when, as often was the case, the rain came in cloudbursts, without driving winds. The verandahs were places where children could play in summer and winter; where laundry could hang to dry in the middle of rain storms; where orphaned lambs could be made pets; where muddy boots and coats could be discarded and stored; where teas could be served to the men; and where one's visitors could be entertained. Furthermore, with the advent of corrugated iron as a replacement for shingles, what more satisfying feeling of shelter could be had, when bad weather prevented work in the paddocks, than by leaning on a verandah post, staring into the rain and hail not more than two feet away, as it thundered on the roof just above.

Although the technical limitations of the construction methods did not allow a free flow of space within the interiors, there is a move toward greater freedom of space in the window design. In Peel's cottages the small openings pierce the thick walls emphasizing their solidity rather than the spaces within and without. In the sitting room of 1888 three tall, grouped windows emphasize the views of the garden, and give an expansive scale to the room which the pug walls could not provide. In the living room of 1900 a bay window is used to the same effect and provides a more marked experience of the interpenetration of inside and outside spaces.

Paraxodically it is in the external *forms* of the house complex that the infinite character of *space* is developed. The earlier roofs hover over the pug cottages and enclose space beneath. The roofs of the brick additions impose a higher, dominant scale and stride out into the landscape. Peel's cottages are boxes suspended in space. The additions of the Richardsons extend with arms folding about garden spaces. The relaxation and freedom of the house is thereby reinforced by its spatial qualities. The spaces of the verandahs and breezeways flow loosely about the complex and provide a bridge between the interior spaces and the surrounding bushland.

In 1924 Lennox Richardson commenced reconstruction of the kitchen block. Eight rooms of Wellard's addition were demolished and Bristow's original bricks provided the material for the new work, which was completed in February 1925. Lennox followed the form of his father's work, and the kitchen wing reinforces all the qualities of confidence, freedom and relaxation which the bushman 'generation' had contributed.

What had started as three rooms of mud and timber had thus grown into a casually but meaningfully related series of pavilions. The growth of the house had occurred with an organic, free-breathing mobility to which modern architects aspire in designing the dwellings of the hedonistic society of Western Australia.

The stables complex was built in 1860. In the foreground are the two-storied men's quarters, with sleeping quarters over a large kitchen. A staircase once led up to the door under the hanging beam.

The stables overlook the orchard and a billabong of the Serpentine River. Arum lilies, and apple, pear, and almond trees survive from the period of the beginning of the house.
Above the stalls is a large hay loft. Here, in 1870, two small boys started a fire while smoking, threatening the entire homestead. The fire was extinguished by bucket brigade from the river.

Madowla Park *Victoria*

Text: E. A. Beever   Photographs: Brian J. Lloyd

In a small cemetery surmounting a sandhill between the Murray River and Madowla Park, a simple headstone marks the grave of a faithful Aboriginal servant.

OR SOME DISTANCE before they finally meet near Echuca the Murray and Goulburn rivers run roughly parallel courses, east-west, three to five kilometres apart. The intervening land, much of it in its natural state heavily timbered with redgum, is rich and fertile but flat and flood-prone. Towards the eastern end of this belt of country the terrain changes, if only briefly and barely perceptibly to the casual onlooker. There low sandhills rising above the flood plain run north-south from New South Wales into Victoria, intersected in turn by the Murray river, a little to the south by the deep Madowla Lagoon, and a little further south by the Goulburn river. The Towro sandhill between the Murray river and Madowla Lagoon gave its name to the local Aboriginal tribe, the Towroonban. Surmounting it, in a small cemetery, a plain headstone commemorates one of the tribe's members, Biddy, faithful servant to the land's European occupiers. This same sandhill, as it falls away gently to the Madowla Lagoon, also provided the flood-free base from which Madowla Park station was to grow.

Among the first white men to explore the region was the youthful Edward Micklethwaite Curr. Already, by the early 1840s, Curr's father held several squatting properties in the Port Phillip district, but as resident manager in Tasmania of the Van Diemen's Land Company, left their operation to his son. From 1841 Curr's centre of activity became Tongala station, bordering the Goulburn river, the homestead located on the same belt of sandhills, just south of the river. Once established at Tongala, Curr quickly explored the unoccupied country to the north, around Madowla Lagoon and from there north-east along both sides of the Murray river. For a time occupying land on the New South Wales side of the river, later to become Sir John O'Shanassy's Moira station, Curr's main acquisition was Lower Moira on the Victorian side, a tract of country exceeding 60,000 acres (24,000 hectares), including what was to become Madowla Park. Lower Moira became an integral part of Curr's essentially migratory system of sheep grazing. As described in his *Recollections of Squatting in Victoria*, during the winter months Curr ran most of his sheep on the Coragorag run, to the south of Tongala; then to Tongala for shearing around September; over to the Madowla Lagoon area until November, when they were moved north and east to the major portion of the Lower Moira run, eventually returning by April to Tongala and finally back to Coragorag.

The oldest part of the present homestead looks out over the deep Madowla Lagoon. The luxuriant garden, originally supplied with rare specimens by von Mueller, provides a striking contrast to the new growth of native gums.

After the death of his father in 1850 Edward Curr divided and sold the squatting empire built up during the previous decade. In June 1852 the partnership of James Murphy and William Looker acquired the licence to the Tongala run and two months later also the adjoining Lower Moira run. In February 1855 the two runs were registered solely in the name of James Murphy. By profession a brewer, conducting in addition by the 1850s a thriving wine and spirit trade, Murphy during that decade took up the twin hobbies of so many prosperous businessmen in Victoria—politics and land. Murphy's political career was brief, undistinguished, even ignominious. His sole action that brought him prominence was to move a vote of no confidence in the Yan Yean reservoir scheme; the motion was defeated and Murphy retired from politics. As a landowner Murphy appears to have been rather more successful and certainly survived longer.

Although he transferred the pastoral licence to the great Lower Moira run to Frederick Bury and Peter Cheyne in July 1859, in September of that year Murphy acquired a pre-emptive grant of what was to become the homestead block of Madowla Park. A Lands Department plan shows the grant as one square mile in shape as well as area, fronting on to the Murray river and extending south from there to include the Towro sandhill, the central reaches of the Madowla Lagoon and a strip of land to the south of the Lagoon. While most of the land was still timbered with redgum, box and she-oak, it nevertheless supported the nucleus of a sizeable farm establishment. The plan shows that there already existed a group of huts on the banks of the Lagoon, on the site of the present homestead complex, a stable and other huts a short distance away, stockyards further to the north-west, and sheep pounds along the post and rail fence forming the eastern boundary of the property. Among the huts close to the Lagoon were almost certainly the original homestead and substantial two-room store, similar structures of untrimmed redgum slabs laid horizontally. The former, in a dangerous state of disrepair, was demolished a few years ago; the latter, though now with windows and iron roof, survives, dusty and unused, but a rich museum of generations of past owners and users.

While James Murphy's purchase marks the beginnings of Madowla Park as a separate property, its major development, first as pastoral and later as mixed farming enterprise owes most to Robert Hill Kinnear and Matthew O'Shanassy. Kinnear, born in Scotland in 1822, sailed for Melbourne in 1839 and quickly established himself in commerce and on the land. In the early 1860s he added to his already extensive pastoral interests the Lower Moira run, including the Madowla pre-emptive block acquired by Murphy. During that decade, perhaps the most prosperous in the nineteenth century for pastoralists, Kinnear was able to build up, with the assistance of deficiencies in selection legislation, a large freehold estate in the Madowla region, operating in conjunction with his licence holding of the Lower Moira run. Subsequently, probably in the 1870s, the Madowla freehold was acquired by the O'Shanassy family, to be operated by Matthew, eldest son of Sir John O'Shanassy, in conjunction with the latter's property Moira across the Murray river in New South Wales. After Sir John's death in 1883 the family properties were progressively divided

Otherwise sober and restrained, Madowla Park displays an unexpected touch of lavatory humour.

or relinquished. Madowla Park, however, remained in the possession of Matthew O'Shanassy until his death in 1900.

Between them Kinnear and O'Shanassy were responsible for the construction of a remarkable collection of station buildings, all of timber and mostly redgum. None is individually outstanding, but collectively they form an impressive tribute to a great nineteenth century working station; to the wealth of the 1860s and the optimism and ambition of the 1880s in particular.

Of the homestead complex, all but the original slab hut survive. Kinnear's residence, a long, low, wide-verandahed structure overlooking the Madowla Lagoon, set the pattern for subsequent expansion in its use of redgum boards for the walls and Murray pine for floors and ceilings, and in its simple functional design. Never intended as a showplace the homestead was from the start a practical unpretentious dwelling put together from local materials. Set a little way back from the homestead were the servants' quarters and kitchen. O'Shanassy considerably extended the homestead as well as erecting a new kitchen, separate guests'

Elegantly furnished in cedar and oak, with floors and ceilings of Murray pine, the dining-room was one of the additions made to the homestead by Madowla Park's second main occupant, Matthew O'Shanassy; it was subsequently enlarged in the present century by the Honourable William Cain.

115

quarters and other homestead buildings. Most notable perhaps is the meat house, built on the principle of a Coolgardie safe. On each of its four sides two pairs of redgum board walls, with insulation within each pair, are set a few inches apart to allow sheets of hessian to be soaked by water from above, and ventilated by narrow horizontal and vertical doors; surmounting the whole is a heavily insulated roof. Centrally placed within the meat house stands a chopping block about a metre in diameter, the stump of a once mighty redgum.

As the homestead complex grew, so too did its acre or more of garden. Kinnear, a friend of von Mueller, obtained from the latter rare and exotic specimens to form the basis of a luxuriant garden setting, as if to compensate for the unobtrusiveness of the homestead itself. Once carefully cleared of all native trees and vegetation it provided, like so many homestead gardens, an apparent refuge from the uncompromising Australian landscape. Much of the garden survives from the nineteenth century, though now overshadowed by a new growth of tall gums on the homestead side of Madowla Lagoon and concealed from the approaches from the Murray river by a stand of peppercorn trees.

A short distance from the homestead complex are located the main farm outbuildings, some of recent construction but the majority built during the time of Kinnear and O'Shanassy. Most prominent is the tall storage tower, once containing the feed to supply the numerous working horses in the stables adjacent to it. Close to the tower a shed houses a great portable steam engine, which powered, among other things, the chaff cutter in an adjoining shed and the conveyance of feed to the storage tower. Close by

Matthew O'Shanassy, racing enthusiast, ran separate stables for his race horses and for his working horses.

are the harness room, still in use, and a smithy with furnace and bellows still in working order. Among other early buildings are what were once the more palatial racing stables including grooms' quarters, dairy shed and, located separately near the eastern boundary of the homestead block, the woolshed. Although largely rebuilt the original frame of Murray pine beams still forms the central spine of this building, and a portion of one exterior wall, of horizontal slab construction, survives from earlier days.

Matthew O'Shanassy, owner of Madowla Park through the 1880s and 1890s and possibly some time earlier, was a quiet unassuming man. In contrast with his Irish-born father, three times Premier of Victoria, he had little interest in politics. Matthew's major interest, as known at least to the public of Victoria, was horse-racing, for which Madowla Park, with its flat and fertile paddocks, and within easy reach of rail transport to Melbourne, provided an ideal property. Apart from his racing stables and associated buildings O'Shanassy apparently operated his own private racing track on the property; evidence of this came to light in recent years when the present owners, ploughing hitherto permanent pasture, encountered a broad oval of heavily compacted ground, the product of countless pounding hooves.

Although relatively unsuccessful in the big races—one Caulfield Cup winner was his sole major triumph—O'Shanassy was an active and well-known figure in racing circles. From 1881 until shortly before his death he was a committee member of the Victorian Racing Club and, in his later years, concentrating more on breeding than on racing, he acquired a high reputation for his brood mare stud at Madowla Park.

A horizontal slab storehouse, originally shingled and without windows, is the earliest surviving building on the property.

The meat house, literally built around an enormous redgum stump used as chopping block, operated on the principle of a Coolgardie safe. Each of the four sides consists of insulated pairs of walls set a few inches apart to allow hessian sheets to be soaked from above and ventilated by narrow horizontal and vertical doors.

The harness room, part of an impressive complex of large timber outbuildings dating from the nineteenth century, still serves its original purpose.

Matthew O'Shanassy, possibly along with other members of his family, also had a great interest in irrigation, and he was one of the first to experiment with the immense potential of the Murray river. Although the exact chronology is uncertain, his first efforts were probably concentrated on a great barge, specially constructed with powerful pumping equipment and a hole in the middle from which water was drawn through long canvas pipes to O'Shanassy property on both sides of the river. Parts of the original piping were removed and are among the more remarkable pieces in Madowla Park's informal museum. The barge itself, what remains of it, lies submerged and deeply embedded in the Victorian bank of the river. Only a short distance away, just east of the Towro sandhill, are the remains of a more permanent irrigation system established by O'Shanassy. A tunnel leading from the river to the present boundary of Madowla Park, still clearly marked by a line of slightly ominous depressions where the tunnel has collapsed, once carried water to a powerful steam pump securely anchored on higher ground. Driven by a 70 horsepower steam engine, it was claimed to be capable of lifting no less than 10,000 gallons of water a minute from the tunnel into the large open channel, along which water flowed south towards the woolshed and from there along branch channels in various directions. At some later date the open channels were supplemented or replaced by large steel pipes: one, still clearly visible, ran parallel with the original main channel; another from the main channel beneath the Towro sandhill, conveyed water to flat land further west.

The still-obvious immensity of the original works conveys again the image of an active, innovative property where social life was almost an afterthought.

Matthew O'Shanassy died in May 1900. During his last years he had not spent much time at Madowla Park, in part because of a near-fatal accident on the Murray river which had resulted in permanent ill-health. After his death the executors of the estate ultimately decided, reflecting the changing times, to subdivide the property for more intensive agriculture. The 5,554 acres (2,200 hectares) of freehold were advertised for sale in September 1903, in ten lots. The choicest and largest of these was the Homestead Block, of some 1,340 acres, the original pre-emptive block with additional land to east and west. The subdivisional plan shows the greater part composed of irrigation paddocks, mostly under lucerne. This 'highly improved' block contained, according to the accompanying description, 'a commodious wooden house, surrounded by a charming garden, picturesquely situated on the Madowla Lagoon, which is as broad as the Murray, and permanent, extensive stables, sheds and outbuildings, the whole being reticulated from an elevated tank, supplied by a hot air pump'. The planned subdivision was a failure and more than a year elapsed before the whole property was re-advertised for sale as a single going concern. On a copy of this second advertisement, held at Madowla Park, the estate is carefully shaded by pencil into zones of 'heavily flooded', 'annual light flooding' and 'occasional'. One area of high ground to the east and the north-south sandhill country alone escape the penciller's shading. Perhaps it is little wonder that the earlier proposed subdivision, each block amply supplied with water but few with high ground, had been a failure.

At the 1904 sale Madowla Park was brought by William Cain, native of the Isle of Man, seventy-three years of age, with a long and successful career as builder and railway contractor, and in his later years as a leading public figure in Melbourne. Mayor of the city during 1886-7, he played an important part in the formation of the Melbourne and Metropolitan Board of Works; later he was to become a Member of the Legislative Council in the newly constituted State of Victoria. Although in the 1890s his personal fortunes dwindled, Cain remained solvent, unlike most leading businessmen, and ultimately rebuilt in part at least his extensive commercial and pastoral interests. After acquiring Madowla Park, Cain generally spent some months there each winter, one of his sons being resident manager of the property.

After William Cain's death in 1914 Madowla Park remained a family estate until 1950 when it was purchased by the present owners. Under the younger generation of Cains a further major experiment in irrigation was attempted, to the south of Madowla Lagoon. Here some eighty-five acres of low hill country were planted with citrus trees, following the contours. Water drawn from the Madowla Lagoon was pumped to a series of concrete tanks at high points and from these down concrete channels to the groves of citrus. As with earlier experiments in irrigation this does not appear to have been notably successful: environment once again was to triumph over even the most vigorous efforts of Man. Yet, as with so much of Madowla Park's history, the visual reminders are still there; some of the tanks and channels, and even a small patch of citrus trees, not heavily yielding, but enough according to the present manager to keep his household well supplied.

A few years ago complete reconstruction of the woolshed was cut short by the commencement of the shearing season. As a result one small section of an early horizontal slab wall still survives.

Eynesbury *Victoria*

Text: T. A. Hazell   *Photographs: Brian J. Lloyd*

EYNESBURY IS A PROPERTY of some 7,000 hectares situated about forty kilometres from Melbourne near the small town of Melton, an area which is rapidly being engulfed by the north-western suburban sprawl of the city. It once formed part of the extensive pastoral holdings of the Staughton family and was, in fact, part of the original Exford run, taken out by Simon Staughton in 1841. At the time of the founder's death in 1863, the estate consisted of more than 70,000 acres (28,000 hectares) of land. After 1870 the Staughton family subdivided the property, amongst themselves, into four sections. These were Exford, Nerowie, Staughton Vale, and Eynesbury, each with its own homestead. As an interesting document in the history of a pioneering pastoral family in Victoria, the original section of the Exford homestead is probably the most intrinsically valuable survivor of the Staughton holdings. Eynesbury, however, is certainly a grander house and it is much larger than the parent homestead.

The Eynesbury homestead was built by Simon Thomas Staughton, the eldest son of the founder of the Australian branch of the family. At the time of the sub-division of the 1870s, the estate consisted of 20,000 acres (8,000 hectares). Widespread local opinion in the early years of this century held that the development of the Melton district was restricted by the size of the pastoral holdings in the possession of so few people. In particular, the size of the Exford and Eynesbury estates was criticized. Haphazard subdivision and, more particularly, the activities of the Closer Settlement Board in fostering more intensive agriculture in the area, signalled the end for the vast Eynesbury estate and reduced it to its present size. It passed from the ownership of the Staughton family in the 1920s and now forms part of the extensive pastoral holdings of the Baillieu family.

The Western volcanic plains of Victoria were one of the earliest settled parts of the colony. They attracted the pioneer pastoral families who both profited from the land and enriched it with the fine homestead buildings, which are so important a feature of man's taming and adaptation of the landscape. The approach to the Eynesbury homestead is through a magnificent forest of grey box trees which must surely be unique in Victoria, both for its acreage and for the maturity of the trees. The house itself is now approached from the rear and it is hard to determine the location of the original track to the main entrance. The house appears as one passes by a beautifully-planned and sited artificial lake, indicative of the care with which the homestead buildings were laid out.

The front of the homestead building, which looks out across a beautiful garden towards gently undulating countryside. The fine proportions of the house and its generous size are most evident.

The former men's quarters, a fine blue-stone building with each room having access on to the verandah, which runs the length of the building.

Both the house and outbuildings of Eynesbury are substantial structures built of bluestone said to have been quarried on the property. The original section of the house is two-storeyed and of very simple design and construction. It was built in the early 1870s and pre-dates Simon Staughton's rise to prominence both as a leading pastoralist, and as a Member of the Legislative Assembly from the 1880s until 1901. He died in 1903, after a distinguished career which included service in the South African War.

The two-storeyed central block of the house forms a very narrow rectangle. Off the wide hallway, on the lower level, there are two principal rooms and several smaller ones. None of these rooms is in its original condition, although some relics of early days have survived in, for example, a marble mantelpiece and some built-in furniture. The staircase is strangely positioned just inside the front entrance door. It is possible that this not entirely satisfactory arrangement dates from an internal re-arrangement at the time of the extensive building alterations of the 1880s. The upper level consists of some six rooms with partition walls dividing the one from the other. The style is very simple indeed and the rooms are almost completely unaltered from their original state. Fireplaces, call-bells, and some built-in furniture, of basic design and construction, are intact. The two-storeyed section is surmounted by an observation platform or belvedere, now accessible only through a manhole in the ceiling. From the belvedere a splendid view is obtained of the surrounding countryside, with its rolling plains and evidences of volcanic disturbances. Under the iron roofing of this central section of the homestead, the original shingles are still in position.

Eynesbury's chief beauty, however, lies in the extensive alterations and additions to the house carried out in the 1880s. They are the work of an unknown architect and builder. The additions are in the form of corner pavilions to the original central block, giving the house a great dignity and style which can only be described as 'Colonial Palladian'. The additions involved the provision of a new roof and eaves for the central block to make it conform with the roofing of the pavilions. At the same time, in the interests of conformity, the original chimney stacks were re-built. The new

A corner detail of the roofing and eaves of the main section of the homestead building.

A view of the rear of the homestead showing the original section, surmounted by the belvedere. The schoolroom was formerly in the room on the right of the photograph, whilst the left-hand pavilion contains the manager's office.

The octagonally-shaped meat house, and its adjoining smoke room, at the rear of the homestead buildings. Both are built in brick and are well preserved.

An interesting detail of chimney stacks, of staggered height, on the central block and south-east pavilion.

Looking south along the front verandah of the house. The well-proportioned timber joinery is in an excellent state of preservation. The verandah flooring is of timber in the central section and of tiles around each of the pavilion fronts.

The main entrance doorway of the stable block showing the building's finely worked bluestone. The attention to detail, evident in all of Eynesbury's buildings, is an outstanding characteristic of the homestead.

and old sections are skillfully tied together in the front of the house by a wide verandah extending the full width of the central block and pavilions. In the rear, coherence is achieved by the provision of a verandah extending around three sides of a court-yard enclosed by the original and later sections of the house. The combination of the early homestead building and corner pavilions is remarkably successful and gives the house an external character and beauty in a unique expression of architectural unity.

One of the corner pavilions is completely detached from the main body of the house, in that it can only be entered from a doorway leading on to the front verandah. It still serves as a billiard room and is almost entirely unchanged from Victorian times. The room is of elegant proportions with walls papered in an interestingly patterned paper of late Victorian 'aesthetic' movement design. Two large cedar leather-upholstered couches, raised on platforms to enable the spectators to see the top of the table, and the full-size billiards table, with Simon Staughton's cue hanging close by, complete the furnishings of the room. The matching pavilion, at the other corner of the house, now serves as a drawing-room but, in all probability, it was a dining-room in earlier days. The remainder of the house has been altered and modernized during the last fifty years, but much of its original homestead character still remains. The manager's office and a very large room, said to have been the homestead school room, occupy the other corners of the building.

The front of the house and part of two sides are surrounded by stone walls, enclosing a beautiful garden which is now fully mature and well maintained—a true oasis of greenery and refinement surrounded by rural land. The stone wall in front, containing the entrance gateway, is a comparatively rare example in Victoria of a ha-ha wall: on the garden side, it is only about two feet high but the outer side drops down to a depth of about four feet. Centred in the gateway, but a good distance away, is a mound of volcanic origin known as Mount Mary.

A canopied walkway connects the rear of the house with the former men's quarters, which have a verandah running along the entire length of the bluestone building. It is a block of fine proportions and its low roof-line is in harmony with the roof-line of the rear of the main homestead building. Enclosing the rear of this area is a stable block, also built in bluestone, and in a good state of preservation. Close to the house is a brick, octagonally-shaped meat room, roofed in corrugated iron with an adjoining smoke room.

By careful attention to planning and proportions, a pleasing union of an original homestead building, of great simplicity and style, with more elaborate additions is achieved in the Eynesbury homestead. The unknown architect and builders have been successful in giving an external character of charm and distinction to make this house one of the most graceful and elegant in the immediate vicinity of Melbourne.

The elevated water tank to the south of the homestead buildings. It is said to be of early date and is still in use.

The stable block at the east of the home-stead. It is a building in a good state of repair and the trellis windows are an interesting feature.

Banyule *Victoria*

Text: Frank Strahan   *Photographs: Brian J. Lloyd*

The entrance leads to a house of twenty rooms. The gently pitched arch is a restrained example of Gothic revival forms of the earlier nineteenth century, a character at variance with the vigorous nature of the pastoralist and explorer Joseph Hawdon, builder of Banyule House.
Through the porch the scene opens to the hall, flanked to the right by the original ballroom, later a sitting-room; to the left is the dining-room, enlarged in 1908 to incorporate the gun-room.

Herbert Allen, who acquired the property in 1942, found Banyule in dilapidation. He set to with renovations, sealed his proprietorship by installing a new front door. Sprigs of a cyprus pine, planted by James Graham during his tenancy of 1860-65, overhang the picture.

To all whom these Presents shall come, Greeting . . . at a Public Auction . . . for the Sale of Crown Lands in Our Territory . . . Richard Henry Browne of Sydney has become the purchaser of the Land hereinafter described for the sum of one thousand three hundred and thirty four pounds Sterling.

THE CROWN GRANT by purchase was dated 31 January 1839. The land, later the site for Banyule, was portion 6, Parish of Keelbundora, County of Bourke. Nine miles north from the newly-found town of Melbourne, its 920 acres (360 hectares) are now absorbed in the Melbourne suburb of Heidelberg. Its purchaser had the popular name 'Continental Browne', given it is said because he had taken the grand tour of Europe and talked of it with persistent enthusiasm.

Closer horizons included grazing land at Yass, near the Murrumbidgee river; but 'Continental Browne' was also known as 'a dandy land agent', of 'persuasive tongue and sanguine predictions'. Property speculation, not visions of homesteads, prompted his Heidelberg purchase. In October 1839 he sub-divided portion 6 as four parallel lots, fronting the Yarra river. This was early recognition that the country of Banyule had the character of an out-station to Melbourne, not a place in the bush. An auctioneer's advertisement for the region in the boom time of the late 1880s encapsulated the concept:

It is so situated as to command a lovely aspect, in which valleys of emerald pasture are contrasted with purple hills, forest clad, while two rivers—the Yarra and the Plenty—introduce into the fascinating scene that light movement, freshness and vivacity of which Australian landscapes are generally destitute. Indeed, nowhere within the same distance from Melbourne would it be possible to find residential sites combining all that is most attractive in the rural scene of England with the social and intellectual advantages procurable in a great and progressive metropolis like the capital of Victoria.

It fits the scene that Banyule has the style of grand houses of England. Built, probably in 1849—certainly by 1852—for the famous overlander and explorer Joseph Hawdon, its elements of Elizabethan and Gothic revival have likenesses to early nineteenth century buildings of Hawdon's native Durham. From the beginning it carried the title 'Banyule House'.

126

The south-west view. A crenellated bay window crowns the entrance arch and porch to the front door on the west façade. Pinnacles marry with chimneys and the upward sweep of moulded parapets. These perpendicular forms carry through to the base and the whole is finely tied with stringed courses. The blending east wing extension of 1908 commences at the mid-point of the second parapet, right. The style combines elements of Gothic and Tudor revival, with Regency forms of the windows. The blind window upper right completes the symmetry.

The east elevation presents the extensions completed in 1908. The ground floor room, left, was built as a schoolroom, converted to a sitting-room after 1942, reverting to childs' use as a play-room in 1963. Its French doors carry through the style of the original ballroom doors, ground floor far left. The upstairs balcony leads right to the new master bed-room, rear to a children's bed-room, converted to a dressing-room in 1965.

Banyule has always been an out-station of Melbourne. The eastward view was the remaining claim to a rural character: the flats of the Yarra River; the Dandenong Ranges banding the horizon. Urban development of the Bulleen-Templestowe region now intervenes, continuing the march of the city.

The building site was a 279-acre lot of Browne's sub-division bought by Hawdon on 10 February 1840. Hawdon consolidated his holding by purchase of adjacent lots. He bought 264 acres to the east from the Melbourne merchant Arthur Hogue on 19 October 1843. On 24 May 1845 he became outright owner of 114 acres to the west, bought in concert with the pastoralist J. S. Bolden two months earlier from William Verner, recently retired Chief Commissioner of Insolvent Estates, Melbourne. He named the whole Banyule, adopting the title given to his lot by Arthur Hogue, and said to represent the word meaning 'hill' in the dialect of the local tribe of Warringal blacks.

Whereas Banyule was built to an appearance and substance of permanency, Joseph Hawdon exhibited a more restless nature. Between 1836 and 1839 he accompanied John Gardiner and John Hepburn from Howe's station on the Murrumbidgee in the first overland drive of cattle south to Melbourne; established the first overland mail route to Sydney; pioneered a stock route from Howlong on the Murray river to Adelaide; demonstrated the practicability of a land route for mails from Melbourne to Adelaide, driving by tandem with a Lt. Mundy 'through the uninhabited country of Australia Felix with as much ease as they might have done through an English Park'.

Hawdon's time at his 'English Park', Banyule, proved almost as transitory. In 1853, after sub-division and sale of a 16-acre portion on the south west corner, he leased Banyule to his son-in-law, Melbourne lawyer Hugh John Chambers, and left for England. He made brief returns to Melbourne through the 1850s before locating permanently in New Zealand in the early 1860s. Whereas he owned Banyule to 1867 he never again lived there. His contact with the property was the correspondence with his business agents, notably the merchant politician James Graham, writing as to tenants, rents, repairs or attempts to sell.

Close though he was in relationship, the tenancy of Hugh Chambers resulted in great bitterness. He acted as Hawdon's attorney, and it was Hawdon's claim that his outlays on improvements, including building a lodge, exceeded agreement as to costs in lieu of rent and that Chambers had improperly charged the balance against Hawdon's account. In November 1857 William Henry Fancourt Mitchell, Legislative Councillor and one time Chief Commissioner of Police, became the new tenant. There had already been police association with Banyule. An agreement of 1855, retrospective to February 1853, leased some six acres along with a dwelling house to the government for a police establishment to train cadets. This land in turn was surrounded by farm land leased to John Nuttall and George Pregg. Further, in 1858, 200 acres surrounding Banyule House were leased to William Nuttall, and west of here lay the leased farm of Messrs Barnes and Edney.

These leases carved Banyule lands among tenant farmers with their beef and dairy cattle, fodder crops, orchards of pears or plums. Meanwhile Banyule House took on the role of gentleman's residence. Mitchell's tenancy covered the house and 'about 40 acres . . . comprising grass paddock in front of the dwelling . . . flower garden, shrubbery and upper part of the cultivation paddock in the rear'. However, distance from town, poor communications and tightness of money made it difficult to place Banyule House either for rent or sale. James Graham's efforts were unsuccessful when Mitchell did not renew his lease in 1860. His answer was to rent and occupy the house himself to 1865, when he withdrew with apologies. A caretaker was placed in possession until October 1867, when Banyule was sold to Dr Robert Martin for the depressed price of £7,500.

Dr Martin did not live at Banyule. In 1874 he settled the property, leaselands and all on Mary McCrae Christie ('Minie') Martin, wife of his lawyer son Robert and daughter of James Graham. Two girls were born at Banyule to Minie and Robert Martin. A diabetic, he died on 14 May 1878; Minie died on 19 June 1889. Of the daughters, Mary Lucy (Marnie) died 6 January 1891; Edith Maude (Mandie) married Percy Warren and by the turn of the century had emigrated to a long life in England. Banyule House had reverted to tenancy in 1886, and Mandie Warren carried through ownership by absentee landlords established by Joseph Hawdon in 1853.

The ivy strung court of Banyule. Robert Simpson, purchaser of Banyule in 1965, created the court, throwing the living focus of Banyule inwards. To the left are the extensions of 1908, bonding to the north-south orientation of the original house. The central window lights the stairway, that to the upstairs right a staff bedroom, and beneath it a staff bathroom. Banyule was originally roofed in wooden shingles, then Welsh slate, half of which, as shown, was later replaced with galvanized iron.

The room was originally the ballroom, a wall-flower function to more recent society, and rarely to be found today. In 1963 it became a sitting-room. It opens across the hall to the staircase which spirals to the upper floor. The restrained Gothic element characterizing much of Banyule is found in the pattern of the door. Behind the camera French doors of Regency style open to the southern aspect.

OPPOSITE *The stance embodies solidarity. Banyule is sheathed in cement render. In 1861 the tenant, James Graham, wrote: 'I . . . had the walls and stonework carefully repaired with the best Portland cement, and the whole painted with three coats of best paint, and it now looks capitally, and will last forever'. Behind the render, the walls are hand-formed bricks, set on sandstone foundations. Rafter timbers show no nail in the construction of this original section. They are locked by dove-tail joint or timber studs. Herbert Allen renewed the window joinery in the renovations following his purchase in 1942.*

Gordon Lyon, farmer and mining investor, stands out as the most notable of the later tenants. He leased Banyule House and 107 acres in 1903. He held the lease to 1 December 1938. As to farming practice, he developed a famous Jersey herd. In the case of the house a growing family caused Frank Graham, uncle and trustee for Mandie Warren to write to her on 4 September 1907 that: 'as the Gordon Lyons find they are getting rather cramped . . . owing to the family increasing . . . Mr Lyon approached me to know if you would make some additions to the house'. Major alterations followed. The east wing was added; the dining-room was enlarged; extra fire places were installed in the drawing and smoking-rooms. These works were completed in September 1908 to plans of the Melbourne architects Klenginder & Alsop, builder G. Curry, price £1,385.

When Lyon's lease terminated thirty years later, much of the Banyule land was leased to Banyule Stud Pty Ltd, and the house remained vacant. Following the death of Mandie Warren and release of the property from entailment, Banyule was purchased by Herbert Alfred Allen on 15 December 1942. He found a dilapidated scene. 'One outdoor toilet served the whole building', he wrote. 'There was no lighting, no garden, no stonework or terraces.' He proceeded with energy, renewing flooring and wiring, along with the front door and window panes of the west elevation. To the north a single-storied detached kitchen was joined to the house and a staff sitting-room added.

131

Banyule's land spanned the 757-acre purchase of Joseph Hawdon in the 1840s. Now it is reduced to two-and-a-half acres. Suburban building flanks this scene; but the foreground has an untamed air, and Banyule House looks angry. It watches the Dandenong Ranges, those 'purple hills' to the east, so often in battle to stay the bruising blow of the auctioneer's hammer.

OPPOSITE The garden walk leads west to the court. Banyule had bad luck with its gardens. Work by successive tenants such as James Graham, an assiduous planter of roses and camellias, was ruined by later carelessness or neglect when the house was vacant. In 1943 Herbert Allen built extensive walks, lawns and flower beds. This section and the court were works of Robert Simpson, in 1965.

Allen sold Banyule in 1958. The property was now part of the Melbourne suburban scene and the new owners were Stanhill Pty Ltd, a company of the property developer, Stanley Korman. In the style of 'Continental Browne' Stanhill quickly proceeded to sub-division. Two-and-a-half acres were retained as a buffer to Banyule House, but outbuildings such as the oast house and barn were destroyed, as was the lodge built by Hugh Chambers. The house again became vacant, remaining so until purchase on 25 October 1963 by Robert Simpson following the spectacular crash of Stanley Korman's enterprises.

Robert Simpson rehabilitated Banyule. The staff quarters at the old kitchen were converted to a flat. Family rooms were re-orientated from the west towards open courts; a garden was developed to the east, a swimming pool and tennis court to the north.

Banyule was advertised for sale by Robert Simpson on 23 November 1974. The property passed to the present owner, the State Government of Victoria, by purchase prior to auction. The site of Banyule is again Crown land. Despite encroachment of suburban building Banyule retains a commanding identity. It retains views of 'emerald pastures' and 'purple hills' of the auctioneer's advertisement of the late 1880s. These were rich subjects for Tom Roberts, Arthur Streeton, and Frederick McCubbin, members of the Heidelberg School of painters at that time. The government's plans build the colour of the past into Banyule. They incorporate public display of works of the Heidelberg School, with Banyule a branch of the National Gallery of Victoria.

Corryton Park *South Australia*

Text: *Harry Plumridge*   Photographs: *Marcus B. Brownrigg*

The front door with its sidelights, seen through the entrance arch between the Doric columns, reveals an unexpected lack of depth compared with the breadth of the house.

AT A CROSS-ROADS ten kilometres east of Williamstown in the Barossa ranges, a finger-post points to Trial Hill, and a gravel road runs off towards the north and into the Barossa Valley. About three kilometres on from the finger-post the road swings sharply to the right and begins to climb. Just before the turn, and facing the traveller, are the pillars of Corryton Park gateway, topped by cast-iron griffins. Through the gates, on a wooded rise 800 metres away, sits the house David Randall ordered built in 1851 and called Glen Para, a name it was to bear for only nineteen years.

The wide single-storey building also has some structural points of difference from when it was occupied by the first owner. A square tower erected by his successor rises above the front entrance. Its stone walling with painted lined joints, and the white sandstone quoins and enrichments of balustrading and urns match the house and lend a finishing touch.

The colonnaded verandah and portico in the Doric order date from 1928. The old shingled roof was replaced many years ago with galvanized iron, but the three-light bay window is part of the original ballroom, as can be seen in the reproduction of a water colour sketch by Mrs Randall now in the South Australian Archives.

The name Glen Para, which has a local application, had been suggested by George Fife Angas, who had recently arrived in the new province to take up his estates. The father of colonization in South Australia had in fact strongly influenced the fortunes of the Randall family. Some years before, David Randall, lately married to Eliza Wickes, a school-master's daughter, had heard that Angas was in the north of England lecturing about South Australia and had invited him to visit them in their Northamptonshire home and give them some advice about emigrating.

As a result, David and Eliza Randall, their two children, Mr Wickes, the St Bernard dog, Hector, and forty work-people, whom David had recruited and whose fares he had advanced, took passage in the ship *Templar* on 24 July 1845. They arrived in Port Adelaide on 24 November. The retinue also included a groom, a gardener and two maids. Eliza kept a journal, which many years later was to find a place in her autobiography. In it she wrote that her husband read the scriptures daily to their 'people' and at the end of the voyage presented Bibles to them and the sailors.

She also observed that the passage to Australia was so pleasant that 'some of us were almost sorry when it came to an end'. The family piano travelled in the saloon, and weekly sing-songs and recitations were enjoyed. Eliza discovered a talent for sketching portraits. Nearly all the cabin passengers, 'including the gentlemanly young captain', consented to sit. An albatross 'with twelve-foot wings' sailed through the stern windows of the ship one fine morning and provided the ship's company with some excitement and the Randalls with a memento for their drawing-room.

The early days after the arrival were spent in exchanging calls with new acquaintances and in settling into the house the Randalls had bought from William Giles, the Adelaide manager of the South Australian Company, of

Stone pillars topped by iron griffins at the entrance to Corryton Park frame the distant house. The house is typical of its period, 1851, when a style was evolving that was later to be recognized as characteristically nineteenth-century South Australian, with some vestiges of Georgian influence.

which George Fife Angas was chairman in London. But David Randall was in a hurry to take up farming land, and in his haste bought 600 acres (240 hectares) of poor land near Port Adelaide. This he sold later without loss and bought 2,500 acres (1,000 hectares) from Charles Flaxman, confidential clerk and agent of Mr Angas, in the undulating and well-watered country of Mt Crawford in the Barossa Ranges. Here a 'dairy and cattle station' was established and soon fifty cows were being milked. The Randalls were followed a year after their arrival by David's brother, William, who had married Eliza's sister, Annie. Mr Wickes, the girls' father, obtained the post of Secretary of the Board of Education.

A second house was bought in the suburb of Walkerville and David embarked on a career of further land buying. Before long his various holdings totalled 6,000 acres (2,400 hectares).

The time had come for the Randalls to move to the country. Early in 1851 while they were staying at Lindsay House, Angaston (one of the Angas houses), an expedition of ten set out for the Barossa Ranges to choose the site for what was to be named Glen Para. They chose a site about a kilometre from David's dairy farm in cool grassy hills, some 50 kilometres from Adelaide by to-day's direct routes. Stone was cut for the house, the heavy outbuildings and flagged paths, from deposits a few kilometres away on the estate. The work began in 1851 but, through various causes, including the rush of labour to the Victorian goldfields, it was twelve months before the owners could move in, and even then there were some half-finished rooms.

David's interests increased and diversified. He grew grapes and made wine, which found a ready market. He bought a valuable property at South Rhine, some kilometres away, where grapes and fruit also grew in abundance. A citrus crop on yet another property near Gawler returned £1,000 in one year. On the home estate he eventually turned to raising English breeds of sheep and 'often paid fancy prices for good rams'.

Eliza's autobiography provides glimpses of the social exchanges which lent colour to her life in the country. The Joseph Gilberts, of Pewsey Vale, were virtually neighbours and were frequent callers, as were the Murrays of Murray Vale and the Warrens of Springfield. On one visit to the Gilberts the horse shied, the wheel of the dog-cart went over a stump and Eliza was pitched over the wheel on to the ground, but without serious injury. On another occasion Henry Evans, the architect of Collingrove and Lindsay House, and his wife, were expected at Glen Para for dinner, but they entered the estate by the wrong gate and got bushed in a paddock twelve kilometres round. They eventually reached the homestead at bed time, 'much troubled'.

The Randalls leant heavily on the Angases for friendship. Eliza confesses in the autobiography that 'the intimacy with that family did more to reconcile me to living in South Australia than that of any whose acquaintance we made in those early days', notwithstanding, presumably, comings and goings with vice-royalty and other exalted persons!

The book records setbacks and sadnesses. Eliza disclosed that both David and his brother, William, lost money in speculation. The Burra copper boom was at its height. Instead, however, of buying shares in the going concern which would yield dividends David bought various bits of land in the hope of making new finds, with predictable results.

Two of the Randall's four children died, Edward, eight-and-a-half, who was an avid reader 'far too clever and in fact beyond his years', and, years later on, the much-prized older son Walter. Cleverness, seemingly, did not kill Edward, in fact, but bronchitis. The son Walter died when twenty, also from the results of a cold caught when he was inspecting a property part-owned by his father, near Port Augusta. Walter and two workmen who were accidentally killed on the property are buried in the Mount Crawford cemetery.

One of the minor disasters of the Randalls had to do with Trial Hill. A bullock wagon coming by way of Lyndoch with a long-awaited load of furniture and china from England came to grief while climbing the steep and twisting track. The wagon was upended, and the precious cargo went crashing over the edge.

In the midst of these sad accounts Mrs Randall relates how her painting of portraits and scenes on silk and ground glass was coming along, and names some of the high-born recipients of her work, including the Duchess of Edinburgh, 'who did me the honour to accept one as a wedding present'.

After nineteen years at Glen Para the strain of managing all his properties began to tell on David Randall, and he decided to sell Glen Para and

Two stages in Corryton Park's history seen through the arched gateway into the front garden: the tower added in 1869 and the re-built verandah of 1928. The walling of the house, like the tower, is local stone with a rougher surface than bluestone and flecked with mica.

The return verandah had originally been trellised, with openings facing the windows. It was widened in 1928 and the trellising replaced with a Doric colonnade designed by J. R. S. Evans, of Adelaide. The blocked quoins of house and tower are of a variety of local white sandstone.

John Wilson, who was a noted modeller of architectural decoration, built this stone walling and arch with dry joints, and the curved balustrading illustrated on page 134, when Mrs K. A. McBean re-designed the garden twenty years ago.

OPPOSITE: *Native stone walling with joints flushed up and ruled, and massive pit-sawn red gum framing from trees felled on the property, gave strength and style to the splendid outbuildings. The coachhouse (on the right) has now been refitted as an additional residence in character with the main house.*

The rear view of the coachhouse, which also houses the blacksmith shop and the old winery, with its doorway at the foot of the long wall. Shearers' quarters are at the left. At the extreme right is a stone oven where bread was once baked.

move to Seacombe House, Brighton. He was greatly interested in colonial free trade and federation and travelled widely advocating these objectives, in the next few years. He was clearly a lavish spender. A contemporary refers to him as a 'true English gentleman who did things well—too well for a pioneer in a new country'. His selling methods showed the impetuosity of inexperience, and he often missed the market.

In 1874 he visited England for his health's sake and with the idea of promoting a company to buy suitably-established vineyards in South Australia. He persuaded the Duke of Edinburgh to place South Australian wines on his table. However, in October of that year he became ill in London and died, at the age of fifty-five.

Glen Para had been purchased in 1869 by William Rounsevell for £15,000. He promptly changed the name to Corryton Park, which had family origins in his native Cornwall, and later had the tower built on the house. Rounsevell was by then firmly established in South Australia. He had started his career in the police force and then set up a livery and coaching business which grew to huge proportions, with contracts for carrying nearly all the mails in the province. At one time he had more than 1,000 horses in harness. He sold the mail and coaching business to Cobb and Co. before he bought the pastoral property.

There were two sons, John and William Benjamin, who were half-brothers. At Corryton Park they acquired a taste for pastoral pursuits. They successfully acclimatized various kinds of English game, and went into sheep-raising with a flourish, as in everything else they did. They exhibited pure merino wool at the Colonial and Indian Exhibition in London. Corryton was soon carrying 3,000 sheep on 2,500 acres (1,000 hectares). Both brothers bought and sold sheep stations in various parts of South Australia. Both served terms in Parliament. John did not seek re-election after one term in the House of Assembly for the district of Light, as he was appointed Government contractor for goods traffic on the South Australian Railways and for the supply of a large quantity of sleepers from Corryton Park. He constructed 800 kilometres of the overland telegraph line north of Port Augusta and did all the cartage for a further 950 kilometres of the line, employing 100 six-horse teams. He was a famous whip. When a circus proprietor visiting Adelaide drove a twelve-horse team through the city, John Rounsevell capped his performance by driving nearly double that number through the same streets.

W. B. Rounsevell was an even more many-sided personality than his brother. He was in Parliament, except for a break of six years, for a total of thirty-one years and, for a term, held Cabinet rank as Treasurer and Commissioner of Public Works. He was a distinguished cattle breeder and judge, a president of the Royal Agricultural Society, a successful racehorse owner, and a pillar of the South Australian Jockey Club. He introduced coursing at Corryton Park, and was the first president of the National Coursing Club.

Life was attacked with zest at Corryton Park in those days. Gay parties and balls abounded, especially during Christmas and the racing season, and the Rounsevells drove across to Oakbank races in a four-in-hand with horn blowing, to the entertainment of the countryside.

Corryton Park passed into its third ownership in 1898, when Mr Charles Gebhardt bought it from John Rounsevell for the Mackerode group of sheep-breeding estates. Eldest son of Gustav Gebhardt, the German settler who had established Mackerode, he had retired to Glenelg because of failing health ten years before. Tiring of the seaside, he came out of retirement, transformed the property and its livestock and, in 1902, bought it from the partnership with his brothers. He stocked it with merinos from Mackerode and with champion rams, and also established a Hereford herd. He finally sold it in October 1919 to Horace George Lillecrapp, who resold it nine months later without having lived in it.

In those days Corryton Park had a fine avenue of gum trees (since demolished) leading up to the house.

When Corryton Park was sold by Mr Lillecrapp in July 1920, it passed into the possession of the McBeans, a pastoral family which had acquired great tracts of land in South Australia, the Riverina and Queensland in the nineteenth century. Lachlan McBean was a hardy and astute Scot, who had arrived in South Australia in 1838 and, after employment in Adelaide with Mr William Younghusband, had begun cattle dealing and droving on his own account, making several overland journeys from the Darling

Inside the stables: the pit-sawn blue gum slabs of the stalls, and the red gum posts and beams supporting the hayloft, are all in their original state.

Downs. He soon amassed considerable capital and bought Baldon Station, near Truro, South Australia, which he converted into a freehold of 24,000 acres (9,600 hectares).

Lachlan, who remained a bachelor, was followed to South Australia by his brother Alexander, who had twelve children. It was one of these, Lachlan Jnr, who bought Corryton Park as a coming-of-age gift for his eldest son, Keith Alexander McBean; having himself succeeded to Baldon Station, Truro, earlier on, and later acquired Glen Devon, Mount Pleasant. Mr Keith McBean went into possession in 1924 and set about putting the estate into first-class condition and replanning the house. Later he added 1,300 acres (920 hectares) from the nearby Pewsey Vale estate, consisting of the Peak Paddock, containing a 600 metre hill, which is now a 'trig.' point, and the Reservoir paddock whence Pewsey Vale once drew its water supply.

In 1936 Mr McBean married Miss Ella Fuller and, since his death in 1969, she has spent most of her time at Corryton Park, giving it her care and supervising her 7,000-acre (2,800 hectare) property near Truro, both of which are managed by Mr James Marshall.

The rounded pastures and fine gums of Corryton Park breathe tranquillity. Looking down from Trial Hill road, which skirts the home paddocks on the north east, the house, among its ornamental trees, with its tower and white enrichments, gives a strong illusion of a country house in the Scottish hills.

'Mount Eliza', named after Mrs Randall, who often climbed it to show visitors the estate, rises behind the outbuildings. Here were planted the orchards and some of the vines which provided grapes for the winery.

Corryton Park has fine trees. At this point the south-east corner of the verandah looks across the incoming drive to the gums on the banks of the stream which wanders through the property. The steps, designed as part of the 1928 additions, were intended as the main approach to the house.

The tower and turret of Holland House, which dominate the front of the homestead. The rubble masonry is offset by English freestone trimming; and the unity of the whole building is maintained by the use of the same castellation and flat-arched Tudor windows as in the south and west facades.

Holland House

South Australia

Text: David Dolan   *Photographs: Marcus B. Brownrigg*

THERE CAN BE LITTLE DOUBT that when Richard Holland named his newly-built residence 'Holland House', in 1854, he was thinking of Holland House in London; for that great Jacobean mansion, the town-house of the Earls of Ilchester, was one of the most famous buildings in the Empire. In his autobiography *Men, Women and Things* (1937) the octogenarian Duke of Portland listed the thirteen great houses which had dominated the mid-Victorian social scene, adding sadly: 'Now, except four, they are closed.' His only consolation was that among the survivors was Holland House, 'perhaps the most interesting and important of all'.

Richard Holland was born at Windsor, New South Wales, in 1815, his father having arrived in Australia in 1806. He came to South Australia and was conspicuously successful with land and stock, and in 1849 he married a widow with three sons. In 1853 he bought the Turretfield Estate near Gawler, and immediately set about building a house for the family he had acquired. This was Holland House, completed in 1854 to the design of James Macgeorge, architect and surveyor.

For much of its life Holland House was known simply as Turretfield, the name of the estate upon which it stands, and one which has an important place in South Australian history and agriculture. In the first years of the colony, the explorer John Ainsworth Horrocks grazed sheep in the area, as he passed through on his way to Penwortham in the mid-north.

The first owner of the land, and the founder of the Turretfield Estate was Henry Dundas Murray, who came to South Australia in 1839. He brought sheep and cattle overland from New South Wales, but found no market for them, so, with a partner, he bought the Gawler Boiling Down Establishment, which rendered down sheep for tallow, and re-established it on his property in 1849. Enormous stockyards and vat-houses were built, but of these no trace remains. At this time there were no white settlers between Turretfield and Gawler, but there were many Aborigines and, in general, relations with them appear to have been quite cordial.

After Richard Holland took over the property Murray moved into Gawler, but after a few years left for New Zealand where he died in 1882. The nearby village of Rosenthal, which can be seen from the tower of Holland House, was growing fast in the eighteen-fifties. The fifty founding German settlers, who had built the charming unpretentious St Martin's Lutheran Church, had swelled their numbers to over five hundred by 1855, only six years after their arrival. In the wartime hysteria of 1918, the name Rosenthal was changed to Rosedale, as part of the anti-German agitation which so shamefully mistreated many of South Australia's most devoted and industrious citizens.

Holland House faces east on to a small lawn area at the top of the main drive. From the deep porch one may enter the passage, or climb the stairs to the balcony below which the vault is situated. The archway on the right leads through to the small rear courtyard.

The modestly-decorated bay window of the south hall has doors which open on to a patio. The steps lead to a steep descent to the banks of the North Para River, where Richard Holland established a garden and grew fruit, maize and sugar cane.

The south front of the house has symmetrically placed windows on either side of the large bay window. From the almost overgrown patio one has a spectacular view of a long bend in the river below.

To the villagers, Holland House must have been a grand mansion, modest though its twelve rooms are even by Australian country house standards. Although its name has led to the obvious supposition that it was modelled upon London's huge Holland House, built in 1607 by John Thorpe, there is no similarity in the architecture. Its Tudor-Gothic style has no resemblance to the Jacobean manner, and its size would make it a 'cottage' on a large English estate.

Nonetheless, it is clearly not without its pretensions, and, as has been observed, Holland could hardly have been unaware of the allusion in its title. With its tower it seems to exemplify the concept that 'an Englishman's home is his castle', and although he was Australian-born, Holland would have made a perfect English country gentleman. His main interests were stock breeding and the turf, and his race horses were successful in several colonies.

Holland House was built on a rise overlooking a sweeping bend in the North Para River. This not only gave it an impressive outlook, but also put it well out of danger of floods—in the middle of the last century there were a number of serious floods in the area. Three bridges over the North Para, one of which was directly in front of Holland House, were destroyed in the sixties, as was the dam of the watermill. The square, Welsh-style chimney of this mill still stands beside the river, a few hundred metres east of Holland House.

James Macgeorge designed Holland House in a mid-Victorian mixture of Gothic and Tudor styles. The dominating feature of the house is its tower and turret—very fashionable at this time because of the association of Osborne, in the Isle of Wight, with the marital bliss of Victoria and Albert, as Professor Joseph Burke has pointed out.

The tower is not large, hardly rising more than a metre or two above the peak of the roofline. It is the octagonal turret which adds grace to what would otherwise be a squat and top-heavy feature. It not only adds height to give a more pleasing proportion, but serves to connect the tower to the main body of the house. The tower and turret are adorned by castellation which matches that which tops the walls on all sides of the house, and this further unifies the overall effect.

Considering the design as a whole, Macgeorge's success is extraordinary. He has wrapped up a square, twelve-room colonial homestead in Gothic-Tudor dress, and made the result coherent. This has been achieved by what might be termed 'consistency in inconsistency', centering in part on an even and admirable rendition of detail by the builders as well as the architect.

The Gothic Revival, the movement which dominated academic and ecclesiastical architecture in the English-speaking world and much of Europe in the nineteenth century, was at its height in England at the time Holland House was built. There the disciples of Pugin were carefully imitating medieval designs and using them in a quite literally religious spirit.

The bay window of the south hall is the most elaborate in the homestead. The archway and the capitals of the columns are decorated with a pattern of formalized leaves and flowers.

The south hall is dominated by a coat of arms set into a panel above the doorway. The heavy door is elegantly framed by thin pilasters which appear to support the crest in its setting.

Holland House does not belong to this phase of the Gothic Revival, but is rather a relic of an earlier, less intense stage of that complex historical mode. It is not so much a small version of the huge neo-Gothic piles the rich mid-Victorian merchants retired to, as of such eighteenth-century follies as Strawberry Hill, Horace Walpole's villa.

Of course there is not the theatrical exuberance of a Strawberry Hill, nor the grandeur of a Fonthill in little Holland House, any more than a Puginian passion for archaelogical accuracy. It has not so much been built in a Gothic-cum-Tudor style; rather it has had the style imposed on it with admirable resourcefulness.

The house, including its walled courtyard at the rear, is stolidly symmetrical. The front with the tower faces east, and the deep-shaded porch contrasts with the bright, light stone walls. The local rubble masonry gives the house a lively and variegated look which can never be achieved with dark or even sandy-coloured freestone used in Eastern Australia. The English freestone trim contains and offsets this textured masonry to achieve excellent balance and interest. The same design executed entirely in freestone would be dull; a more elaborate and decorated style would become messy with rubble masonry walls.

There are few if any South Australian precedents for Holland House. The distinctive local variation of the neo-Gothic style, based in part upon the use of rubble masonry, was emerging in church building by the late fifties. But the colony was only seventeen years old when Holland House was commenced, and the leading domestic architect was George Kingston, with his highly individualistic style. Holland House pre-dates any of his efforts in a comparable mode of building.

Macgeorge seems to have been aiming to produce a house which would evoke rather than reproduce an English gentleman farmer's residence. His design seems to be based on a vague nostalgia for the old country, rather than any passion for medieval manor houses.

Writing in 1933 the Rev. W. Gray mourned the loss of the 'beautiful park with magnificent gums' which had surrounded Holland House at the turn of the century. But a sketch by J. G. O. Tepper, made in 1868, shows the house alone on a bald hill, and the same impression is given by a photograph of 1872. Clearly, when Holland built his homestead it was a determined statement of what he was intending to achieve on his land. It was a defiant link with the buildings of 'home' that rose on that commanding site above the North Para river in 1854.

Holland House could not have been less like the traditional Australian homestead, 'verandahed-about' and sitting on flat land like a ship at sea. And yet, in the methods he adopted to develop his farm, Holland was not bound by conventions imported from the mother country. He was a leader of the colony when it came to agricultural methods, and there is nothing of mock-gentility in his image as it has come down to us. One of his legendary feats was to fight off an angry bull while armed only with a stick; and one writer has described him as a 'big, powerful, John Bull type of man'. For much of his life he was a Justice of the Peace.

One of the most interesting features of Holland House derives from its first owner's closeness to his homestead. Off to the side of the tower porch,

beneath the stairs up to the balcony, is a crypt which is now as empty as the day it was built. Holland had expressed the wish to be buried there by a Church of England clergyman, but there were problems involved as it was not consecrated ground.

The difficulty of reconciling church doctrine with Holland's wish had to be faced when he died on 25 November 1881; and this episode brought the somewhat mysterious Rev. Alfred Sells into the story of Holland House. Sells, the amateur artist whose watercolour views of South Australia, painted during the decade he spent here, are such an invaluable record of the colony's years of growth, was then rector of Lyndoch and Williamstown. He, whose own life was to continue as a succession of tragic bereavements, found a way around the problems and conducted the funeral in the south hall of Holland House, and Holland was interred as he had requested. His stepson bought the house at a high price so that Mrs Holland could end her days there.

Unfortunately the double coffin of cedar and lead was not airtight, and some time after Holland's death his continued presence on the premises was all too apparent. The vault was opened, and the body was removed and re-interred at Gawler.

The south hall of the homestead, where the funeral was held, is the only room of any pretensions in Holland House. Over the doorway from the central passage there is a large coat of arms in the central one of three shallow arched niches. A substantial wooden folding door divides the south hall from another room of nearly equal size, where heavy wooden shutters are fitted to exclude the heat.

The imposing doorway feature is balanced by the decorated bay window recess, which from the outside dominates the south front. A dutch gable surmounts the bay window, which is flanked on either side by groups of two and three arched windows set rather closer together than the windows in the tower.

On the western side the arrangement is less formal, and the lower part of the wall is punctuated by the entrance to the spacious cellars. At the rear of the house a doorway leads through the wall to the enclosed courtyard with its charming outbuildings only a few metres from the house. This unpretentious area is interesting for its contrast with the house, with which it is nevertheless perfectly integrated.

Holland House continued as the home of members of the first owner's family until Margaret Holland's death at eighty-two in 1898. During the later decades of the century Holland's stepsons continued racehorse breeding, and farmed the Turretfield Estate as well as running Bookmark, Chowilla and Calperum stations which Holland had acquired. After their mother's death, her sons sold off all the original household furnishings in a two-day auction, and no trace of these has been left.

After one or two brief tenancies, the estate was purchased by the South Australian Government, and in 1908 the Department of Agriculture established a stud and dairy farm which was the forerunner of the present Turretfield Research Centre. Turretfield was one of the few state farms to be retained by the Government in the depression of the nineteen-thirties, when so many others were closed or sold.

The view out from the passage, through the front doorway and the tower porch. The Tudor arch in the base of the tower is echoed in the shape of the stained glass around the door. A second, smaller arch above the door is more Gothic in proportions.

Richard Holland had been an innovator in agriculture and sheep farming, being the first land owner in the colony to build an underground water storage tank, and among the first to erect wire ring fencing—as early as 1853 in fact. It seems therefore appropriate and pleasing that in its second century Holland House should be the centre of an institution devoted to the development and prosperity of farming in Australia.

Since 1908 Holland House has been the home of the officer-in-charge of the Turretfield Research Centre. One of its occupants, the late John R. Goode, was especially noted for his devotion to the house. During his period of residence he undertook extensive research into the homestead's history and the lives of its first owners.

The fabric of the house has been well preserved, and the cluster of new buildings in its vicinity does not spoil its views or its unique character. Without doubt, the true spirit of Holland House is still living.

From the balcony beside the tower one overlooks the Turretfield Estate upon which Holland House stands. In the distance is the town of Rosedale, or Rosenthal, with the spire of St Martin's Church.

Gulf Station *Victoria*

Text: Mark Richmond   *Photographs: Brian J. Lloyd*

The south wall and cool verandah of the original Gulf Station homestead. Built of vertical slabs, this building, with its lofty hipped roof, adjoins the present homestead. It has been used as a kitchen, and has a bakehouse with brick oven and chimney; the brick-paved verandah is supported by solid tree-trunk posts.

SEVERAL TERMS HAVE BEEN USED to describe this magnificent section of the Yarra Valley, not far from Melbourne. Some are more lyrical than others, but each is apt. The Yarra Basin at this point is walled by the escarpments of a semi-circle of mountain ranges, from the Christmas Hills spur on the west, north to the Great Dividing Range, and east then south to the mountains behind Healesville, where the Upper Yarra emerges on to the plain.

The Aboriginal name for the area was Billanook, but it soon became known as Yarra Flats, probably from the time of surveyor Robert Hoddle's explorations there in February 1838. Charles La Trobe saw it as 'Vale of Yarra' during a visit in 1851. Three years later, with money won on the Diamond Valley goldfields, James McPherson put up a homestead in the area, and named his property Yarra Glen. But Yarra Flats remained the official title until a public meeting was called in 1888, at which local residents—many of Scots origin—preferred 'Yarra Glen'.

In this 'vale of Yarra', close to the river, nestles the small township of Yarra Glen, splendidly dominated since 1888—not by a church spire—but by the tower of the Grand Hotel. And just to the north-east of the town lies the Gulf Station property, with its rich array of aged timber buildings. There is no record of the reason why this was named 'Gulf' Station; but anyone looking down from Big Hill or other vantage points above this part of the middle Yarra, can readily see a veritable riverine flood-gulf, with floodwaters at times backing up along the Dixon's and Steel's Creek courses towards the landblock of the Great Divide.

The most remote outbuilding on the property is the shearing shed, with post-and-rail fencing leading to the sheep race and penning yards adjacent to the shed, which itself is a timber frame clad with weatherboards.

151

Detail of lapsed joinery in the fourteen-bail former milking shed, the eastern section of the largest outbuilding, which also contains a smithy and large hayshed. Like other buildings on the property, it has well-preserved shingles beneath the present roofing iron.

The facade and gable-end of the domestic stables, facing the homestead area. It is constructed of massive vertical adzed slabs, with a lean-to on one side.

It may seem surprising that this river country was first settled from the high country to the north and the west, rather than through a logical flow of settlement outward along the Yarra Valley from Melbourne. However, the earliest pioneers were among those many who overlanded south from the settled areas of New South Wales in the second half of the 1830s, while the advantages of the area were soon discovered also by men who had landed at Melbourne, and who moved out to farm at Kangaroo Ground and other parts of the Diamond Valley.

The piggery at Gulf Station, showing the farrowing pens; the styes are immediately beyond, to the north.

OPPOSITE
The working (or 'west') stables: a five-stall weatherboard structure. The gable-end of the smithy can be seen beyond, with the rear of the domestic stables roof further east, surmounted by the old-established trees of the homestead garden.

Interior detail of the domestic stables, showing a variety of slab, post, and shingle construction.

Amongst the bands of overlanders were the Ryrie brothers, whose father grazed land in the Monaro District. Following an advance party, they established the Yering station in 1838, and set about growing beef and dairy cattle and bullocks. They also planted vines, bottling their first vintage in 1845, thereby pioneering here an industry which was to flourish subsequently in the expert hands of the de Castella brothers, Guillaume de Pury, and the Deschamps family. These Swiss gentlemen and their families migrated from the province of Neuchatel on the recommendation of Charles La Trobe's wife, herself a native of that province.

Among the early settlers who descended to the Yarra from the high country to the west were the Bells and the Armstrongs, who built the present Gulf Station. With a background of agricultural and pastoral experience in Scotland, they were among passengers who disembarked in Melbourne in October 1839. William Bell had with him his wife Agnes, and their three sons and two daughters. Thomas Armstrong was single, but married Dinah Bell in 1841, and at about the same time entered into partnership with his father-in-law.

For a short time after their arrival, William Bell and his two elder sons worked in the Melbourne building trade, but soon moved out to the stringybark area of the Diamond Valley (north-east from Melbourne) to cut building timber. It was not long before they established landed interests: Bell and Armstrong had a pastoral lease near Eltham by 1841. Further out, at Kangaroo Ground, James Donaldson had settled on a small but rich volcanic patch surrounding Memorial Hill. Beset by bushrangers, Aboriginal marauders and natural dangers, he felt compelled to subdivide: a classic example of rural urbanization for the purposes of mutual protection. Thus Bell and Armstrong took up land at Kangaroo Ground, and Bell's elder sons, John and Thomas, were also established landholders there by 1848.

From the 1850s onwards, Bell and Armstrong, and the Bell sons, were also involved with a number of leaseholds and freeholds in the Yarra Flats area. They would certainly have visited there earlier, following the bullock track cut by the Ryries to meet up with the Heidelberg track to

The old school-house, of vertical slabs, with trunk-posted verandah. At the back is a weatherboard lean-to roofed with Redcliffe brand iron sheets.

Melbourne, for carting produce and stores to and fro. But it was possibly not until 1851 that they realized the value of having land on both the high and the low country. On 'Black Thursday', in February of that year, the Bells and Armstrong saved their stock from a disastrous bushfire by droving them down to John Dickson's Gulf Station. They subsequently acquired land from Dickson, and erected the present buildings over a period—the dates are not yet firmly documented—spanning the late 1850s and early 1860s.

It seems that they and several other Kangaroo Ground and Christmas Hills settlers perceived that a satisfactory symbiosis could be established between the low and the high country: the high country a refuge, when necessary, from Yarra floods; the low country a relief in times of drought and bushfire on the scrubby ranges above. This relationship was enhanced for a time when the Yarra Flats farmers opened up what is still known as Buttermans Track, for the purpose of marketing dairy produce to diggers on the northern Diamond Valley goldfields.

Interior detail from the shearing shed showing the wool press manufactured by Donald & Sons, of Rushcutters Bay, Sydney. Other items within the building include branding irons, wool-bale stencils, and a Cooper shearing machine.

The buildings on Gulf Station are disposed, not in a cluster, but in a functionally-distanced ribbon from east to west along a gentle rise. The most easterly of the buildings are the homesteads, comprising the current residence, which is linked by a covered way to the original slab homestead, to which is attached a bakehouse, with a rustic lavatory close at hand. Facing these are the handsome domestic (or 'east') stables, flanked to the south by the kennels (originally a fowl-house?) and piggery, and to the north by the butcher's shop. Further west is the station's largest outbuilding, a complex encompassing milking shed, smithy, and hayshed; next, the working (or 'west') stables; then, to the north, the old school building and, to the south, the slaughterhouse and sheep-dip; and finally, a fair distance removed to the west, the shearing shed.

There is no record of architect or builder for Gulf Station. But there can be little doubt that both functions devolved upon William Bell and his sons—after all, they had first worked as builders in Melbourne before moving to the Diamond Valley, where they gained further experience with indigenous timbers while cutting out stringybark along the creeks.

The basic materials used are local gum and stringybark. The modes of construction embrace both horizontal and vertical adzed slab, as well as split paling and weatherboard walls, peeled log and tree-trunk members and supports, split shingle roofing, floors of brick, cross-cut log and timber, and post-and-rail fencing. Wood was also used in various types of joinery, and in fittings such as latches.

The buildings not illustrated here include the butcher's shop (containing a massive chopping block) and the kennels, both basically of vertical slab construction; and the present homestead. This last building is of considerable interest and charm. Of some ten rooms, its variety of roof lines and materials suggests that it was built in three stages, ranging from the part-slab section joined by covered way to the old homestead, through a major central section of verandahed weatherboard, to a southerly section which features a gabled bay window with stained glass and Edwardian shingle wall cladding. The collection of buildings represents not so much a vernacular architecture as a pragmatic adaptation of local timbers and other materials to 'bush' skills already possessed from British precedents, or quickly acquired, by many of the incoming settlers.

It is probable that William Bell Junior lived on Gulf Station, while his father continued to live up at Kangaroo Ground until his death in 1870. The property remained in the hands of the Bell family until it was taken up under Soldier Settlement by Mr J. Smedley shortly after World War Two. His widow still owns it, and her daughter and son-in-law, Mavis and Don Fellowes, at present occupy and work the farm, whittled down now to sixteen hectares.

Gulf Station is of immense historical value, comprising as it does such an extensive group of surviving timber structures, and one in which such a variety of early structural crafts may be seen.

The forlorn skeleton of a eucalypt stands in front of Gulf Station's slaughterhouse, built of horizontal slabs battened on to posts. Connected to the back of the building is a sheep-dip, still used by a neighbouring farmer.

Kingsford *South Australia*

Text: Dean W. Berry   *Photographs: Marcus B. Brownrigg*

The date panel reading 'A.D. 1856' is boldly carved; however, the surrounding moulding with dentil enrichment is delicate indeed and indicates the work of an experienced mason.

'THIS MORNING WE MADE an excursion on foot along the North Para, to visit Mr Stephen King, an old colonist about six miles from Gawler Town.' This reference, in *Colonists, Copper & Corn* edited by E. M. Yelland, is to the builder of Kingsford at a time when he was supervising the construction of his new home.

The reference continues: 'We had still several tiresome hills and two gullies to pass to reach Mr King's sheep-farm, whose buildings and fences struck us as being in much better order than those we had seen near Gawler Town. We partook of Mr and Mrs King's hearty hospitality, which included some very good wine; after dwelling upon a few old colonial reminiscences, dating back to the earliest period of the Gawler Survey, we walked out to notice a substantial stone building in progress, as Mr King's future dwelling, of two floors, with spacious sitting rooms. When finished this will certainly be one of the best houses in the colony though costly.'

Before we examine Kingsford in detail we should perhaps know something of Stephen King, the man who was undoubtedly the author of the project and possibly its designer. Stephen King Snr, as he was known, contributed a notable share to the pastoral pioneering of South Australia. He was also the son of a Stephen King, and was born at Kelby, Lincolnshire, on 17 August 1806. Having decided to emigrate he made the voyage to South Australia in the barque *Orleana* (Captain Cameron) which left Liverpool on 5 October 1838, 'with forty cabin passengers and forty-four emigrants'. The vessel had an extremely quick passage for those times. She got to King George's Sound from Liverpool in eighty-five days, and must have broken the record to South Australia had not easterly winds prevailed for the rest of the journey.

The captain 'favoured' the Adelaide press with the latest English newspapers, in one of which it was stated that if emigration to South Australia proceeded as rapidly as was then contemplated there would soon appear an announcement that the island of Great Britain was 'to let'.

The *Orleana* arrived on 15 January 1839. (Mr King died on the same day forty-three years later.) He spent his first weeks in Adelaide camped in a tent with his family on the north parklands.

It is possible that Stephen King's career in the land of his adoption was largely influenced by friendships made on the voyage out. Among his fellow passengers were Henry Dundas Murray and John Reid, who, on the last day of the month in which they landed, obtained a special survey of

A luxuriant growth of ivy covers massive walls of hard, deep-biscuit-coloured stone relieved by white painted windows of Georgian design. The ivy aesthetically welds the porch to the main building.

4,000 acres (1,600 hectares) on the junction of the North and South Para Rivers.

The application for this valuable special grant was made on the recommendation of the first Surveyor General, Colonel William Light. Its ownership was not confined to Messrs Murray and Reid, but was also extended to Messrs Stephen King, Henry Johnson, William F. Porter, Patrick J. and Robert Todd, J. L. Patterson, James Fotheringham, Thos Stubbs, and John Sutton and the Rev. C. B. Howard, who wisely took Light's advice. The neighbourhood had previously been occupied by a Mr Horrocks as a sheep station. The proprietors of the special survey caused the town of Gawler to be laid out and named, and one can understand why Reid Street, King Street, Murray Street and Orleana Square are included in its nomenclature. 140 acres were set aside for streets, parklands, school, churches, cemetery, market and other public purposes, of which Stephen King's contribution was eighteen and three-quarter acres.

A brass bell with a Scandinavian history hangs from a wrought-iron bracket under the verandah which protects the garden entrance.

OPPOSITE *The garden entrance under the east verandah overlooks the tennis court. The photograph shows the rugged nature of the stone walling. In springtime almond blossom adds enchantment to this area.*

The main house is roofed with slates as once was this charming dairy. The white paint of the woodwork with its black iron-work contrasts pleasantly with the warm colour of its stone walls.

The syndicate enlarged their holding to 20,000 acres (8,000 hectares) and Mr King settled on his portion of the survey about five miles further up the North Para River, where he established the estate known as Kingsford; he also held runs further north. His first house, built by the ford which gave the property its name, is now a ruin. It was his second building venture which developed into the charming Georgian mansion known today as Kingsford and it was from Kingsford that Stephen King's son—Stephen King Jnr set forth at the age of nineteen years to join John McDouall Stuart's exploring party, the first to cross Australia from the Southern Ocean to the Indian Ocean.

The house and its outbuildings and woolshed nestle in the folds of the hills; however, as the land falls away to the south there is an extensive view down the valley of the North Para River towards Gawler.

Built in 1856 the house is Georgian in character and is constructed of a warm, biscuit-coloured stone thought to have been brought out from England as ship's ballast. The walls are taken up above the roof line to form a parapet which surmounts a heavy, primitively-moulded cornice above which the ridge is barely discernible. The carriage approach to the house was originally from the east over the old ford, but now it is from the main road on the west. When this change was made the large bay-fronted room on the southern facade was abandoned as the principle entrance and an elaborate porch in the Gothic manner added on the west. (Recently the opening to the porch has been filled in with an outer door.) A heavy growth

of ivy on the walls of the main house has helped aesthetically to weld the florid Gothic architecture of the porch to the simple Georgian facade of the house.

It is interesting to note that, although the stone of which the house is built is extremely hard, it has proved capable of lending itself to fine detail as the date panel on the south front indicates. The date 'A.D. 1856' is boldly carved; but the surmounting moulding with dentil enrichment is delicate indeed and indicates the work of an experienced mason.

It is doubtful if the building was architecturally designed. Rather, it would appear to be the result of a discerning owner working with a stone-mason who was calling on his recollection of work carried out in the old country. Certainly the joiner who made the main staircase had not forgotten the finer points of his craft.

The garden entrance under the east verandah overlooks the tennis court and here there is to be found a brass bell suspended from a wrought-iron bracket. This bell has sentimental significance for the present owner, having been sent to him from Scandinavia by a grateful former farm employee.

The north or 'hot' side of the house has, on both floors, been planned to accommodate rooms of lesser importance. (Here the Englishman can be seen adapting his needs to meet changed climatic conditions.) Bathrooms, store rooms and the kitchen have northern aspects and adjacent are the outbuildings necessary in the early days for the satisfactory functioning of a residence on a pastoral property. These buildings are constructed of materials similar to the main building, as the dairy, situated between the kitchen and the stables, indicates.

Unusual features abound in the central hall of the house. The floor is flagged with large slabs of slate with a 'patina' from years of wax polishing. (In the illustration the occasional Persian rugs have been removed to show the paving.) In a narrower section of the hall is the present main entrance from the Gothic porch. In a wider section at the opposite end are the stairs to the first floor, while in a central position is a large built-in cedar buffet, beyond which is a door to the kitchen. In point of fact, the buffet encloses stairs to the cellars. By lifting up a section of the top of the buffet, and opening a gate in its end, easy access is obtained to the cellars. A combined chute and steps from the garden enable the cellars to be filled with farm produce.

It was in these cellars that three bushrangers who 'stuck up' the station were eventually found. Curran, Hughes and Green were their names. The first two were executed in Adelaide—'Hughes fighting the executioner and causing a dreadful scene on the gallows', according to the chronicles of the day.

When it was realized that the road on the west of the property provided a better approach to the house than that which came over the old ford from the east, it was decided to change the entrance from the bay-fronted room on the south to an existing doorway on the west. At this time the elaborate Gothic porch was added to give protection and dignity to the facade.

The main staircase, built in cedar, is the principle item of joinery in the house. It may have been that the Gothic detail used in its design influenced the style in which the entrance porch, added years later, was built. However, the Gothic revival, current in England, was often a source of inspiration even in connection with buildings mainly Georgian in character.

This cedar buffet is the dominant feature of the main hall. Its scale is large as it houses the cellar steps. Conveniently nearby is the kitchen door. In the distance can be seen the present main entrance from the Gothic porch.

The timber detail throughout the house is, in the main, restricted to doors, architraves and skirtings. However, the main staircase provided the joiner with an opportunity to display his skill. As was fashionable at the time, Gothic detail was introduced, as can be seen in the timber arches of the stair balustrade and the moulded handrails and newel caps.

The building of Kingsford was certainly carried out most ably under the careful guidance of its first owner, Stephen King Snr, who did so much to pioneer the pastoral industry in South Australia. The property then became famous for the Hereford stud that its second owner—John Howard Angas—built up there. Angas was the son of George Fife Angas, one of the founding fathers of South Australia.

Unusual features abound in the central hall of the house. The floor is flagged with large slabs of slate with a 'patina' from years of wax polishing. In the illustration it can be seen that the flap in the top of the buffet has been lifted and the door opened to give access to the cellars.

Ownership subsequently passed to Messrs Clement, McNeil and Foster, and then in 1924 back to the Angas family in the person of Sir Keith Angas, a great-grandson of George Fife Angas, who, however, never lived in the house. Later, Frederick and Alfred Scarfe, Dan Cudmore and others became its owners.

Today, Kingsford is in the hands of Mr A. S. Fotheringham, a descendant of one of the shareholders in the original special survey. Great praise is due to Mr and Mrs Fotheringham for the way in which they have restored the building and for the sympathetic manner in which it is maintained.

Wonnerup House *Western Australia*

Text: Noel Stewart and Mollie Lukis   *Photographs: R. V. Penrose*

THE EARLY HISTORY of the south-west of Western Australia is epitomized in a small cluster of buildings set among tall tuart trees and peppermint gums some six kilometres north-east of Busselton, at a short distance from the glistening blue-green waters of Geographe Bay.

Known as Wonnerup House, the main buildings and about two-thirds of a hectare of land were acquired by the National Trust in 1972 and officially opened by Her Excellency Lady Hasluck, wife of the then Governor-General (Sir Paul Hasluck) on 4 November 1973. Since then two additional hectares of farm land and several out-buildings have been purchased.

Western Australia's earliest historic houses are perhaps not of great architectural merit, but they are impregnated with the personalities of those who built them and reflect their courage, endurance, adaptability, neighbourliness and steadfastness.

The young man who planned this pleasant old house in 1859 was George Layman II. His father, George Layman I, had arrived in Western Australia in October 1829, just a few months after the colony's establishment, having migrated two years earlier to Van Diemen's Land with his elder brother Charles. George travelled to Fremantle on the *Orelia*, landing with only sixpence in his pocket. He soon found employment and this subsequently took him to Augusta, which was then being settled by such pioneering families as the Bussells, Molloys and Turners. He was assigned some land there, where he made his first home after his marriage in Perth in 1832 to Mary Ann Bayliss. When the Bussell family moved north to the Vasse River in 1834 Layman decided to follow and, in 1835, established his wife and two little daughters in a small cottage on the Vasse River near Soldiers' Point, several miles from his new grant. Most of the settlers had built their homes fairly close together because of the ever present danger of native attack—something George had already experienced when walking the 200 miles (320 kilometres) from Augusta to Perth shortly after his marriage. He was speared in the leg by a native and is said to have carried the barb until his death a few years later.

By May 1837 George Layman was ready to transfer his family to his property, which he called Wonnerup, the name given to the area by local natives. On 20 May he wrote to the Governor, Sir James Stirling, thanking him for providing additional military support, which had made the move possible, and adding: 'I have erected a hut and brought my things over. Tomorrow I remove my family and cattle.'

Wonnerup House, built in 1859, is typical of so many of the houses built by Western Australia's first settlers—a long narrow structure surrounded by wide verandahs from which all the rooms were entered. These early pioneers literally carved their homes from the surrounding countryside. The limestone of which Wonnerup House is built was quarried nearby; the timber was cut from adjoining forests and its design was most likely drawn on a home-made jarrah table by candlelight—and the candles would also have been homemade.

BELOW *In this side and back view of the building, as in the front view, the importance of the verandah posts is clearly apparent. The regularly-spaced verandah posts are a feature of this type of house and those at Wonnerup are distinguished by the decorative carving at the top. The section at the end is an addition for a bathroom and laundry made some time after the completion of the main building.*

Around the walls of the drawing-room hang photographs of members of the Layman family. The large cane chair on the left was a favourite of George Layman II and is remembered by some of the older generation of the family as 'grandfather's chair'. Only a few pieces of the original furniture are now in the house; in the main it has been furnished by the National Trust in a manner appropriate to the period.

Three months later Layman was again in correspondence with the Governor, informing him that because of the hostility of the natives the settlement was in a state of semi-starvation. However his isolated little family managed to survive and in May 1838 a happy event occurred—the birth of his first son, George Layman II, who was destined to spend the rest of his long life at Wonnerup and to establish firmly the prestige of the Layman farm and family. His father did not live long to enjoy the company of his growing son as he was speared by a native after a minor altercation on 22 February 1841 and died almost immediately. So ended the short career of a brave settler. His death was a sad and unnecessary occurrence as he and other settlers in the vicinity were by now regularly employing natives as herdsmen, shepherds and for other farm pursuits and, in the main, relations between blacks and whites had become fairly friendly.

A year after George's death his widow married Robert Heppingstone. The marriage was a happy one, but was cut short by another tragedy with Heppingstone's death by drowning when his whale boat was swamped in 1858.

Once again Mary (Layman) Heppingstone was widowed. She was held in high esteem in the district, and when Georgiana Molloy was dying in March 1843 she asked that her three-months-old baby daughter be taken to Wonnerup so that Mary Heppingstone could care for her—which she lovingly did for over a year. There was a pleasant sequel to this incident at the opening ceremony of Wonnerup House in 1973, when Lady Hasluck presented a beautiful mahogany workbox inlaid with brass as a memento of Georgiana Molloy; saying she was sure Georgiana would be happy to think her workbox would be preserved in an environment she had known so well, and in which her infant daughter had spent the first year of her life.

This room was built as a kitchen and generally used as such, though meals were often cooked in the kitchen of the older house and served here. In the late 1890s it was converted to a dining-room and a small adjoining room used for cooking. By this time the daughters of George Layman II were entertaining more formally and the new arrangement was more convenient.

The carved panel over the mantel is the work of Clair Layman; more fine examples of her wood carving are to be found on furniture in other parts of the house.

After Robert Heppingstone's death, the main responsibility for maintaining the Wonnerup property fell on the capable young shoulders of George Layman II, then just 20 years of age. In 1859 George married Amelia Curtis, for whom he built the main house which now stands on the property. The 'new' Wonnerup House is pleasantly shaped and built on a flat site with the front elevation facing north. The rooms are not large, but are of pleasing proportions and comprise three bedrooms, entrance hall, drawing-room and dining-room. Crossing a wide lawn from this main homestead one arrives at the older dwelling, of which the date is uncertain. An atmosphere of cosy solidity and comfort somehow pervades this interesting old house, primitive as it is. Leaving its stone verandah one passes through a little wooden gate near the old original well to reach the substantial barn with its well-preserved horse stalls, harness-room, lamp-room and hay lofts. A nearby 'smithy' is in process of restoration.

As soon as George and Amelia were married in 1859, the young bride commenced a diary, only fragments of which, unfortunately, remain. There is, however, sufficient in it to give some indication of the daily farm

In nineteenth century houses in Western Australia most bedrooms, as well as the living-rooms, had fireplaces, and this was the case at Wonnerup House. The bedrooms had built-in jarrah wardrobes similar to the one which can be seen here beside the fireplace. Originally all the rooms were entered from the verandahs but over the years modifications have been made and the rooms are now connected by inside doors.

activities—cheese-making, fencing, searching for straying cattle, collecting stores, boring for artesian water (Wonnerup is well-endowed with this), rearing and killing pigs, kangaroo hunting, making additions to the house, receiving innumerable visitors and attending weddings and funerals. By 1879 there was a school on the property. Amelia mentions in her diary that the children had been examined by two members of the District Board of Education. The small wooden school house and teacher's dwelling, just across the road from the Wonnerup entrance, have been acquired by the National Trust and restored.

As the years went by Wonnerup House was noted for its hospitality and it also became one of the outstanding dairying properties in the district. Getting his produce to market was Layman's greatest problem. During the four years he represented the Sussex district in the Legislative Council (from 1884–8) he constantly stressed the need for railways in the growing colony. Eventually a line to Bunbury was built, and opened in 1893. To get to Council meetings in Perth, George Layman had to ride the 150 miles (240 kilometres) on horseback, as did his sons when attending Bishop

A number of alterations were made inside the house over the years. Some, like the doorways for internal communication, were for convenience; others to repair damage. In a letter from Mrs Layman to her daughter Clair in 1904 she mentions that as the ceiling in Clair's bedroom had fallen down both it and those in other bedrooms had been replaced by ceilings of stamped iron.

A huge olive tree, believed to be about 100 years old, is prominent between the main house and the older dwelling on the left: a long narrow limestone structure containing a series of small bedrooms, an office, a dairy and a large all-purpose room used as a scullery, kitchen and washhouse, with an open fireplace where meals were cooked in the early days. The fireplace is flanked by a bread oven on one side and a copper on the other. Four large homemade wooden troughs occupy the opposite wall. A long jarrah table, butter churn and wooden clothes basket, also all homemade, indicate the self-reliance and improvisation so necessary in pioneering days. Next to the scullery is the dairy, which has a deep cellar for storing cheeses and other farm produce.

An overall view of the main buildings on the property BELOW RIGHT shows, in the foreground, the stone barn built early in the century to replace the old stables which stood between the house and the entrance gates. Wonnerup was renowned for its horses, as George Layman was a keen breeder and fine horseman. He sent several shipments of horses to India in the seventies and also despatched a number to Western Australia's north-west when that area was being opened up. By 1887 Layman held 1,000 acres (400 hectares) of freehold land, mostly fenced and divided into paddocks, and 6,000 acres (2,400 hectares) under pastoral lease. He had 200 head of cattle and horses, was milking 40 cows twice daily and had achieved some success with wine-making and root crops.

This mahogany workbox brought to Western Australia by Georgiana Molloy in 1829 was inherited by her second daughter Mary, who took it to England after her marriage in 1855 to Lieutenant (later Sir) Edmund Du Cane. The box passed eventually to Mary's granddaughter, Dorothea Pullen, who gave it to Lady Hasluck, by whom it was presented to Wonnerup House when she performed the opening ceremony in 1973.

Hale's School. He took an active interest in all district affairs and was a member of most local organizations, from the Agricultural Society to the Volunteer Corps and the vestry of St Mary's Anglican Church, Busselton, where his father had finally been laid to rest after having been buried under a tuart tree close to where he was killed in 1841. George and Amelia Layman had been married in this lovely little church in 1859 and it was there, 50 years later, that a special service was held to celebrate their golden wedding. They were the first West Australian-born couple to have a golden wedding, and their son, George Layman III, who predeceased them, was claimed to be the first child born in the colony of West Australian-born parents.

Following the golden wedding church service in 1909, a merry gathering of family and friends took place at Wonnerup House, where the large number of presents the couple received included, according to a contemporary newspaper report, 'a handsome silver-mounted, rubber-tyred buggy and harness from sons and sons-in-law'. By this time George Layman's kindly temperament and solicitude for everyone's welfare had earned him the title of 'the grand old man of the South-West'. The published list of guests at the golden wedding celebrations reads like a roll call of the pioneering families of Western Australia.

By 1912, following the death of James, the youngest son of the family, the management of the Wonnerup farm was in the hands of the aging Mr and Mrs Layman and their four unmarried daughters, Clair, Ida, Stella and Nina. All the Layman sisters were accomplished horsewomen and good judges of stock, and it was their interest and determination which kept the property together during their lifetime. They were all colourful personalities and played prominent roles in district affairs, as well as being unusually adventurous. They were among the first women in the district to ride bicycles, and in 1907 Clair Layman caused something of a sensation by riding her horse astride at the local show.

The sisters carried on at Wonnerup after the death of their father in 1921 until the 1940s when a nephew, Ivan Webster, went to live there and gradually took over the management. In 1962, following the death of the last of the sisters, Miss Stella Layman, the property was sold, after 120 years of Layman family ownership.

When the National Trust bought the property in 1972 the task of restoring the buildings, which had fallen into disrepair, was entrusted to a local committee, chaired by Mr J. M. Butcher, which worked with enthusiasm and dedication to carry out the recommendations of the Trust's honorary architect, the late Mr Marshall Clifton. The result has been an outstanding success. Since its opening Wonnerup has attracted thousands of visitors who come not only to admire the pleasant old buildings and their charming surroundings, but also, perhaps, to pay tribute to the men and women who pioneered this lonely countryside so many years ago.

The balustraded parapet to the roof of Para Para is capped by large urns which are decorated with swags. The original stonework is in excellent condition and has been meticulously restored.

Para Para *South Australia*

Text: Judith M. Brown   *Photographs: Marcus B. Brownrigg*

PARA PARA WAS BUILT by the Hon. Walter Duffield who arrived in South Australia in 1839 at the age of twenty-three with only £60 in his pocket. He began work immediately, carting wood from Mount Lofty down to Adelaide by means of a bullock team. In the following year he was put in charge of Mr Jacob Hagen's property on the Para River at Gawler where he stayed for seven years before deciding to strike out on his own. On 20 September 1847, he moved into a small brick house in Finniss Street, Gawler, and bought the Victoria Flour Mill.

In 1851 Walter Duffield bought the 450-acre (180-hectare) Para Para estate—Para Para being the native term for the merging of two streams, in this case the North Para and South Para Rivers. That same year the exodus to the goldfields caused the price of flour to rise from £12 per ton to £37 per ton and the astute miller was able to buy up large tracts of land, one of which became the Princess Royal run, while at Koonoona Station he established the famous merino stud. He also began to build his 'dream home' which he called Para Para. The design was basically Georgian but Duffield added a curious mixture of adornments. To shade the lower rooms he built a typically colonial verandah with a sloping roof, while the front door was covered by an imposing portico sporting Corinthian pillars and a balcony. The design of the porch was continued to the roof of the second storey which was flanked on either side by large urns decorated with garlands of flowers. French windows led from the downstairs room on to the verandah, and were matched by similar windows on the second storey.

The inside was magnificent. On the right-hand side of the entrance hall was the dining-room, and here Walter Duffield excelled himself. The walls were superbly decorated with what at first glance appeared to be wallpaper but on closer inspection proved to be a hand-painted design. The lower part of the walls had a series of rich wooden panels and each one was decorated with a separate painting of flowers or fruit, highlighted by gold leaf. The cornice was richly ornate, as was the heavy cast-iron rose from which hung a massive chandelier, and the doors bore an intricate pattern in gold leaf. Altogether there were twenty-three rooms in the house, the *pièce de résistance* being the ballroom. This room had an imported cedar floor with Corinthian pillars around it, and a simulated marble niche in which stood a statue of Queen Victoria. The walls were hung with valuable paintings. Although the house was two-storied, the ceiling of the ball-

The portico is enriched with square Corinthian columns. This photograph shows the excellent detail in volutes and acanthus leaves.

A reporter from Gawler's newspaper The Bunyip *wrote in 1867 that Para Para was such 'an imposing looking structure' that a visitor may suppose 'that he is looking at some public building'. As many as 4,000 people at a time attended the numerous fêtes and garden parties held in the spacious grounds.*

Light pours from a domed ceiling down into the ballroom through this unusual circular gallery. Here the chaperones could sit in comfort to watch their charges dancing below.

The entrance hall leads straight into the ballroom which has an imported cedar floor. In the centre of the opposite wall is a simulated marble niche in which stood a statue of Queen Victoria.

room was a dome set in the roof of the house from which hung another chandelier. A circular cedar gallery where guests could stand to watch the dancers below surrounded the second storey, and a cedar staircase led to the upstairs bedrooms. The kitchen was outside, the stables had been architecturally designed, and there was a lodge at the gate.

It was not until 1862 that the Duffields were able to move from the cottage in Finniss Street, and to mark the occasion, they gave a garden party at Para Para which was attended by the Governor, Sir Dominick Daly, and his daughters. The garden was fully established, for Walter Duffield had begun planting both trees and vines when he bought the estate in 1851. In the front garden were pines of the Californian, Mexican and New Caledonian species which had adapted so well that they caused not only local, but colonial interest. Amongst these was a variety of shrubs from the Northern Territory, and 180 varieties of roses. Added to this were 10,000 orange trees, an apple orchard, banana trees, the Bengal citron, Lisbon lemon, and olive trees, a green-house, and last, but not least, an apiary containing six hives, in which small glass cases had been provided for the bees to deposit the honey, which was 'by that means enabled to be brought to the table in its primitive state'.

The Gawler River had originally wound through the estate and although its course had since been altered, two plateaux remained. On these Walter Duffield planted vines from which he made excellent wines, and the cellar at Para Para boasted Chasselas, Frontignac, Tokay, Muscat and Pedro Ximenes, all made from grapes grown on the property. The soil at Para Para is sandy loam with a clay sub-soil, and as this tended to make the water drain quickly the grapes were grown on the flat. Until then the French style of planting vines on slopes had been used in the colony. A well on the estate sank to a depth of almost eighteen metres and a horse was constantly employed pumping the water.

When the Duke of Edinburgh visited South Australia in 1867 Kapunda and Gawler were chosen as the two country towns he should visit. When it was discovered that the Royal Party was ahead of schedule, an impromptu visit to Para Para was arranged and His Royal Highness was met by Mr Duffield and his daughters, Louise, Ellen and Emily, who served refreshments of fruit and wine. The Duke of Edinburgh then went for a stroll in the garden and 'made the hearts of the young ladies happy by inserting his autograph in their albums'. During his next visit to South Australia in 1869 His Royal Highness accepted an invitation to lunch at Para Para which nearly ended in disaster when the family butler, Mark, imbibed too freely before the Royal party arrived.

Para Para was the scene of many other gatherings. In the same year that the Duffields moved there, a 'Grand Brass Band Contest, Picnic and Rural Fête' was held in the grounds to mark the fifth anniversary of the Institute, while in January 1874, three train-loads of Oddfellows arrived from Adelaide for a picnic at Para Para and the final crowd was estimated at 2,000. In December of that same year nearly 300 employees of *The Advertiser*, *Chronicle*, and *Express* gathered at Para Para, while as many as 4,000 gathered at the mansion in 1881 when the first military demonstration by the non-commissioned officers of the volunteer military force was held.

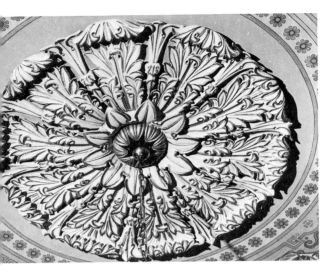

The ceiling of the dining-room is graced by an ornate cast-iron rose from which hung a massive chandelier. The Duffields entertained frequently and lavishly, and the Duke of Edinburgh attended a luncheon at Para Para in 1869.

Mr Frank Cork recently engaged the Austrian master painters Josef and Werner Ott in the restoration of Para Para, and the rich art-work in the walls and cornices can now be seen. BELOW RIGHT

Delicate patterns of leaves, flowers and fruit are painted in gold leaf on the panels of imported cedar in the dining-room. Note the high skirting board. The walls above the panel are painted in intricate designs which at first glance appears to be a decorative wallpaper.

Walter Duffield bought the Union Mill from the Harrison brothers and also established mills at Snowtown, Wallaroo and Port Pirie. He continued to expand his pastoral interests and it was said that all his business deals were 'marked by strict integrity and honour'. He was a local director of the Bank of South Australia from 1859–73 when he accepted a position on the Adelaide Board, and was also a director of the Adelaide Marine and Fire Insurance Company. He sat for eleven years in the House of Assembly and for seven in the Legislative Council, and was associated with the second, third and fourth South Australian parliaments before he was defeated. He returned to the Legislative Council in 1870, holding office as Treasurer in both the Hart and Boucaut ministries, and during this time he was responsible for bringing in an act requiring all dogs to be registered. He was a foundation member and ardent supporter of the British and Foreign Bible Society for twenty-six years. The first meeting of the Gawler Racing Club was held at Para Para on 23 January 1879, and £400 was given in stakes. Plans for a meeting in the following year were completed and the stake raised to £500, when ill health forced Walter Duffield to cancel the meeting. He was loved and respected by all and *The Bunyip* wrote of him: 'In his private life he endeared himself to many and thoroughly earned the admiration of the whole district, and when his reason was impaired and he was compelled to give up all business and political pursuits, the sorrow was general for miles around.'

For the last few weeks of his life Walter Duffield suffered extremely bad health, so much so that *The Bunyip* declared 'on Saturday afternoon it was reported in Adelaide that he had left this world. Although this was not true, early on Sunday morning he did die.' He was sixty-six years old. At 3.00 p.m. on 6 November 1882 a coffin of plain cedar left Para Para covered by a cross, a wreath made by Mr Malcolm's children, and three wreaths made by Walter Duffield's five daughters. His son, Mr D. W. Duffield, organized the funeral arrangements and the hearse was preceded by a

procession of workmen from Para Para who were followed by the chief mourners. All shops in the district were closed as a mark of respect, and flags flew at half-mast.

Para Para remained in the Duffield family until 1924 and during these forty-two years it saw a great variety of tenants, among them Mr Lewis who taught the piano and the Misses Nott who ran a 'School for Young Ladies'. Then on 31 October 1923, F. W. Bullock & Co. of Adelaide, offered the estate for auction in the Forester's Hall at Gawler. The grounds had been divided into thirty-two lots, the sizes varying from two to forty-two acres. Only fourteen of the thirty-two blocks were sold, for Para Para was not what it had been. Gone were the vineyards and orange groves, gone was the botanic garden that Walter Duffield had so carefully nurtured, and the house showed the wear and tear of many uncaring tenants. The mansion was offered at auction with the outbuildings and fourteen acres of land, but was passed in at £1,400, although the lodge with seven acres was bought by Mr A. Lillecrapp for £800. Finally, on 25 February 1924,

These magnificent double doors lead from the dining-room into the entrance hall. Although the house was virtually empty for sixteen years and was damaged by vandals they did not destroy the main features, and the restoration work revealed the artistry of the original decoration.

Para Para was bought by the estate agent Henry Woodcock, from Walter Duffield and Kenneth Duffield, grandsons of the original owner, but Mr Woodcock only lived for another three months, dying on 22 May 1924, and once more the great house became host to a stream of tenants, some authorized and some not. Vandals forced open doors and broke windows, while children played in the garden by day and possums wreaked havoc at night.

In 1939 the *Adelaide Chronicle* reported, 'In the centre of the building the huge ballroom, once famed for the colourful dances held beneath the high domed ceiling, is falling into decay. The spiral cedar staircase and the circular balcony above the room are dilapidated, the walls are stained and chipped. The rooms are dark and silent with the exception of a few on the ground floor, occupied by an old gentleman whose sweet peas are famed throughout the district.

'Equally famed gardens, once the pride of the town, are now a mass of weeds and prickly pear. The orange grove in the valley, where once golden fruit hung in luscious bunches, has almost disappeared and workmen's cottages scattered across the estate have been reduced by Time to ruins.'

In 1940 tenders for demolition of the property were called and it was then that Mr Leslie Cork of Gawler South, and his wife, Edith, decided, against the advice of all their friends, to buy and restore Para Para. Reconstruction began immediately and by 1 March 1940, *The Bunyip* was able to report: 'Mr Cork is highly pleased with the splendid workmanship revealed in the old home, the only crack in the building is said to be due to the earthquake experienced about thirty years ago. It is Mr Cork's intention to renew the lower storey, giving residence of six or seven rooms, and will later pay attention to the second storey. Old Gawlerites will be glad to know that the historic home is not to be lost to the district.'

The stables were architecturally designed, and the attractive old stone work can still be seen. When the Duke of Edinburgh arrived in Gawler in 1869 Walter Duffield was running late to meet him, so he jumped the six-foot railway gates on his magnificent white charger which was kept in these stables.

The groom lived above the stables and reached his room by this staircase. At one time part of the land and these stables were used as the headquarters of a thoroughbred stud run by Sir Sidney Kidman's brother.

Leslie Cork died in 1959 and his wife in 1964, and Para Para passed to their son, Mr Frank Cork, who lives there today. He has carried on the work of his parents and engaged the Austrian master painters Josef and Werner Ott, who restored Ayers House, to work on Para Para. The superb artistry of the original craftsmen can now be seen. In the dining-room the delicate tracery on the walls and doors has reappeared, and the individual designs on the wooden panels stand out clearly. The cedar floor and gallery in the ballroom shine with polish in the light that filters through the domed ceiling. The outside has been meticulously restored and the architectural details stand out clearly.

In May 1973, Mr Cork lent Para Para for a concert given by the world famous violinist, Brenton Langbein, who was born at Gawler. A programme of chamber music was given in the ballroom and some of the guests sat around the gallery of the second storey from where they could look down on the quartet. The acoustics proved to be faultless and Brenton Langbein said, 'It was marvellous to bring life again to Para Para, a house I have always loved'.

Not only the people of Gawler, but everyone in South Australia, should be grateful that Mr Frank Cork's devotion has both saved and restored this historic house which was once famed as a show place throughout the entire colony.

Longerenong *Victoria*

Text: George Tibbits   Photographs: Ian McKenzie

Longerenong, designed in the picturesque Gothic villa style, faces east, and was once approached through a long avenue of trees. It is unique among early homesteads in Victoria in that it probably draws directly on American sources for its design.

L**ONGERENONG HOMESTEAD** is a jewel-like exception among country houses in Victoria. Both its location and style come as a surprise and a delight. It stands on the banks of the Yarriambiac Creek which flows through the flat plains of the Wimmera, a sparse wheat growing area in north-western Victoria. At the time the house was built in 1862 this area was a remote sheep grazing frontier well beyond the limits where such a polished architectural design might be expected. Indeed, the region remained isolated until this century. The appearance of such a joyful example of the picturesque gothic villa style in this strange, somewhat desolate, Australian environment, has been described by one sensitive visitor as 'surrealistically unusual'. Such a style of course is rare in country houses in Victoria. Among the pastoral pioneers of mid-century Victoria, Gothic seemed to hold little interest as a homestead style.

The house was built on a vast grazing run by Samuel Wilson (1832–1895) who had come to Australia from Ireland in 1852 to join his brothers, who had been in Australia since the early forties. The vast open country around Longerenong had been settled by squatters who began establishing sheep stations in the area after 1842. The Longerenong run was first taken up by William Taylor and Dougall McPherson in 1844. At that time the run was some 193,000 acres (77,000 hectares). The early pastoral settlement of the Wimmera was done at some risk. During the years 1844–5 it is reported that large numbers of sheep were taken by the Aborigines from the runs held by Taylor and McPherson: more than a third of the sheep were taken from the Polkemmet station and destroyed. However, William Taylor later reported that he found the local Aborigines to be 'the best shepherds in the district'.

By 1852 the brothers Alexander and Charles Wilson had the licence for Longerenong which had been reduced to about 153,000 acres (61,000 hectares) after the Ashens station had been split off around 1844. Both Taylor and McPherson, after leaving the Wimmera, established fine houses near Melbourne: William Taylor built Overnewton at Keilor, and Dougall McPherson built Bungeeltop at Ballan. By 1862, the original Longerenong run was further subdivided to form a smaller Longerenong Station, and St Helens, Green Hills, Marma Downs, and Kirkwood stations, all owned by the Wilson brothers, came into existence as a result of this subdivision. Samuel Wilson, who had joined his brothers in 1856, occupied Longerenong, and in 1862 set about to build the homestead. Six years later, Samuel purchased the Longerenong Station from his brothers for £40,000, and by 1871 he had acquired all the surrounding property holdings of his brothers' partnership.

It is believed that the original buildings at Longerenong were slab huts. An early print of the nearby Ashens homestead shows a slab hut and it is presumed that the remains of a similar hut at Longerenong is one of the original buildings dating from the early 1840s. Beyond this, nothing remains of those early days.

Samuel Wilson, for whom the present house was built, remains one of the most remarkable and successful of pioneering settlers in Western Victoria. He was the youngest and sixth son of an Irish farmer and land-owner of County Antrim, and he was named after his father. He was born at Ballycloughan on 7 February 1832. During his schooling he is reputed to have shown remarkable gifts for engineering and intended becoming an engineer, but on leaving school he went into linen manufacture with a brother-in-law. When Samuel was seven, two of his elder brothers, Alexander and Charles, migrated to Sydney. Two years later they were joined by a third brother, John, whereupon the three formed the partner-

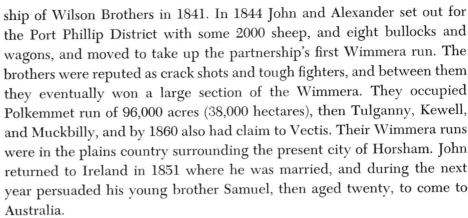

While the homestead is formally designed around an axis, many of its features, such as the oriel window on the first floor, the bargeboards, and the groups of windows, each introduce variety and delight. They each stand against the framed background of soft red bricks which set the overall character of the house.

ship of Wilson Brothers in 1841. In 1844 John and Alexander set out for the Port Phillip District with some 2000 sheep, and eight bullocks and wagons, and moved to take up the partnership's first Wimmera run. The brothers were reputed as crack shots and tough fighters, and between them they eventually won a large section of the Wimmera. They occupied Polkemmet run of 96,000 acres (38,000 hectares), then Tulganny, Kewell, and Muckbilly, and by 1860 also had claim to Vectis. Their Wimmera runs were in the plains country surrounding the present city of Horsham. John returned to Ireland in 1851 where he was married, and during the next year persuaded his young brother Samuel, then aged twenty, to come to Australia.

Samuel's first venture was in trade serving the goldfields. From the sale of goods on the diggings he made a considerable profit, enough it seems to join in partnership with his brothers in the Wimmera. He took management of Kewell Station with about 20,000 sheep. Here he gained pastoral experience. In 1856 the Wilson Brothers partnership acquired the extensive Longerenong run. Within four years the profits had paid for the purchase of the licence. The success was due to the skill of Samuel Wilson who constructed dams and water holes along the Yarriambiac and Wimmera Rivers and dug irrigation and drainage channels across the country. He turned the run into valuable grazing land.

In 1861 he married Jeannie Campbell, daughter of the Hon. William Campbell, MLC, pastoralist, financier, and conservative politician. In June of the next year Samuel laid the foundation stone for the Longerenong homestead. Samuel Wilson was an active member of the Acclimatization Society, and at Longerenong he had extensive gardens laid out in which he attempted to transplant the European flora to the Wimmera plains. He kept deer, Angora goats, ostriches and camels. The camels taken on the Burke and Wills expedition were acclimatized at Longerenong.

In 1869, a year of great drought, the Wilson Brothers partnership was dissolved, and Samuel acquired the entire Longerenong Station property. However, Wilson and his wife did not stay very long at Longerenong. By 1869 the homestead was occupied by a manager, John McLean, who had moved to Longerenong from Coree Station near Jerilderie in New South Wales. The death of their first child, who is buried on the property in a well-marked grave surmounted by a carefully preserved tombstone, has been suggested as the reason for the brief occupation of the Longerenong homestead. It would seem that other forces also may have led Wilson to move. It has been remarked that 'despite his enormous wealth, Wilson's hunger for land was insatiable'. Speculative considerations may have induced him to consolidate his holdings in good quality areas, and he may have aimed at achieving this by selling the Wimmera holdings, and taking up good quality land in the Western District. At any event, he sold and invested in the properties of Mount Bute, Marathon, and Corangamite, in the Western District. It was during this period of rearrangement that he acquired the historic Ercildoune property near Ballarat, to where he and his family moved. By the end of the seventies he held 117,452 acres of freehold in Victoria, about 150,000 acres of freehold in New South Wales, and about 2½ million acres in runs in Queensland.

Samuel Wilson played an active part in social and philanthropic movements in Victoria, and was elected to the State Parliament in Victoria. In 1874 he made a donation of £30,000 to the University of Melbourne for a new Examination Hall, known for ever after as Wilson Hall, designed by the architect Joseph Reed and begun in 1879. He was knighted in 1875, returned to England, where he rented Hughenden Manor, which Lord Beaconsfield had occupied before his death. In 1885 Wilson was elected to the House of Commons. He revisited Australia in 1894 and had returned to England only a few weeks when he died in his sixty-third year. He was a remarkable man of many talents, great enterprise, and boundless energy.

The homestead which Wilson built is dated by the foundation stone which he laid on 30 June 1862. John Tepper, a German from Prussia, visited the homestead in 1872 and recorded in his diary: 'Mr Samuel Wilson, I have been told, spent thousands of pounds on homestead and gardens (£30,000 or more).' Samuel Carter, in *Reminiscences of the Early Days of the Wimmera*, recollected that Samuel Wilson erected a very fine two-storied brick residence in 1863, suggesting that the homestead was completed during that year. The earliest known recording of the completed building is found in the diary of J. J. Westwood *Journal of Eight*

The present dining-room was once the drawing-room. The ground floor rooms each have a large bay window beyond a plain Tudor arch. The pressed metal ceiling was added at the turn of the century, and it is not known what the original ceilings were like.

Throughout the house, beautiful cedar doors, with fine Gothic pointed arches and cusping, create an impression of refined elegance. From the landing outside the central upstairs drawing room the superb divided stairway can be seen below.

Coming from outside into the hall at Longerenong one stands in a deep subdued brown light facing the top-lit stair. The overwhelming experience is to turn and face the entrance door. A brilliant radiance of unrivalled effect is created by the stained glass. The emphatic British motifs in the glass rather contradict possible American influences in the design of the house, and inspiration may have come from earlier English pattern books of the 1830s.

Years Itinerancy in Australia as a Minister of the Gospel who noted on 21 October 1864:

> Drove 8 miles to Mr Samuel Wilson's station, Longerenong. Since preaching on this station three years ago a fine brick mansion has been erected, with first class stables, men's huts, and all the conveniences of an extensive station; a large garden in front of the house is also being well laid out.

No contemporary newspaper records referring to either the design or the erection of the homestead have been found. It is assumed that Samuel Wilson himself was responsible for the design, which bears striking resemblances to American houses illustrated in Andrew Jackson Downing's *The Architecture of Country Houses*, first published in New York in 1850. The designs in Downing's book were by the American architect Alexander J. Davis. Wilson's interest in engineering, and his known concern over design details during the building of the Examination Hall at the University of Melbourne, make it possible that he might have known Downing's book and adapted ideas in it to his own needs. It may of course be that Wilson derived his house directly from English sources, just as the American designs were themselves derived from English models and were described by Downing to be in the 'English Cottage Style'. The American architectural historian Myra Orth has recently observed, after visiting the homestead, that '. . . nowhere does one find what one finds at Longerenong except in Downing'.

The house stands on a low flat sandy stretch right on the banks of the Yarriambiac Creek, and the eighteen-inch load bearing brick walls of the house have had to be set on stone walls which extend down some twelve feet through the river sand, to where the footing blocks can stand on a firm sandstone foundation. Under the centre of the house is a cellar eighteen feet square. The ceiling of the cellar supports the marble tiled floor of the elaborate stair hall which rises above. Rough beams eleven inches by three inches support closely-spaced floor joists of the same size. This sub-floor structure is braced by herring bone struts. All the timber work in the cellar ceiling is oregon. The walls are granite blocks which rise up to about three feet below the cellar ceiling from where the brickwork of the house above begins. The bricks in the house may have been made on the property; they vary in size, and are a soft salmon pinky red in colour. All the walls which are not load bearing are lathed and plastered on a six-inch oregon frame. The most impressive constructional feature in the house is the magnificent stair which rises from a central flight in the stair hall on the main axis of the house. It divides and returns around above to a spacious landing from which the entire stair can be seen below. From above, a soft light falls through a patterned glass skylight, and gently illuminates the enclosed hall of the stair.

The rising central stair on the ground floor faces one of the most superb stained glass entrance surrounds in any building in Victoria. It is set within a broad Tudor pointed arch, an arch motif which repeats throughout the house. The entrance hall and stair hall are bathed in a deep, soft brown light, but from around the entrance door there radiate the most beautiful and intense glowing colours: deep reds, intense blues, transparent yellows.

These stained glass panels have emblematic insets and one of them features Samuel Wilson's monogram. The glass is reputed to have been imported from Brussels.

On either side of the axial entrance hall and stair hall there are impressive doors opening into the various rooms on the ground floor. These large cedar doors are set in moulded cedar architrave surrounds. The doors are panelled and each one features a pair of finely-wrought pointed arches with cusping. This trefoil motif is repeated in the cast-iron balustrading to the stair and in the balustrading of the exterior of the house, and on some of the fireplace surrounds. The quality of the design of the cedar doors, and the repetition of the motif through the house, suggests a real care for detail on the part of Samuel Wilson. It would have been the result of carefully prepared plans and forethought before building commenced.

The two principal rooms are on either side of the main axis at the front of the house. They each have a pair of doors, one opening into the entrance hall and the other into the stair hall. Both mirror each other, and each has a large square bay window at the end. From inside each room this square bay is framed by a Tudor arch. It has been proposed that the room on the right was the drawing-room and the one on the left, the dining-room. In both rooms the stone fire surrounds are mounted with Samuel Wilson's crest, the lion rampant. This device occurs on all the nine fireplaces in the house, and was probably intended on the escutcheon set on the over-sailing courses of the corbel to the first floor oriel window. At some time early in this century all the ceilings within the house were replaced by pressed metal ceilings. There is no surviving evidence as to what they were originally like. Today the use of the two principal ground floor rooms is reversed, and the original dining-room, with its grey-mottled marble mantelpiece, is a living-room, and the former drawing-room is now used as a dining room. Originally, meals would have been brought into the house from an external detached kitchen, through a rear entry hall on the left side of the stair hall. Adjacent to that rear hall was the butler's store, which also opened into the breakfast-room, immediately behind the former dining-room. The room behind the former drawing-room was a library. Both the breakfast-room and the library follow the formal pattern of the front rooms: both have a deep square bay window which is separated from the main space of the room by a broad Tudor arch. Adjacent to the library, immediately behind the stair hall, is a room which was the manager's office. It had a rear access door onto the back verandah, and from the office one could enter either the library or the stair hall and the main rooms at the front. The planning on the ground floor is exceptionally skilful in its disposition of functions, its interconnection of those functions, and its concern with the social distinctions between various activities and the social standing of the participants.

Upstairs were the bedrooms and dressing-rooms, on either side of a central private drawing-room, which is the upstairs room on the main axis under the main gable and with the oriel window. The room behind the stair hall above the manager's office was a nursery. The rooms upstairs once opened out on to a promenade deck surrounded by a Gothic trefoiled cast-iron balustrade. The effect can be seen in old photographs. In recent

The hall and stairs are the central features in the house. All the rooms on both floors are symmetrically disposed around this space. Something of the restrained character of the homestead can be judged from this fine space. The eye is constantly drawn to small items of detail which are enhanced by the simple white surfaces against which they are seen.

The central room upstairs has a pictur-
esque oriel window opening off it, and
from within it is seen through a Tudor
arch. The room was once a private draw-
ing-room, but is now used as a principal
bedroom. In the 1870s it was used as a
schoolroom. The antique Dutch bed has
been entirely restored by Mr John Gregory.

years, when the deck deteriorated beyond repair, the cast-iron balustrade
was taken down and placed along the ground floor verandah. The old
deck can no longer be used, and is now merely the roof to the verandah,
which runs around the front and sides of the house.

The plan of the house is rigid in its symmetry. The upstairs rooms match
each other exactly on either side of the main axis. Downstairs, this precise
mirror of spaces around a central axis can be seen within the front of the
house, and is strikingly clear on the outside. It is only in the central area
behind the stair hall on the ground floor that the rigid symmetry breaks
down. Such formal axial planning is a feature of the picturesque Gothic
villa style, and pervades the model plans in Andrew Jackson Downing's
book, and in the designs of Alexander J. Davis. Another much admired
example of this style in Victoria is Norwood, near Maryborough, designed
for Alfred Joyce by the architect Leonard Terry. At Norwood a similar
formal axial layout is evident, but it is at Longerenong that one sees this
formality most completely realized.

Externally the internal planning is clearly expressed by the intersecting,
steeply-pitched, picturesque gable roofs with their decorative barge
boards. Apart from the barge boards, the details around the exterior are
chaste and without conspicuous ornament. The central Tudor arch to the
porch, the surrounds to the sets of triple windows, the chimneys, and the
quoin work, are without ornament altogether. The timberwork to the
verandah is equally austere, with merely a decorative fretwork reference
to the trefoil cusping found elsewhere in the house. Both outside and inside
there is a chasteness of expression and bluntness in detailing which, in the
Gothic revival of the 1840s and '50s, is taken to be 'realism'.

For many years after Samuel Wilson left Longerenong, the property was in the hands of the Bullivant family. In 1908 the property was broken up and sold for £4/10/- an acre. At about the time of World War I, the homestead was occupied by the Delahunty family. In 1920 it was purchased by Mrs F. B. Gregory, and today is still in the Gregory family, being occupied by both Mr and Mrs John Gregory, and Mr and Mrs David Gregory. Surprisingly, they are descendants of two people who were at Longerenong in the nineteenth century: Thomas Davey, who was a store-keeper at the station, and John McLean, the manager between 1869 and 1878. John Gregory's wife, Ethel, is a grand-daughter of Thomas Davey, and both David Gregory and his wife Marigold are descendants of John McLean.

It is the Gregory family to whom we must be grateful that such a superb and uncommon homestead not only survives, but also has been well cared for and kept in excellent repair. They have spent many years of effort in retrieving the house from decay, and in repairing and restoring its fabric. Time has not been kind to the extensive outbuildings and the fine garden that was established by Samuel Wilson. Today, there is very little left of the well-cared-for park which surrounded the homestead, and the settlement of outbuildings has disappeared leaving little trace. What little has remained is carefully guarded. But the exquisite house remains as a reminder, to paraphrase Andrew Jackson Downing, of those who appreciate 'dignity and elegance . . . who value accurate and elaborate artistic effort'; an exquisite house 'for a family of domestic tastes but with strong aspirations after something higher than social pleasures'.

The wide verandah runs around the front and sides of the house, and features in the centre a fine Tudor arched porch. The cast-iron railing was once the balustrade to a promenade deck above the verandah.

The Springs *New South Wales*

Text: R. J. Chivell   Photographs: Kerry Dundas

Built in the late 1850s The Springs is a well-proportioned timber homestead set low to the ground. In the foreground is one of the springs after which the property was named. In this view a glimpse of the schoolhouse, the boys' bedroom and the homestead from the north can be seen.

Bᴏᴏᴋ ᴇᴀʀʟʏ 1840s, when David Donald occupied a pastoral run of 23,120 acres (9,250 hectares) known as The Meadows in the Wellington district near Dubbo, the unauthorized occupation of Crown land extended well beyond the accepted defined boundaries of rural settlement. There had been an early Act of Council in 1833 designed to ensure that such occupation should not continue so as to create any title for the occupiers, and the 1839 Land Act was another in the series of attempts to regulate the activities of the squatters. It provided for the subdivision into districts of the areas beyond the Nineteen counties and for the appointment of Crown Land Commissioners to act as representatives of the Crown in property matters. In addition, Commissioners were to resolve disputes between squatters and the Aborigines and to collect licence fees, as well as providing a small force of mounted constables to assist with the maintenance of law and order. Lawrence Vance Dulhunty, an early settler who took up land on the Macquarie River near the present site of Dubbo, was appointed the first Crown Land Commissioner for the Wellington District on 21 May 1839, and David Donald's run was notified in the *Government Gazette* on 19 February 1840. By the 1846 Land Act and Regulations, proclaimed on 1 May 1847, the Governor was empowered to grant leases of runs for grazing and pastoral purposes for terms of up to

BELOW: *The garden fence, the shepherds' huts and the early slab dwelling shown in late 1850s drawing have gone, but the homestead and other outbuildings remain substantially as in this view, believed to be the work of A. C. Baird's daughter, Kennedy.*

An essential element in keeping the whole building cool, the wide inviting verandahs of The Springs also serve as the means of access to the small rooms at either end. Many of the formally laid-out garden beds around the homestead have been replaced with lawns and shrubs.

fourteen years with provision that if, during the term the property was offered for sale, the tenant would have first right of purchase. Until that Act, licences to depasture stock had to be renewed annually and, as there was no assurance of renewal, licensees were only prepared to effect such improvements as were absolutely necessary. Without some security of tenure they were generally reluctant to build permanent buildings on their runs.

200 acres (80 hectares) of The Meadows run was taken up in 1846 by Arthur Campbell Baird as a lease. He called it The Springs, after the several clear water springs which water the area. A Scotsman from Ayrshire, Baird had arrived in Sydney with his wife Isabella and eldest child Thomas as passengers on *The City of Edinburgh* in August 1837. Their second child, Kennedy McIntosh, was born at Bathurst in November 1838 before the family came to the Dubbo district, and their younger son, David Donald, was born in May 1841 during the period his father was working as an overseer on The Meadows.

In January 1853 David Donald entered into a partnership for a term of ten years with Arthur Campbell and Isabella Baird. This involved several other station properties as well as The Springs, and provided that the stations were not to be sold at the end of the term without the consent of all parties. David Donald died in 1861, thus terminating the partnership, and Baird, to finalize the partnership account, instructed Richardson and Wrench to sell all the stations together with the stock. There appears in the *Sydney Morning Herald* of Wednesday, 2 October 1861, one of a series of advertisements offering several properties for auction. The Springs was described as having an area of some 20,000 acres (8,000 hectares) of well-watered and thickly-grassed country suited for either cattle or sheep with a frontage of about seven miles to Little River.

'. . . The improvements consist of the homestead, a capital dwelling-house of 10 rooms, woodlined and oil painted throughout, back and front verandahs, kitchen, store and cellar, a garden, orchard and vineyard of about 1½ acres, a cultivation paddock of about 70 acres, a grass paddock of about 150 acres, stock yard with swing-gates, hay shed 60 feet by 14 feet, men's huts, etc.'

The homestead was not sold at the auction on 15 October 1861 and family information would suggest that Baird resolved to remain on the property, treating it as the nucleus of his pastoral and grazing activities. He followed the traditional squatters' course in the appropriation of Crown lands around the original lease, which he purchased for £201 in 1866 after survey. A grant dated 8 June 1866 was issued in his name pursuant to the 1861 Crown Lands Alienation Act.

The 1861 legislation provided for the selection of parcels of vacant land of between 40 and 320 acres (between 16 and 128 hectares) which could be occupied by settlers upon part payment of a fixed price of £1 per acre, the balance being due within three years. So long as the land had been the

David Donald Baird had seven sons and six daughters. As the family grew it became necessary for a schoolhouse and extra bedroom accommodation to be built. Fortunately no attempt was made to enlarge or alter the homestead itself.

One of the principal rooms opening off the central hallway is the main bedroom. Much of the furniture and the fireplace surround are of Australian cedar. There is some fine embroidery on the Dexter rocking chair.

bona fide residence of the selector for that period and certain other conditions relating to improvements were complied with, the selector could then take title to the land. Should he decide to postpone indefinitely payment of the balance due he could continue to occupy the land but would receive no title. The well-advised squatters soon learnt how to take advantage of the provisions of the legislation in moves to increase their pastoral holdings. Baird borrowed heavily to finance purchases of surrounding land and additional stations or runs. He was able to offer several nearby properties as security but it would appear that he over-committed himself in his own and in assisting his sons' speculative land dealings. As part of a family arrangement Baird was himself financially assisted by his friend John Strahorn (the owner of Wandoo Wandong, another well-known property near Obley), to whom The Springs was transferred in July 1867. John Strahorn's daughter, Jane, had married Baird's son David at Wandoo Wandong on 7 January 1867. In January 1873 Strahorn sold the property to David Donald Baird who, with his family, had continued to occupy the homestead and to manage this along with other family properties. In June of the same year David's father transferred to him a pastoral run of 320 acres (128 hectares) adjacent to The Springs, which had been selected in May 1873. It was from this base that David, after the death of his father on 10 October 1881, when his father's other lands passed to him, set out to develop and improve the property. In 1871 his older brother, Thomas, purchased Dundullimal, another well-known Dubbo property, from William Walter Brockelhurst, and thereafter does not seem to have been involved at all with The Springs.

David continued in his father's well-advised steps and was able to increase greatly the area of his properties by taking full advantage of amendments to Crown Land legislation and regulations designed to promote rural settlement. In the family papers there is a considerable correspondence with the Minister for Lands requesting reservation of adjacent areas, to ensure supply of water necessary for the occupation of The Springs, and to protect improvements made to the property. By 1885 he controlled an area of 11,740 acres (4,700 hectares). In 1895 he took up an additional 1920 acres (768 hectares) on a twenty-eight year Conditional Lease and again, in 1897, a further 527 acres (210 hectares) under Licence. Towards the end of 1898 he owned or controlled some 15,600 acres (6,250 hectares) under various titles and tenures, while The Springs had become one of the leading and largest pastoral and grazing establishments in the area.

Over the years the Baird family were highly respected and became well known for their generous hospitality to visitors and travellers and for their interest in community and agricultural affairs. They were also enthusiastic supporters of the Presbyterian Church, and Arthur Campbell Baird was the first Elder appointed when the Church was established in Dubbo in 1873. The silver trowel used by his wife, Isabella, for the laying of the foundation stone of the first St Andrew's Church on 16 December 1874, is still at The Springs.

Although no longer used as such the kitchen outbuilding is kept in good repair. Within the huge whitewashed fireplace are several cranes supporting a variety of boilers, a camp oven and a hot water fountain. An eight-tiered cast-iron pot rack stands between the fireplace and a smaller fireplace. Further to the right, but not illustrated, is a baker's oven.

A Brittania steam engine used to power the shearing gear until the 1930s.

A collection of buggies, traps, sulkies and drays used by several generations of the Baird family.

David Donald Baird died on 26 July 1901. Some indication of his popularity and the esteem in which he was held can be seen from a funeral notice which appeared in the *Dubbo Liberal* on Wednesday, 31 July 1901. After giving some details about his family it noted that the cortege was one of the largest ever seen in the district, extending nearly one-third of a mile and consisting of some eighty vehicles apart from horsemen. He left a widow, seven sons and six daughters. Only four of the children married and subsequently had children. The daughters who married were Kennedy McIntosh Baird (born 1870) who married Fenelon Selwyn Chalmers MacCulloch in 1891; her sister Ruby Baird (born 1883) who married Norman Edwin Lane in 1915; and the youngest daughter Violet Rose Baird (born 1884) who married Thomas Henry Tourle in 1916. Arthur Campbell Baird (born 1873) married Rhoda Gee in 1901, and there were two children of the marriage. Arthur's children have no interest in the property now, as his interest was purchased on his death by other members of the family. The other children all continued to live either with their mother in the homestead or in cottages on the property.

David Donald Baird did not make a Will, and Letters of Administration were issued in October 1901 to his widow and two of his sons, John and David Rivers Baird. Administration of the extensive estate was protracted and the family found it necessary for other members to be appointed as administrators over the years, the last of these being David Donald's grandson Thomas Donald Tourle. Although still run with adjacent properties owned by the family, the total area of The Springs has been reduced with Closer Settlement and Soldier Settlement action to some 1,485 hectares including the homestead block. It is now controlled by a private company made up of the various descendants of David Donald Baird.

Although the exact year of construction of the homestead is not known, it is clear from the 1861 auction advertisement that the existing homestead and many of the outbuildings were then completed. Also, it would follow from the description that the property was then well established, with its own vineyard, orchard and garden. Something of what it must have looked like can be seen from an interesting pen and ink sketch which now hangs in the sitting-room. It is understood that this unsigned sketch of the homestead complex from the west is the work of Kennedy McIntosh Baird, from the late 1850s. An early dwelling, which has since disappeared, of vertical split logs with bark sheet roof secured by cross saplings tied through to the rafters, is shown on the extreme right to the north of the kitchen. The store and other outbuildings extending behind the homestead can also be seen.

All the buildings other than the early dwelling had timber shingled roofs, which have since been replaced by corrugated iron, while all the chimneys were cement rendered early this century to arrest deterioration of the brickwork. The ledgers and other station records do not indicate when construction work commenced, but do show that in the early 1860s many tradesmen were employed on improvements to the property. Towards the end of 1866 there was a flurry of activity by builders like Edward Jamison, Matthew Cavanagh, Benjamin Lewes and John Irvin, who were working with plasterers and others to ensure all would be ready

when David Donald Baird brought his bride to live in the homestead after their marriage in January 1867. The whole family, including David's parents, lived in the homestead. As the family grew and its needs changed additional buildings were constructed nearby, but not so as to alter the building. Set on a rise to the south-east is a two-roomed uncoursed rubble schoolhouse, later used as bedrooms, and closer to the homestead is a large weatherboard dormitory built as bedroom accommodation for the boys.

The well-proportioned homestead is set low to the ground on a foundation of iron bark logs. Its practical design reflects the Georgian love of symmetry and is a good example of the manner in which the architectural traditions, so well known to the early settlers and the builders they employed, were adapted to deal with the hot dry Australian climate. Opening off a wide, airy central hallway are four large rooms, and under the eight-foot-wide verandah which extends right around the building are a further six small rooms. Both the dining and sitting rooms have french doors opening on to the northern verandah. The other large rooms and all but one of the small rooms were used as bedrooms. The small room in the south-western corner was the office, and is still used as such. The only significant alterations which have been made are the conversion of the two small bedrooms on the western side for use as a kitchen and bathroom. In the large rooms there are brick fireplaces with simple cedar surrounds. Much of the joinery is original and care has been taken to ensure that necessary replacements over the years are sympathetic with the original design. Interior walls are lined with twelve-inch wide tongued and grooved boards with slightly narrower boards forming the ceilings. Many of the six small-paned windows which run in timber grooves and are held open with metal clips, remain. The outer-face of the walls is sheeted horizontally with six-inch weatherboards chamfered at the base. Among the early family furniture which remains is an Australian cedar four-poster bed, the other bedroom furniture, and 'a cottage pianoforte in an elegant

One of a complex of rude timber outbuild-ings around the homestead. These include a kitchen, station store, washhouse, meat-house and a long barn now divided into a coachhouse, winter stables, a small grain store and the open summer stables. To the left can be seen the rear of the drop log construction barn.

rosewood case', which cost £75 when purchased in July 1876 from Elvy and Company of Sydney. With it is a numbered certificate from Sebastian and Pierre Erard of London, inventors and manufacturers of the instru-ment. Little remains of what was once an extensive formal garden. This has been replaced with well-kept shrubs and lawn. Under the pepper trees at the back of the homestead are several unusual flower beds made from hollowed out eucalypt logs.

To the west of the homestead is a series of unpretentious, rude timber outbuildings. They are forthright, no-nonsense buildings, each with a specific utilitarian purpose: a kitchen, station store, laundry or washhouse, meathouse, saddle and harness room, and a long building once probably a barn, but now divided into a coach house, winter stables, summer stables and a small grain store.

Separated from the main building by a thirty-five-foot-long, corrugated iron covered walkway is the kitchen. Its construction would suggest that the present building is an early twentieth century replacement. Vertical slabs are set top and bottom into shallow grooves cut in large log sleepers to form the walls. There is no ceiling. The walls of the building are not lined and thin timber battens have been used to cover the gaps between the slabs and to exclude the weather. On either side of the entrance door are small, six-paned sash windows. To avoid the glare of the afternoon sun, these have not been repeated on the western side. In front of a huge white-washed open fireplace is an eight-tiered cast-iron pot stand, and hanging within is a variety of boilers, a hot-water fountain and a camp oven. To the right of the fireplace is a baker's oven. Apart from the well-scrubbed pine table, the room now has very little furniture. Although it is kept in good condition, it is no longer used, as a modern kitchen has been built into the main building.

On the same axis and directly behind the kitchen is an earlier split log construction building, part of which was used as the station store. From here the numerous shepherds and other hands employed on the property were issued with supplies of food, clothing, spirits and other provisions, in part payment in kind for services rendered. A shallow groove has been chiselled into the length of the base sleeper to take the split logs which, butted together, form the walls. The tops of the posts have been tenoned to fit into mortices cut into plates which run around the wall under the roofline. Like most of the other outbuildings the joints in the store are well fitting; the whole being wedged and pegged into rigidity without the use of nails. Beneath the store was the cellar, which has now been filled in. In the store is a varied accumulation of scales, containers and other general household equipment. The part of the building closest to the kitchen was used as a laundry or wash house and contains several early fittings such as a large mangle, a manual washing machine, and two tubs set in pine frames.

Behind the store and running west away from the homestead is a further group of outbuildings. Adjacent to the store is a butcher's room complete with chopping block and a large walk-in gauzed meat hanging area. The small separate saddle and harness room which comes next has in recent years been repaired in weatherboard. Perhaps the most interesting of this group is the next building, a long one divided into four areas. Unlike the other outbuildings, it is constructed of horizontal slabs dropped into grooves cut into vertical uprights supporting the corrugated iron roof. The first section is a coach house or barn now used to store a magnificent collection of buggies, sulkies, and drays. Then come the winter stables, long since disused and altered to accommodate vehicles, a small grain and food store and, at the end, the open summer stables. There is also the small verandahed slab building illustrated which is believed to have been used as a shelter for poultry. Away from the group is the shearing shed and in a shed adjacent to this is a large Brittania steam engine, still in excellent condition, and formerly used to power the shearing equipment.

Built when supplies of glass, paint, lead, nails and other hardware were both difficult to obtain and expensive, the settlers resorted to the natural building materials around them. The iron bark and stringy bark eucalypts, weathered silver grey over the years, have proved both extremely durable and resistant to decay. The exceptionally good condition of the homestead and outbuildings reflects the interest the Baird, and now the Tourle, families have shown in their care and maintenance.

As pioneers themselves, through their marriages into other early squatter families and through their interest in community affairs, the Baird family was an important element in the development of the Dubbo area. The descendants of Arthur Campbell Baird are conscious of the historical significance of the homestead and are preserving it as a memorial to his pioneering spirit.

ABOVE: *An interesting massing of the chimneys to the kitchen fireplace, baker's oven and the washhouse. All the chimneys on these buildings and the homestead were cement rendered early this century to arrest further deterioration of the brickwork.*

A feature of numerous early Australian homes is the covered walkway. Kitchens were detached both to remove the noise of servants and to minimise the possibility of fire damage to the homestead.

Beltana Station woolshed, built of stone before the turn of the century. The sign on the roof is to assist aircraft. It signifies twenty-two miles to Leigh Creek airfield.

Beltana *South Australia*

Text: Ashley Cooper   Photographs: S. H. Gilbert and G. W. Prosser

SIR THOMAS ELDER, GCMG, pioneer pastoralist, merchant and philanthropist, died in 1897 at the age of seventy-eight after playing a leading part in the development of South Australia. His partnership with his brother-in-law Robert Barr Smith eventually became the successful stock and station organization, Elder, Smith & Co. Ltd.

The sponsorship and founding of the Beltana Pastoral Company was one of Sir Thomas's most satisfying activities. His achievements include the camel-breeding depot he established at Beltana Station, which was of great assistance to a series of expeditions of exploration of the vast unknown inland of Australia. From the seventies onwards, leaders of expeditions were invited to select their camels at Beltana, where every hospitality was accorded them. In fact their expeditions were in many cases made possible by the financial backing of Sir Thomas Elder.

During this time a string of sheep and cattle runs extending from Beltana, situated east of Lake Torrens, to Kanowana on Cooper's Creek were being steadily improved by Elder in association with his colleague Peter Waite and managing partner Nathaniel Edmund Phillipson. At the time of Sir Thomas's death the partnership owned the pastoral leases of Beltana, Mount Lyndhurst, Murnpeowie, Cordillo Downs and Kanowana (the last named was sold in 1914). In 1893, 320,844 sheep were shorn and 26,000 head of cattle were depastured on this vast tract of semi-arid country. Since then the onset of prolonged droughts and the sustained depredations of rabbits and wild dogs have greatly reduced stock numbers. In his will, Sir Thomas, who was a bachelor, bequeathed his holding in the Beltana Pastoral Company to his eighteen nieces and nephews.

Beltana Homestead verandah: the house was built of bluestone in 1874 and except for interior amenities and a well-established garden, has been substantially unaltered since that time.

204

The view from the terrace of Beltana Homestead. In the foreground is the tree-lined Warrioota Creek, beyond which is Mount Phillipson, named after an early managing partner.

Beltana Station, 500 kilometres from Adelaide, today is some 1,700 square kilometres in extent and runs 8,500 sheep and 1,500 cattle. It lies almost beyond the limits of the northern Flinders Ranges. It has a prominent landmark in the steep range of hills known as Mount Deception which offers good pasture for sheep on the slopes and in the foothills. From here the plains extend in the direction of Mount Torrens. The pasture is saltbush, blue bush and various herbage. Beyond Mount James outstation is the well-known sandhill country, which produces nutritious, quick-maturing plants after rain.

Warrioota Creek, the main waterway, runs through the now largely deserted Beltana township, on through the broad valley past Beltana Homestead, well marked by red gums, and ends in Lake Torrens.

The eastern verandah of Beltana Homestead, showing the french windows which open from the master bedroom.

Pastoral settlement in the northern Flinders commenced in the early 1850s. The property, which was to become known as Beltana, was taken up from the Government in 1854 by John Haimes under Waste Lands Lease. The sheep run was then 195 square miles in area at ten shillings per mile, to run for 14 years from 1 January 1855. To meet Government requirements, Haimes' lease was promptly surveyed, the surveyor engaged being John McDouall Stuart, who was to become famous for his crossing of Australia south to north in 1861-2.

In the late fifties, when John Haimes was working Beltana, Thomas Elder began to cast his eyes on the pastoral north. In 1860 he rode out to Lake Hope, beyond Lake Gregory, with J. McKinlay's party, who were seeking to relieve Burke and Wills's tragic situation in the region of Innamincka on Cooper's Creek.

McKinlay's party included four camels brought over from Victoria. Observing their great utility on the journey as far as Lake Hope, Elder and his associate, S. J. Stuckey, became greatly interested in the possibilities of importing camels to Australia. As a result, Stuckey travelled to Karachi in 1862 to make investigations on their joint behalf.

Meanwhile Elder was increasing his holdings in the northern Flinders Ranges and beyond, and in April 1862 he took the decisive step of acquiring the Beltana run. In 1867 the run was consolidated in Lease 1710 to run for twenty-one years: 532 square miles at two shillings and sixpence a square mile per annum.

Like all pastoral pioneers in the Far North, Thomas Elder encountered disastrous losses in the early days. In 1864–5 the newly-established squatters suffered the worst drought in living memory. In the Great Drought, as it came to be known, it has been estimated that 235,000 out of 270,000 sheep perished.

Notwithstanding seasonal problems, Elder pressed on with his project to import camels to South Australia. 109 animals were safely landed at Port Augusta in 1866. They were taken first to Elder's Umberatana Station and later to Beltana Station. Here camel-breeding began, with Afghans to assist in the husbandry.

In the late sixties N. E. Phillipson was occupying a responsible post on Beltana Station. In 1870 he was appointed Manager. In June 1869 a second stalwart of early South Australian pastoral enterprise, Peter Waite,

207

The machinery shed in Beltana Station yard. Note the pillar of natural timber.

The famous TE brand, being the initials of Sir Thomas Elder. This brand dates back to 1870 and is still in use.

appeared on the Beltana scene as Superintendent of Thomas Elder's northern runs.

A fascinating diary discovered in the South Australian State Archives records events at Beltana Station from 1867 to 1876: the building of the manager's house in 1874; the frequent extreme heat; visits by the partners; and details about horses, horsehandling and horsebreeding.

The references to sheep, shepherds and shearers are enlightening. The station diarist wrote on Friday, 22 April 1870: 'Ant. Earthmann came in to report the loss of his whole flock, lost off camp the night before last.' Next day the diarist said, 'I returned, having camped last night with sheep . . . found all hands more or less drunk.'

There is a good piece of bush psychology in the next entry: 'Sent out sugar to all the shepherds, their tents being so old, would not keep rain out.'

Just before the Christmas of 1875 Johnson and McLeod came to the Homestead 'for Christmas presents', which betokens a benevolent employer, even though their wages were about twenty-five shillings per week.

Transport was an all important aspect in the Far North in those days, as it remains today. The wool clip was transported to Port Augusta by horse drays, bullock wagons or camel teams, there to be shipped to England and Europe by a fleet of ships.

Camels were of value in many ways. In May 1872 they were being used for carrying posts over the range at Beltana. Shortly afterwards Phillipson had six camels in a wagon, and in 1875 camels harnessed to a dray were 'shaping first rate'.

Ernest Giles, whose expedition to and from Western Australia in 1875 and 1876 was transported by camels supplied by Beltana Station, wrote in his journal: 'In case of any future attempt only one gentleman in the whole of Australia can supply the means of its accomplishment and to him the country at large must be in the future as it is at present indebted for ultimate discoveries. Of course that gentleman is the Hon. Thomas Elder.'

Elder's continuing desire, as revealed in his letter to Captain Lindsay, leader of the Elder Expedition of 1891, was 'to fill up the map of Australia' and establish what pastoral potential existed in the arid Centre.

As the nineties progressed, the depressed condition of the pastoral industry caused much heart-burning and enquiry in Adelaide. The main problems were poor wool and stock prices, severe droughts, the abnormal increase in rabbits and wild dogs and the insecurity of tenure of the pastoral leases. The volume of wool exported dropped by fifty per cent and the value of a bale of wool was only £8.

In July 1894 A. G. Downer gave a lecture in Adelaide on the pastoral question, in which he said:

'Others—only too few in number—have been successful by the possession of skill, energy, perseverance, in short, by living on and being absorbed by their work, by bringing to bear on the industry abilities which would have been successful in any walk of life, and by having been backed by outside or almost unlimited wealth . . . thus enabling them to develop and live through periods that to others would have meant failure.'

The office and store on Murnpeowie Station.

Downer's words could well be a pen picture of the Beltana partners, with whom he was closely acquainted. Phillipson and Waite lived and worked in the northern pastoral environment and their achievements were safeguarded in bad times by the wealth of Sir Thomas Elder.

For positive impact on the development of the Beltana properties, Phillipson looms larger than life. He it was who rode the far-flung runs as far as Kanowana and Cordillo Downs, laid out the woolsheds, the homesteads and the mustering yards, and planned the orderly provision of the waters. As evidence of the confidence of Elder and Waite, Phillipson was admitted to full partnership in 1877, ultimately reaching the status of managing partner.

Phillipson had a great instinct for direction. Men had to keep their eyes skinned if they were slacking on a job out on the run because he would emerge from any point of the compass in his horse-drawn buggy.

On one occasion 30,000 sheep from Momba, a Barr Smith station in New South Wales, were being auctioned at the Burra. The bidding started for a

The shearers' quarters on Beltana Station. They have been modernized and made very comfortable.

reasonable parcel and they were knocked down to Phillipson. 'How many will you take?' asked the auctioneer. 'The lot,' said Phillipson, and there was almost a riot.

If Phillipson worked energetically at executive level, Peter Waite was virtually Managing Director of the partnership and frequently visited the group of Beltana stations. To Waite is attributed much of the impetus in enclosing sheep paddocks for better watering and pasturing. This was a tremendous advance on the archaic and time-consuming shepherding of the flocks. The 265-ton shipment of fencing wire which Waite imported from England in 1870 and 1871 is frequently recalled in any review of pastoral pioneering.

Peter Waite also pressed on with well-sinking and dam excavation and, later, the drilling of artesian bores.

In 1895, Waite was writing to *The Register* on the benefits of judicious expenditure on further water improvements and subdivision of paddocks in the light of close observation of needs. He spoke of his enthusiasm for smaller paddocks to conserve dry feed, particularly to nurture ewes and new-born lambs in the absence of rain. He also reiterated his belief in the necessity to spell salt and other bush to avoid destroying Nature's 'haystack' in the Far North.

Thomas Elder received the honour of a knighthood in 1878 and nine years later his work was further recognized with the bestowal of the GCMG.

For the new Company formed in 1898, the first two decades of the century were bedevilled with droughts. As early as December 1900 the Directors, Sir J. Lancelot Stirling, Peter Waite and T. E. Barr Smith reported they did not feel justified in paying a dividend in view of the outlook. Rain was urgently needed and there was trouble with wild dogs and rabbits. As the drought intensified, Peter Waite reported to shareholders, in June 1902, that the weakest of the lambing ewes had died at lambing and all young lambs were dead. There was heavy mortality from wild dogs entering from unoccupied country and sheep were being sold off as extensively as possible.

Except at Cordillo, no horses were being worked on the runs, the men being mounted on mules, donkeys or camels. The donkeys were hardy animals which proved a boon during these bad seasons. Used for riding, as pack animals, in teams, in carts or buggies, they worked where horses would have starved.

So drastic had the drought become that by 1903 the whole of Beltana and Mount Lyndhurst was unstocked and the remaining 17,000 sheep were depastured on the northern end of Murnpeowie. The Cordillo sheep numbers were reduced from 66,000 to 7,000.

Following the drought, Beltana Run was unstocked from 1903 until 1909. This gave the salt and other bush a chance to regenerate and, in any case, the property was untenable until a vermin-proof fence was erected to check the inroads of wild dogs.

In spite of the bleak outlook from 1900–1910 steps were taken to overcome the difficulties. These included the erection of additional vermin-proof fences by the Company.

In 1913 the General Manager, Morton Beach Ive, transferred his headquarters from Murnpeowie to Adelaide. His strict standards of decorum at Murnpeowie are recalled. He insisted that a tie be worn for dinner by the jackeroos as well as himself. Great was his discomfort one night when he realized he had offended against his own rule.

Edwardian decorum was observed even with ablutions in the bush. M. B. Ive wrote to the Beltana overseer in 1908 thanking him for returning his pyjamas. 'I think I left them hanging up in a tree. I got them wet when bathing.'

The Company moved with the times, and in 1911 an I.H.C. motor buggy was purchased for £176/10/- for use on the runs.

There are echoes of World War One in the Company's records. The Murnpeowie letter book mentions in 1916: 'A recruiting sergeant is here and four men are going down to Quorn for examination.' Owing to the number of station book-keepers who had enlisted, the Company's accounts were running late that year.

Sheep numbers were high in 1925; a total of 194,299 sheep and lambs being shorn on the Company's stations.

The November 1942 dividend was the first since 1928. The lean years in between resulted from a combination of bad seasons and the slump in the price of wool as a result of the world-wide trade depression.

The 1931–32 wool-selling season was destined to end with values at the lowest level in living memory. Beltana realized only 5·95 pence for fleece wool at the wool sales in November 1931.

Hardy donkeys and mules were still in constant use by the station staffs, but the mules in many cases lived up to their reputation of being stubborn, vicious and hard to handle. They would gleefully gash or kick an unwary handler. However, everyone on Beltana in those days remembers the

The cairn to commemorate the setting out of the Giles exploring expedition to Western Australia which left Beltana Station on 6 May 1875. The wool shed is on the right.

The Mount Lyndhurst homestead, which has been extensively modified in recent decades to meet modern needs.

remarkable intelligence and tractability of 'Nimrod'. Ridden by Bert Napier, he was almost human in mustering the sheep.

The best general rain for years fell in November 1937 and sheep numbers picked up; a double lambing yielding 31,000 lambs.

With the outbreak of war in 1939, news came through that all wool sales were cancelled and the British Government would purchase the Australian clip. As a result growers were soon receiving more favourable returns.

On 26 November 1941 the Company received a severe blow with the death of the Chairman, Mr T. E. Barr Smith. T. E. Barr Smith Jnr, later to become Sir Tom Barr Smith, was elected to the chair in his place.

Owing to lack of feed and the dry tracks leading to the main shearing sheds in 1945, it was necessary to resort to shearing in the paddocks. In more recent years this problem has been met by the erection of outlying crutching sheds with three-stand shearing machines.

Wool prices were on the rise in 1947. In June the average was 24 pence per pound and by December it had risen to 33 pence. Sheep numbers were restored to 40,000 and the Board was able to report that 'last year saw the start towards recovery which has continued this year'.

In 1950 the wool boom was gaining momentum and the Company's wool clip was sold at very profitable prices. The spiral continued and in June 1951 Mount Lyndhurst wool sold as high as 144 pence per pound.

There was a fairly severe recession in prices in the following year when the 1952 clip realized little more than half the previous year's exceptional earnings. Gradually wool prices reverted to a more normal level.

In 1960 the Company acquired its own boring plant but had no early successes on Mount Lyndhurst, or Murnpeowie. Of seven bores drilled, six were salt.

Careful attention is given each year to the selection of rams from Collinsville with wool of medium staple, showing bulk, density and style. This will help to maintain the increase achieved in the average cut per sheep over the last few years.

The Company suffered a sad loss in 1968 with the death of its Chairman, Sir Tom Barr Smith. The present Chairman is Mr R. M. Barr Smith. The other Directors are Mr T. E. Barr Smith and Mr H. A. E. Gosse.

Good rains have fallen in the last few years, enabling much easier pastoral management.

Some years ago the late Dr C. T. Madigan, a notable geologist and modern day explorer of the Simpson Desert, expressed most clearly what the people in this narrative have had to contend with.

'The history of the country is made up of a series of long droughts broken by short periods of comparatively heavy rain which put the land into good heart for a year or two, from which happy state it slowly but inevitably falls away until the next rain comes, and these cycles of long droughts and short rains control the occupation or desertion of the holdings. Some stations and managements have lasted out several cycles, some have closed finally after one, some have been reoccupied after long breaks.'

The Beltana Pastoral Company and its people can take pride because they have never lost heart and have never failed to return.

MOUNT LYNDHURST

Mount Lyndhurst sheep run, 3,600 square kilometres in extent, is situated 48 kilometres east of Lyndhurst siding. Slightly eastward of Beltana Homestead the Flinders Ranges take a broad sweep north-eastwards towards Mount Serle and Freeling Heights, which overlook the southern hills country of Mount Lyndhurst run. Mount Lyndhurst itself has been described by a northerner as merely a pimple on the landscape.

The beginnings of Mount Lyndhurst run date back to 1869 when Sir Thomas Elder took up the property under pastoral lease. It was then undeveloped country, 1,600 square kilometres in extent. The average rainfall is 150 millimetres but is extremely variable.

Some years ago the Mount Lyndhurst woolshed (illustrated) provided welcome nourishment for the gardens being established at the neighbouring coal town of Leigh Creek. There was a vast accumulation of sheep droppings under the battens of the floor of the woolshed; these were removed and conveyed by motor truck to Leigh Creek.

The Beltana stations have been famous over the years for their hospitality and have seen a number of vice-regal visits.

The visit of Sir Malcolm and Lady Muriel Barclay Harvey in the early 1940s, accompanied by Mr Tom Barr Smith, presented problems, as Sir Malcolm set off separately to visit Beltana and Mount Lyndhurst stations, while Lady Muriel headed for Marree in a separate vice-regal car to open a nursing home next day.

Cordillo Downs woolshed. (Photograph: South Australian Pastoral Board)

Broncho branding of calves with the TE brand on Murnpeowie Station.

The Mount Lyndhurst woolshed, where 28,000 sheep were shorn last year. OPPOSITE

The interior of the Mount Lyndhurst woolshed. OPPOSITE BELOW

The old shearers' quarters on Murnpeowie Station. The boldly-painted name is to assist aircraft.

After a late night at Mount Lyndhurst Homestead it was an exacting task next morning to awaken Sir Malcolm so that he could keep his mid-day appointment with Lady Muriel at Marree. Bathroom facilities were more primitive than at present and Sir Malcolm's bathtub was filled with hot water from a distant copper no less than three times before he was awakened to take the plunge. It is to be hoped he was able to keep his appointment at Marree.

MURNPEOWIE STATION

MURNPEOWIE STATION lies 130 kilometres north-east of Lyndhurst Siding and covers almost 9,500 square kilometres. At present it runs 10,300 Short-horn cattle and has an establishment of 200 horses. Its average rainfall is 120 millimetres.

Originally the run was known as Blanchewater. However, Blanche-water's pre-eminence in the eighties and its spectacular horse-breeding activities were to suffer an eclipse in the early nineties when a decision was made by the partnership of Elder, Phillipson and Waite, to shift the head-quarters of the run to a new homestead at Murnpeowie on the Twins Creek—the name Murnpeowie meaning a watering place for bronzewing pigeons. Murnpeowie has become known colloquially over the years as 'Mumpyowie'. Murnpeowie woolshed, built sturdily of stone, bears the date 1890 and was erected for £2,002 with stands for forty-two blade shearers.

By September 1894 sheep numbers on Murnpeowie had grown to 106,000 at the shearing, yielding 340 tons of greasy wool. The substantial stone homestead (which has been extensively remodelled during the present régime of the Napier family) and the rest of the station buildings, were erected at the same time as the woolshed.

Today the ruins of Blanchewater Homestead lie remote on the banks of MacDonnell Creek south-west of Lake Blanche and west of Mount Hopeless outstation. The massive posts of the original horseyard, with their wide-staring joggle holes, stand like sentinels there.

The Hon. John Baker, MLC, was the founder of Blanchewater Run. In 1857 he took up two blocks each of 100 square miles (260 square kilo-metres) along the MacDonnell Creek. This was promptly followed by further large acquisitions in the area.

Thomas Elder's interest in the Blanchewater region commenced in 1860 when he acquired leases in the Mulligan country east of Mount Hopeless.

John Baker survived the Great Drought of 1864–65, but his herds of cattle were undoubtedly decimated. When he died in 1872 the unexpired portion of the Blanchewater leases was transferred to Thomas Elder.

A vast area of over 10,000 square kilometres was then consolidated into what a station manager described as the 'Blanchewater Horse Stations' on a pastoral map dated about 1885. The area covered is virtually that which became known as Murnpeowie Run in the nineties and has con-tinued more or less intact until today. The map is endorsed: 'Carrying capabilities 20,000 horses', but there may have been a little bravado in this assertion.

The area was described by Chief Surveyor Cornish in 1882 as consisting chiefly of broken tablelands, surrounded by extensive redstone plains intersected by numerous creeks. 'During favourable seasons this tract produces an abundant growth of Mitchell grass—a coarse but very valuable grass—cotton and saltbush, and other good herbage. These, however, cannot always be depended on as the seasons are very irregular.'

The development of Blanchewater soon got under way after Thomas Elder's purchase. The Beltana Station Diary of 13 June 1873, records the Manager, Phillipson, as drafting horses for Blanchewater, and twenty-one were started for their destination four days later. There was continuous dray and camel traffic between Beltana and Blanchewater and, on 4 September 1874, a man named Wedlock is recorded as starting for Blanchewater with Pride of the Mount, who was one of the progenitors of the famous TE horses.

The Blanchewater manager wrote to Phillipson in May 1885:
'I see you have offered 600 horses for inspection here. Our men will muster all the way in. The horses are very wild and our working horses are breaking down fast.
21 August 1885: I am turning Bismarck into St Mary's paddock with twenty-five really good mares.
5 October 1885: Pamphlet I like very much. He is a good boned big upstanding two-year-old. Patchwork is a handsome horse, small, but good.
21 June 1886: If you think a team of four black colts, light, active and very well matched would bring a fair price as a four-in-hand team—I have them in the Worlatandinna paddock.
25 January 1887: The mares with Planet are all doing well, he is a great foalgetter. Barber's Dam has a foal by Planet, a perfect little gentleman.
15 February 1887: A great portion of my lads are laid up with falling off horses.'

Cattle raising was also a profitable activity on Blanchewater. In November 1874 Kingsmill, the overseer at Beltana, was cutting out bulls for Blanchewater; two years later Long, the manager of Blanchewater, was arriving at Beltana with a mob of cattle.

Young Alec Ross, safely back from the Giles Expedition to Western Australia and anxious to learn more about cattle, was sent to Blanchewater in 1878 to gain experience under G. P. Long. Telling of his early experiences at the time of the unveiling of the Giles Memorial Cairn at Beltana Homestead in 1930, he remarked that Blanchewater was carrying 4,000 horses and that any young fellow there soon had to learn to ride.

Blanchewater Homestead was an impressive complex of buildings. The pastoral map of 1885 mentions in its list of improvements a manager's house, men's quarters, store, smithy, outbuildings and stockyards. An 1888 Field Book of the Department of Lands describes 'Government House' (the manager's house) as being 'of three rooms, walls of rubble masonry 18 inches thick and plastered, hip roof of galvanized iron, floor of slate flags, calico ceiling, in all valued at £55'.

The heyday of Blanchewater and its horses seems to have been in the eighties, when up to a thousand foals were born each year and received the TE brand, which was becoming famous all over Australia.

These vivid dunes occupy the southern and western areas of the Cordillo Downs run. Their inter-dune corridors receive the flood-out and drainage from the residual landform watersheds. The wild flowers are crotalaria: *common name rattle-pod.*
(Photograph: South Australian Pastoral Board)

The rear view of the old shearers' quarters at Murnpeowie Station.

217

The harness room at Murnpeowie Homestead, which is very actively used. Note the branding irons hanging from the roof.

The Blanchewater horses were sturdy and tough. They performed admirably in drawing Cobb & Co. coaches in the network of services in inland Australia. They were used widely for stock mustering horses and were also sold abroad for remounts for the Indian Army, often through the medium of Jules Gascard, a shrewd dealer in horseflesh. In Adelaide, horses from Blanchewater were widely sought after for riding and carriage use before the advent and development of the automobile, and old timers recall that doctors in those early days found TE horses most useful buggy horses because of their stamina. It can safely be said that the TE brand came to be regarded as a guarantee of equine excellence.

Consequent on the move from Blanchewater to Murnpeowie there was a clearing sale of Blanchewater horses in September 1891. The catalogue listed 932 brood mares with categories of fillies and colts, 'hunters' hacks and medium draughts all in splendid condition', a total of 3,309 horses, as well as 'valuable sires, both thoroughbred and draught'.

Murnpeowie Station carried on the tradition of breeding good horses,

218

although on a much more limited scale. Even today, Murnpeowie has its establishment of 200 saddle horses, with its brood mares carefully selected each year for mating with a good stallion.

In 1906 energetic, and eventually successful, artesian boring was commenced on Murnpeowie, which is at the southern extremity of the Great Artesian Basin.

The bores had the great virtue of opening up additional country in the vicinity of the streams they created, which were assisted with drains.

A year later Murnpeowie and Mount Lyndhurst were drought-stricken; so badly that horsebreaking was out of the question. Even the lion-hearted are sometimes daunted. M. B. Ive, the General Manager, told W. T. Johnston, the boring contractor: 'There is not much chance of any further boring in this country. The country simply isn't worth it.'

Machine shearing of sheep was introduced at Cordillo and Murnpeowie in 1907. In 1913 a Ruston-Proctor engine was purchased for machine shearing at Mount Lyndhurst.

An old-time method of generating power was Peter Waite's use of numerous steam traction engines, a few of which remain as museum pieces on Murnpeowie and Mount Lyndhurst. These traction engines were used for pumping, driving shearing machinery and sawing wood.

In the early 1940s Murnpeowie was having its troubles with wild dogs, particularly after the vermin-proof fences were badly washed out by the torrential rains of February 1944. Because of the acute shortage of fencing materials, the Board approved the General Manager's recommendation in July 1946 that, until supplies were procurable, Murnpeowie should be

The horsebreaking yard at Murnpeowie Station. Horses are still used extensively here for stock mustering.

A gate in the dog fence which runs across the far north of South Australia. It prevents the encroachment of dingoes on sheep flocks.

Flat top mountain, Cordillo Downs. Characterized by undulating expanses of Mitchell grass and intersected by gidgee and minnaritchie timber lines on the creeks, these gibber-strewn landforms comprise a major proportion of the Cordillo Downs country, which is renowned for the breeding of livestock sound in wind and limb.
(Photograph: South Australian Pastoral Board)

stocked with surplus cattle from Cordillo. The cattle proposition turned out so successfully that Murnpeowie never again reverted to sheep.

There was a natural increase of 4,000 calves in 1956, the Company having been favoured with a succession of reasonable seasons since 1946. Natural increases mean calf branding, and the method of broncho branding is used on Murnpeowie and Cordillo Downs. There is a four-man team: the man on the broncho horse lassos the victim in the mustering yard and drags him across soft sand to three men at the operations point.

There the calf is thrown and branded with the red-hot TE branding iron; while earmarking and castration of the bull calves are completed in a matter of seconds. The throughput is up to one hundred per hour and the mob, mothers and calves, are then returned to their pastures.

CORDILLO DOWNS

SITTING ON THE TERRACE of Cordillo Downs Homestead when the sun is setting and a thousand white cockatoos scream and chatter in the tattered old gum trees above the Station waterhole, one can sense the feeling of history attached to the place. Sturt's Stony Desert, a vast expanse of gibbers, stretches out on all sides, while not far away, at Nilpi waterhole, local legend has it that Burke and Wills buried their instruments.

It is with a feeling of admiration that one thinks of Cordillo's years of survival in this far-away north-east corner of South Australia: ninety-two years under one management, which began with Peter Waite taking up pastoral leases of the area in 1883—Cordillo Downs, 'where we get some of the fag end of the Queensland rains', to quote N. E. Phillipson before the Pastoral Lands Commission in 1898.

This is a hostile land where mirages reach their ultimate in deception and disillusion, in a heat which shimmers and distorts the distant red table-topped sandhills. Yet for fifty years men husbanded sheep with great success and, of all miracles, scoured the wool clip with elaborate machinery alongside the station waterhole. This is the place of which the *Sydney Mail* published a picture in 1926 showing a mountain of wool, 45,000 fleeces, piled ready for scouring.

It was in 1941 that the battle against wild dogs was given up and a vital decision was made by the Company's Board: to abandon sheep and stock with Shorthorn cattle instead. Since then Cordillo has never looked back.

The Cordillo Downs pastoral lease was originally taken up in 1878 by stockholder Edgar Chapman of Adelaide for a period of 21 years at two shillings and sixpence per mile. It was transferred to Peter Waite in 1883, and recorded as having no Crown improvements; it was a new block.

Development in the characteristic Peter Waite manner soon began. The Cordillo Downs Diary of 5 February 1883 records that well sinkers had commenced to timber the well and that the dam sinkers were on the job.

A. E. Witherby, the Manager on a salary of £300 per annum, who had earlier been on Beltana Station, wrote on 27 March 1883: 'two policemen came today with returns to be filled in. I return . . . 28 horses, 580 horned cattle, 10,312 sheep, 1 camel.' A month later he was writing, 'I got one room of the hut done up and roofed with canvas for Mr Kingsmill to use. Am planing up the bed-frames myself.' (This was Kingsmill, manager of Mount Lyndhurst Station, and previously overseer on Beltana.)

A few days later Messrs Phillipson, Kingsmill and Chippendale arrived. An energetic drawing up of plans and measuring for station improvements ensued; plans for horse and cattle yards, a station kitchen and a woolshed: the famous stone woolshed with its heavy buttressed walls.

The wild dogs soon showed themselves to be a menace. Bitten and dead sheep were found regularly and the howling of dogs was heard at night.

The camel teams were indispensable to life on Cordillo. Targe Mahomet was in and out regularly with his camels, bringing supplies from Mount

Cordillo Downs homestead; the original house since the station was settled. The semi-circular roof was designed to economize on roofing timbers. (Photograph: Ashley Cooper)

The office and store on Cordillo Downs Station. (Photograph: Ashley Cooper)

Lyndhurst and Beltana and returning with bales of wool. 'Gool Mahomet arrived on 5 June 1884, with pack camels fetching rations, wire, horse-shoes, etc. having done the trip from Beltana in twenty-four days.'

The year 1885 saw the remarkable feat of transporting and installing the extensive machinery for the station wool scour. This move was dictated by high transport costs. The partners considered it more economic to scour the wool at Cordillo than to incur 'dead freight' on greasy and sandy wool on the 600-kilometre haul by camel train to Farina; the scouring getting rid of perhaps 40 per cent of extraneous matter. On 15 July Mr Witherby was 'putting up and fitting the boiler'. On 6 October the machinery was unloaded from the wagons and was, apparently, set up efficiently because six months afterwards the diary records 'wool scouring finished'.

On 4 April 1889, the diary first mentions the mail coach driven by H. McKenzie. It soon met trouble at Toorawatchie where it broke up and the station had to revert to packhorses.

In July 1890 a schoolmaster, William Sturdy, started at Cordillo at twenty-five shillings a week.

These were the roaring days of Cordillo Downs. A fine map still in existence shows the station as extensively improved, with sub-division paddocks, and well watered with wells, dams and 'permanent' water holes. A very large capital sum for those days, £34,000, had been expended. The wool scour was the most expensive item. In 1890 85,000 sheep were shorn, giving over 1,000 bales of scoured wool.

A vast change had taken place by July 1893 when David Waite, Inspector of Runs for the partnership and son of Peter Waite, wrote that Cordillo was devoid of any feed: the dry stumps of Mitchell grass which were the 'haystack' there. 'I did not handle any sheep. They were too poor and weak to give one a fair idea of what they are.' Cordillo, he added, was quite safe from rabbits as they could not stand the hot stones in the summer time.

Peter Waite sent a first-class manager by the name of A. J. McDonald to Cordillo in 1898 to reorganize the place. He sent an urgent call for wind-mills, or 'air-motors', as these innovations were then often called. Wind-mills proved to be a boon on all the Beltana properties.

At this stage Cordillo had a bad time with influenza, or 'dingo fever' as the Manager called it. 'We are all pulling through the effects of influenza and the empty coffin built by Mr Hack has not yet been called into service —I think we will loan it to the Spaniards as a "torpedo boat".'

In 1907 steps were taken to fence with netting the 7,800 square kilo-metres of the consolidated property of Cordillo Downs, the sandhill country of which was infested with dingoes. As a preliminary, M. B. Ive, the General Manager, and David Waite rode the proposed line of fence from Haddon Corner to the south-east extremity of the station.

In 1928 the seasonal outlook was bad. The Cordillo Manager reported in November that feed was non-existent and that the sheep had nothing but water. The rams were being shepherded outside the netting fence and given a daily issue of Meggitts nuts. The stock losses on all runs since the 1928 shearing exceeded 50,000.

Following the decision to switch to cattle in 1941, the building-up of the Cordillo herds was pressed on. In 1942 1,000 dry cows were purchased at 65 shillings a head, and fourteen Nalpa bulls at 30 guineas a head. The first bullocks en route to the Adelaide saleyards were walked to the railhead at Cockburn in May 1943 and the General Manager reported that the mob included some nice beasts.

Cordillo Downs experienced falls of over 150 millimetres in February 1944, further favouring the cattle project.

However, by the end of 1946 drought conditions were hitting Cordillo. It had received 125 millimetres only in the preceding 2¾ years; the waterholes had given out, and the cattle were on reserve country served by wells and bores. Mobs totalling 2,800 had been travelled down to Murnpeowie. This substantiates the belief of the original partners in the value of owning widely-separated stations whereby relief could be provided for any station within the group which had been hard hit by missing the rains.

A great aid to stock control today is the development of motor truck transport of cattle from Cordillo Downs to Murnpeowie and the railhead, whereby the stock arrives in good condition.

Cordillo Downs, situated in the north-east corner of South Australia, is now 7,700 square kilometres in extent and runs over 6,000 cattle. Its intermittent rainfall is described as being an average of 150 millimetres a year, but that has been greatly exceeded in the last couple of years.

Cordillo Downs has experienced severe vicissitudes in the course of its history, but today gives no signs of closing down. It is still vigorous and enterprising.

223

Mount Talbot *Victoria*

Text: Neil Clerehan   *Photographs: Brian J. Lloyd*

The original homestead was constructed in wattle-and-daub. However, it may well have had, as a nucleus, the house Robert Officer prefabricated in Van Diemen's Land in 1839. The remains of the early house were destroyed in the 1950s.

Mount Talbot homestead presents a front elevation of simple classical proportions. The traditional verandah stops short of the south side but returns around the right (north) elevation. In recent years, this section has been glazed.

IN 1862, WHEN CHARLES MYLES OFFICER decided to build an elaborate house for himself and his family on his property at Toolondo, he chose an architect who was the building surveyor at Hamilton. Such a choice had obvious advantages. The consultant was relatively close, living south across the plains in the prime Western District. Furthermore he would doubtless have been familiar with the problems of building in the inhospitable Wimmera. Such a choice is, ironically, not available to many rural communities today. The long slow decline in farm prosperity has, to a great degree, stripped country towns of their professional class. Architectural and engineering practices are still listed in regional telephone directories, but the numbers almost invariably indicate metropolitan offices. Few architects practising today in country areas can claim to be as professionally involved with their locality as was young John Shanks Jenkins in 1862. Similarly his client, even by 1862, had had a relatively long association with the Wimmera.

Charles Officer was a son of Dr (later Sir) Robert Officer, who had bought the Toolando property from a T. M. Airey in the year 1847. Sir Robert Officer founded a family which went on to earn many distinctions in Tasmania and Victoria in the fields of politics, welfare and medicine, apart from farming. Robert Officer was born in Dundee in 1800 and arrived in Hobart Town in 1822, already a qualified surgeon. His life in the new colony was a dramatic combination of medical practice (in the private and public spheres), farming, land dealing and public service. He was attracted to the burgeoning colony across Bass Strait and made many trips to Geelong either to sell stock or, venturing further up into Port Phillip Territory, to buy or lease properties.

It is known that in 1839 he ordered and had prefabricated an eight-roomed house. This he shipped across the Strait. He may well have used this structure to settle the land he bought in the Wimmera. This land, 100 square miles of it, was to become the Mount Talbot property.

Before the permanent stone house came to be erected twenty years later, Robert Officer's sons had had to buy back the land as the result of a complicated but not fully recorded series of deals. Early family records are not complete and many descendants doubt whether the original Robert Officer in fact lived at Mount Talbot for any length of time. For one thing his career in Tasmania would have kept him fully occupied. He served in the Legislative Council from 1853 to 1856, and then in the newly-formed lower House until his retirement in 1877. He became the speaker in 1861. He travelled extensively between States and bought and ran many properties. His eldest son, also Robert, managed Mount Talbot until 1854.

The entrance facade of Mount Talbot faces east. The evenly-spaced upper windows line with the larger openings of the lower floor. This, the main facade, has a classical symmetry, framed from certain angles by huge trees which ante-date the homestead.

To assist him in his pastoral ventures, Dr Officer recalled two other sons (he had six) from university in Edinburgh. When Charles went to Mount Talbot, the third son Suetonius, some three years younger than Charles, went up to manage other family properties in the Riverina.

Charles was born in Tasmania. After he returned from Edinburgh University, and took over the Wimmera property from his elder brother, he made plans to build the homestead which still stands today, and is now the home of his great-grandson, Mr Derek Officer and his family.

The original house had grown either too small or unacceptable to Charles Officer. In this he was following a well-established tradition. All over Victoria wattle-and-daub houses were either being abandoned or altered to such a degree as to be unrecognizable. A few good seasons had brought prosperity to rural Victoria. This was not a stable period but soon the American Civil War was to have a dramatic effect on the rural

225

A single-storeyed wing containing the domestic offices extends west from the main two storeyed block.

economy, just as another American military operation (in Korea in 1950–51), was to bring unprecedented wealth to the Australian woolgrower nearly a century later.

The original Mount Talbot homestead may well have contained as a core the house prefabricated in Tasmania by the family's founder. After the completion of the new homestead in 1863, the older house fell into disuse and decay. It was not destroyed until the 1950s—a watershed decade which saw many significant rural buildings destroyed before their owners (and the community) realized their worth.

The old homestead stood to the east of the extensive outbuildings and the new house was built further to the east again. A little to the south of the site of the first house stand the remains of a chimney. An earlier building, possibly even a house, may have stood there. The second Mount Talbot homestead consists of the main two-storeyed block, containing four main rooms on each floor and a single-storeyed wing, stretching back to the west and containing the domestic offices opening on to a generous south-facing verandah. Thus, on a room count, with eight or nine main apartments the house was modest for its time but, as events turned out, perfectly in keeping with the twentieth-century standards.

The homestead is situated in an extensive garden with many fine old trees, including a handsome citrioda (lemon-scented gum) and several Lagunaria Patersonii (the pyramid tree, or Norfolk Island hibiscus).

The main block, flat-fronted and symmetrical, is bisected by a wide (three metres) hall. The two main rooms give off this hall, and towards its west end a two flight stair rises to serve the upper floor. The architect chose to give the two front rooms a far greater ceiling height (approximately five metres) than the rooms behind them. This dual ceiling height is reflected in the form of the upper floor. The second flight reaches the lower level of the upper floor and a third flight is necessary to reach the higher section (above the front rooms). This flight extends across the full width of the hall giving a short but spectacularly wide stair. Again the unusual ceiling arrangement is further reflected in the roof form. The front section is covered by a transverse hipped roof. The back half has two gabled roofs forming a variation of the M roof which was almost universal on Victorian houses along with its internal, inevitable and vulnerable gutter.

The main facade of the house contains five evenly-spaced openings on each floor. Each is spanned with a single stone lintel, and in the few cases where the lintel failed (probably during construction) steel plates were carefully introduced to carry the load. The verandah was, by the 1860s, a popular device in Australia for sun shielding and providing summer living space.

At Mount Talbot it does not carry through the facade's symmetry. Sensibly it eschews the sunless south elevation but returns along the north wall. This sun-facing section was later glazed. The original sloping verandah soffit with exposed beams has been ceiled. The verandah floor, already well into its second set of planks, will soon be replaced. The next floor, with the reversed cost-ratio of labour to materials will, of necessity, be concrete. Similarly, the delicate timber dentils which once trimmed the verandah have over the years been removed and not replaced.

A two flight stair rises from the wide central hall. The front upper rooms are reached by a further flight. The third flight is the full width of the stair hall. This is an unusual device which provides high ceilings to the two lower front rooms.

The house has grand dimensions, but a down-to-earth quality in its form, construction and detail. It was an eminently suitable solution to the physical and human problems posed and the solution bears the hall mark of the times and of its architect and his values. He was born in Scotland in 1854 and served his articles with the Aberdeen firm of MacKenzie & Matthews. He emigrated to Melbourne in 1854 and soon involved himself in architectural competitions.

These were then the traditional method by which young architects working in offices could achieve fame and begin practice by themselves. In Jenkins' case the system was to work well but it was to take a long time. He entered the competition for the design of St Andrew's Presbyterian Church in Carlton. He won the second prize. The winning design in that

A service building constructed in pink, hand-made bricks called the Brick Store stands to the north of the homestead.

competition had an interesting history. It was built in Carlton, but nearly sixty years later it was carefully dismantled and re-erected, more or less faithfully, in Camberwell in 1938.

In 1855 Jenkins moved to Warrnambool, and then to Port Fairy, where he became Town (Building) Surveyor in 1858 at the age of twenty-four. Obviously Jenkins' interests were very much centred on the administration of the building process rather than the more esoteric aspects of construction. In 1860 he became Building Surveyor at Horsham, where his private commissions came to include the Officer homestead under review, and numerous small but important public buildings such as the Gaelic School, the Presbyterian Church and the Mechanics' Institute.

When he received the commission to build a grand house at Mount Talbot for Charles Officer, the existing wattle-and-daub cottage with the traditional shingle roof was left standing. A suitable building stone was fortuitously discovered on the property near the chosen site. It is a sandstone laced with ironstone and of an unusual brown colour. Further to the west, sandstone was in general use, but the preferred Victorian materials of the time were either brick or basalt. A contemporary report was very critical of the colour of the stone and falsely assumed that, because it did not fall into any readily assessible category, it was expected to be the base for a more acceptable finishing material. It is extremely unlikely that either the owner or the architect had ever considered stucco or external plaster as the final finish.

The stonework is of excellent quality both as to material and workmanship. Each ashlar is dressed and squared and the main walls are laid in regular courses. At each corner there was an attempt to introduce a different texture, and below each main window the wall thickness is reduced to form a recessed panel externally. Furthermore, the joints of the main blocks are tuck-pointed. Even in those days no owner would consider such an expensive trimming were he also considering covering the wall with stucco.

The house was built from a mixture of local and, despite the great distance from the coast, imported materials.

On its completion in 1862 *The Hamilton Spectator* described it in the arch prose which was still being used a hundred years later to describe grand houses: *'We learn that a fine villa [sic] residence in the Italian style of architecture, where broad eaves and projections are so suited to the requirements of this sunny land, has been recently completed for C. M. Officer Esq.'* The reporter stressed the unpopularity of the stone used by ascribing to it extraordinary architectonic powers—'the colour is not calculated to bring out the proportions of the building in the best manner', and repeated, or perhaps even started, the false story of the ultimate finish for Mount Talbot by suggesting that *'as the building is intended to be stuccoed at a future date, this objection is of little consequence'.* This persistent rumour of future stuccoing was probably not entirely based on prejudice.

Farm machinery from a past era stands in an adjacent paddock. In a garage a 1920 Peugeot stands on its original tyres.

The Furphy was originally a water tank (pictured here) and made by the Furphy brothers in Shepparton, but the name has since become incorporated into the Australian language. The symbols, generally thought to be Arabic, carry a temperance message from the manufacturers in Pitman's Shorthand ('Water is God's gift; beer is a concoction of a devil; drink water').

The outbuildings, some of which antedate the stone homestead, are constructed in local timbers. Galvanized iron replaced the original shingles.

A bay window in the south wall is, and probably always was, plastered externally. There may be two reasons for this unexpected introduction of external finish. The bay window, which was not repeated elsewhere, may have been the result of the client exercising his external right to order last-minute changes and additions. The resultant need to execute angles in the stonework may have been beyond the skill of the masons—or even frustrated by the very nature of the stone itself. A second reason for this small, solitary use of external plaster could have been water-penetration in this south-facing area during or soon after completion.

Another minor, unique and inexplicable detail is the window in the north wall of the upper front bedroom. The fenestration in this wall consists of an ordinary double-hung window, similar to its companions, but it is in this instance alone flanked by narrow matching windows.

This tripartite arrangement was to become a common feature of later Victorian houses, but it was usually employed to add emphasis to the windows of the main rooms and never used by itself on a minor elevation.

When the house was completed, the local paper listed the principal sub-contractors, but omitted to mention the name of the builder. This omission could be explained had the owner acted as contractor or, what is more likely, if this role was taken by the mason.

The names listed give testimony to the most important trades used in the construction. Those responsible were a Mr Wakefer of Fulham, who was the mason. Messrs Scott & Adam were the plasterers. Mr Ewing of Hamilton painted the house, and Messrs Friend & Taylor of Hamilton were credited for the bell-hanging. This was the way of describing the intricate but not unusual task of reticulating a system of wire-operated service bells from all main rooms to a bell-board located near the large kitchen.

In listing those responsible for the crude but effective mechanical communication system, the local reporter was unconsciously forseeing the changes in residential design. Were the house built today, the principal structural trades would receive scant editorial attention. Great detail would be given about the mechanical installations, which would certainly include heating and cooling, cooking equipment and inter-communication systems.

The outbuildings contained all facilities to operate the large property. The blacksmith's forge was an important unit in the self-contained industrial complex.

To the west of the original house and the original cottage, the out-

buildings are constructed in timber. Probably they were erected, dismantled and extended continually over a very long period as the needs of the property varied. With one notable exception they were built in various forms of frame construction. There is one transverse wall in masonry. Certainly it lacks a few refinements, but in general, it matches the stonework of the 'new' house.

As there was neither a structural nor a functional need for a stone wall in this position, it could well be that this sample of stonework was erected as a guide to what was offered by the masons and what was expected by the owner in the forthcoming construction. Such an arrangement, called an 'actuality specification' has reappeared today after almost a century's disuse. A builder will provide a small prototypical section of the building he is engaged to build. Building the section may show him some of the problems to be encountered and it will certainly show the client what to expect.

A few years ago a section of Melbourne's tallest building, BHP House was constructed in a steel-yard in South Melbourne for this very purpose, and a few years earlier a complete bay of BP House in St Kilda Road was built in a builder's yard in Hawthorn. Both of these sections are still standing and the stone stable wall at Mount Talbot may well have been their predecessor.

In 1870 John Jenkins moved on from Hamilton. He became the Shire Engineer of Mount Rouse. His versatility was typical of his generation and reflected his broad training. He was to practise as an engineer, architect and surveyor—a versatility which contemporary educators are trying to recapture and inculcate into the present generation of building and architectural students.

In 1876, again presaging the inevitable move by the successful professional men from rural centres to the metropolis, Jenkins was appointed Building Surveyor of the City of Richmond. This area at that time would have been one of the most rapidly developing areas in Melbourne—an outer suburb changing from market gardens and low density housing to high density settlement and industry. In that position, he entered a competition for the design of the bridge proposed to link his city with Hawthorn, across the Yarra to the east. For some reason best left uninvestigated, the City Engineer's design, although it was placed second, was accepted, and the Swan Street Bridge was built accordingly and as such it stands today.

John Jenkins, shortly after this surprising politico-professional success, reached the plateau of architectural success—he was able to open an office in Chancery Lane, a block of Little Collins Street with an unofficial but pretentious title.

He was now a principal in the firm of Jenkins & Grainger (his partner's son Percy was to attain great heights in his own calling but was never to lose an interest in his father's profession). In the early 1880s the firm entered yet another competition for the design of an important bridge. On this occasion, their design won and between 1886 and 1888 John Shanks Jenkins, the young man from the bush, saw his design for the new (and present) Princes Bridge built.

A simple pump driven by warm air was once used to provide water from the adjacent lagoon.

Kolor *Victoria*

Text: Robin Grove   Photographs: Ian McKenzie

YOU COULD OF COURSE simply transplant your environment, as they did at Ercildoun: elms, and heliotrope, and ivy for the picturesque 'baronial' style; Adam fireplaces, Hepplewhite, Sheraton—a gentleman's Arcadia set down in the plains near Learmonth. But transportation of the Old World is not the only way to colonize a place. And if you travel the Glenelg Highway west to Hamilton, the settlers' changing attempts to adapt themselves to their land are brought home. For the highway, palindromically named, bisects the State, curving over the Western District. There is no better approach to Kolor.

For the first few miles out of Ballarat, gum trees crowd together, trunks shaggy with last year's bark. The towns have upright Yorkshire names—Linton, Scarsdale—and an architecture in keeping: two-storeyed houses in vicarage-red and pale-clay brick stand square; trellised with sweet-peas and perpendicular roses. Even in wood and a single storey, banks and shopfronts aspire to the vertical, through skinny Doric pilasters. There is an earnest, up-and-coming air about these goldrush towns, still on their best behaviour, though faded now to the dun of the mullock-heaps behind them. Even their milestones are self-important, primly incised like tombs.

Westward, the road descends; and the trees thin out, as the vast flow of the plains picks up the highway and carries it on, bending and swerving in slow rhythm. Instead of the narrow up-and-down facades of the gold-diggings' style, these townships sprawl, low-slung. Their few buildings trail away on either side of the road, to peter out as the horizon takes over. Horizontal, in fact, here replaces vertical, through water-surfaces, reservoirs, lakes that fill the hollows of the landscape and reassemble on ground-level, prone, reflections of the sky overhead. Perspective flattens out, Eucalypts themselves, natives of the place, appear marooned in this great grass ocean. And set in such spaces, homesteads and cottages seem the more widely scattered: as though the stress fell, not on their common ground, but on the pioneering separateness of this house, this outbuilding, or that.

The drawing-room bends away from the glare of summer light which still beats down outside despite the shelter of trees, a hawthorn avenue, a shrubbery and verandah. Inside, the cool unhurried sweep of cornicing girdles a room proportioned to the needs of conversation, handwork and repose. Here the curve, the arch, the oval repeat their forms in structure, furnishing and decoration; petals curl away from the ceiling's plaster rose, to be answered by the marble foliage of the fireplace. It is a room in which to forget for a time the sheepruns and paddocks of the district which enabled Kolor to be built.

232

Archway passes into peak then pinnacle here, as Kolor thrusts upward with a vigour increased by the length and bulk of bluestone which holds aloft these sturdy chimneys and lifts the bluff dominating tower. From here, the widest point of the carriage-drive, the planes of the facade advance, retreat and turn away in military order, and even the cypress flares assertively against the sky.

No wonder, then, that cottages only a hundred yards from the road, but with south-west Victoria at their back, look to the traveller like entire social units, indifferent to their neighbours. Each house, self-sufficient, has its cowshed and chicken pen, its vegetable patch alongside; at the front will be flowers and shrubs, often expertly tended; on another site, the owner's fuel-supply and repair-works face a rubbish-dump, municipal in its proportions, where demobilized Holdens and Chevvies lie dishonoured on their backs. The ramble of buildings, truculently renewed in galvanized iron, asserts an ethos of private property, in which the vastness of the countryside is confronted by the rights of independence to do, or make-do, as it likes.

        ✸   ✸   ✸   ✸

South of this highway, and halfway between the start of the Western District and the South Australian border, the twin cones of Mount Rouse break upwards from the plain. An extinct volcano, its stark neck and

234

shoulders loom eerily in that landscape, while knucklebones of basalt sink into the soil at its base, half-lost in bracken. Out of these stones, the landholders' fences have been built—and sometimes abandoned, too expensive these days to repair; bluestone is likewise the foundation of solid Penshurst nearby: population 551 in 1890, and a German meeting-place, as shopsigns ('Uebergang's', 'Schramm's') still testify. Above all, though, the bluestone of the district has literally been the making of Kolor.

Here, independence rises to its height. The house, invisible from below, is set on a shelf of mountain-side. From the road, you wind through a tunnel of hawthorns, oaks and pepperinas—Somerset-thick in springtime —to be landed suddenly on the brief driveway in front of the door. Behind you, a few large European trees, with sheep huddling underneath, curious at the visitor; opposite, a flight of steps, arches, roofs pitched and valleyed: but dominating everything, the great curve of the verandah, swinging wide, only to rush the eye with greater force up the shaft of the tower.

Latticed ironwork, rounded pedestals, and a rhythmic procession of ornamental bearers round the conical, pagoda-like roof give an oriental opulence to the verandah's open gallery.

With its grand effect thus, dramatically, made, Kolor allows the visitor to move slowly. Cut into a block at the right of the steps, an inscription reads:

THIS STONE
WAS LAID BY
J. TWOMEY SEN^r
A.D. 1868

John Joseph Twomey was born at Meenveragh, County Cork in 1793, and came to Port Phillip in 1843. Together with his brother he had taken up land near Penshurst, and already by 1868 they had built two homesteads, Langulac and Banemore, there. The land on which Kolor was to be erected, however, was not so easily gained. From 1838 to 1842 the Mount Rouse run had belonged to John Cox, first store-owner at Port Fairy some thirty miles away, and evidently a dashing fellow. All the worse, therefore, that in 1842 La Trobe's government announced that it was requisitioning the land to establish a settlement for Aborigines. Unrecompensed, Cox was obliged to cede his holding, and the Aborigines, who previously had harassed and murdered station-hands on the property, were now reinstated under La Trobe's protectorate. 'It was no trifling loss,' writes Boldrewood. 'Even in those days the "Mount Rouse stones" was an expression which made the mouth of a cattle-man to water. It was the richest and best fattening run in a rich fattening district.' The irony was that, within a few years, the Aboriginal settlement failed: its 'prosaic, joyless prosperity', to quote Boldrewood again, 'told on health and spirits' —to such an extent that by 1851 hardly a beneficiary remained. At this point the land-licence might again have been offered to Cox, but Superintendent La Trobe—tired of philanthropy, perhaps—arranged for the grass-right to be leased to the highest bidder. In general, £200 or £300 annually was then thought fair; for this run, however, the Government held out for more; and the figure finally accepted from Messrs J. and D. Twomey was an astonishing £900 *per annum*. 'This was rental for the waste lands of the Crown with a vengeance.' Yet the speculation paid off: the property was fenced; undisturbed, the sheep multiplied; and with the lands of Mount Rouse swelling their purses the Twomey brothers were able eventually to buy almost all the freehold. Today Kolor commands 320 hectares.

By 1867 the battle for squatters' tenure was over. Those who had profited from land and recompensed the Crown were now lawful owners of their acres, and the confidence felt in proprietorship is expressed in the strongholds they built. From Portland Bay up to the Great Dividing Range the mansions spread. Squatters were kings, not of grass castles only, but of cedar and bronze, marble and stone *palazzi*.

As such homesteads go, Kolor is imposing, but hardly stylish like Monivae, or the grand Italianate Werribee Park. Take the honeycomb of bedrooms and sitting-rooms at the back, and the house appears not to have been architect-planned at all; on the other hand, from the verandah's magnificent sweep, the entrance and formal rooms at the front, it is impossible to imagine that the edifice just grew. Rather, two styles meet here—meet, but refuse to combine.

Comings and goings in a large house that must accommodate visitors and staff as well as family give new importance to passageways, porches and vestibules. The entrance-hall at Kolor, with its coloured carpet of tiles, combines the two Victorian virtues of durability and imposingness. Five doorways, each with its own doormat of tiles, lead out from it (bracketed in the mirror, the dining-room can be seen); the skirting-boards are cedar, while overhead a skylight of patterned glass lifts the eye upward into the shaft of the tower.

After the colour and sheen of the entrance-hall, the dining-room is plain, even austere, as though to concentrate attention on the sober business of food and drink. A black clock commands the room from a black mantelpiece; even the swags and brackets of the window-bay, twin to those in the hall, are transposed into a minor key. Grandeur is lent to the room by the lavish doorway openings, with their cedar architraves twenty inches deep.

Finely-worked pillars, striated, half-engaged, and set in a square-cut niche, lap their tongues down either side of the entrance steps which march to the foot of the foundation stone. Cathedral solidity contrasts with the domestic flower-beds and bushes.

Thus, in its general living-quarters, Kolor resembles the settler's cottage of the District, where rooms straggle through one door to another, as afterthoughts proliferate and are added. In this part of the building ceilings may be lofty, but the effect of improvisation remains. Once through the dividing door, however, and those reminiscences are left behind. The floor of the entrance-hall is laid with polished encaustic tiles (Maw & Co., Broseley), their terracotta, gamboge and aquamarine as teeth-gritting as coloured chalks. Overhead is a pyramidal skylight of moulded glass—thick as a jamjar it looks, with its close-pressed pattern of flower and leaf. Swagged brackets in the doorway, gilding, and a formidable plaster rose, complete the mid-Victorian decor. Yet even this opulence does not define the house. For Kolor conforms to no ideal: rather, its distinction is in its self-confident breaking-free from coherent standards of taste. It has everything. Or, if not quite everything, then a wonderful miscellany of styles, orchestrated over the grand design of the verandah's base, and up to the masculine tenour of the tower.

Between these two, there is all the scope in the world for variety. For one thing, the weight of the buttressed foundations looks practically medieval. The archways of the porch, on the other hand, are in triumphant Italianate style. Yet Italianism in turn is carried to excess, with arches everywhere: repeated on either side of the steps, caught up on pedestals of the verandah-posts as they swing round their curve, and receding through the door into the house. Brought indoors this way, one realizes suddenly that the great drawing-room on the right is itself an arch, laid flat on the ground: thirty-four feet long. Its rounded end, lightened by three high windows, faces you as you enter from the hall, and bold medallions in the ceiling are answered by the scrolls of the fireplace—carved into such delicate fernery that the marble here and the plasterwork overhead seem to have exchanged properties: like the arches, simultaneously upright and in ground-plan: a through-the-looking-glass effect. All this is held in the bend of the verandah's arm; whereas on the other side of the entrance-hall the dining-room has a fireplace of its own—severe and glossy black, this time—past which the eye is led to another group of

windows, forming, not a second semi-circle to match the drawing-room, but a more conventional, self-sufficient bay. The asymmetrical variation is typical, and one reason why Kolor is exhilarating, although so large.

Close cousin though Kolor is to Narrapumelap, the deserted, lion-crested mansion forty-eight kilometres away, no architect for it has been found; and that seems appropriate in its way, since the house feels as unplanned yet purposive as any self-contained cottage on the highway. Besides, what invariable need of an architect was there, when the craftsmen who built the mansions of the District were so highly skilled? At Kolor their workmanship creates something new out of the rigidity of bluestone, so that instead of the squared-off rectangular look which the material usually enforced, walls swing out like heavy sails catching the wind. You would never guess that (as the architect of Mount Noorat told Niel Black) there are things that cannot be done to bluestone, for here they are, visible in finest mason's detail.

As you leave the front rooms of the house, however, and pass back through the dividing door, realism asserts itself in a different form again. Upper-class high living as against down-to-earth cooking, butlering, and everyday accommodation, is marked by the step to a lower level. Quite correct. No forty-two inch doorways here, on the stairway leading to the tower; servants and menfolk were expected to negotiate this bare narrow corkscrew, while ladies (and Kolor was built in the widest period of the crinoline) occupied themselves in full dress. Going downwards the other way, the double cellar with access from outside as well provided cool storage for perishables (though if the Twomeys were wine-drinkers, they made small provision for themselves). A working-day simplicity prevails here, and even the tower's mezzanine makes a low attic bedroom, with space for boxes and trunks round the pyramid skylight of the entrance-hall below. But it is from the topmost level that the full extent of Kolor and its surroundings can be seen. No doubt these towers, common to many Western District mansions, might serve for observation-posts in the bushfire season. More significantly, though, they rise over the pitch and dip of the household's roofs, and make sense of the whole building, by imposing a viewpoint on it from above. Seen from the right angle, even the most oddly individual structure can amount to a visible society, where grand rooms and skimpy ones, house servants, children, and owners, all have their place, and private property itself becomes part of the District's agricultural way of life.

Kolor has had few owners. The Twomey family continued to hold it until 1928 when, their last son having been killed in World War One, it was sold to Andrew Rentsch. Over the next twenty years or so, minor alterations were made to the garden at front and back, but the house remained intact and was sold to Hugh Robertson in 1949, from whom it was bought by Mrs Stanley Gardiner in 1955. To accommodate, now, three generations of Gardiners some rearrangement of rooms at the back has been made: the old slate-floored kitchen has become a sitting-room for the family; a set of doors has been moved, and the storeroom serves as a child's bedroom. But the alterations have only revealed more clearly that Kolor is meant, vigorously, to be lived in.

Hobnail chimney-caps, deep-set arrow-slit windows, and a strong geometry of bluestone glower down on any idle approach to Kolor—a contrast to the restfulness of the paved verandah OPPOSITE *that bends invitingly around the house's western wall. Shaped by chisel, worn by feet, mortised, mortared, pointed, stone is everywhere, even when unseen: rubble, for example, between the sixteen-inch thick walls.*

Chimneys, tower and peaks stand sentinel looking out across the plains of the Western District to scattered townships and mountain humps. Even the rooftop of Kolor dips, sweeps, pitches in bold asymmetrical patterns fishscaled with slate: a grey complement to the volcanic cone of Mount Rouse which alone overtops the building.

Leschenault *Western Australia*

Text: Charles Staples   *Photographs: R. B. Penrose*

L ESCHENAULT WAS BUILT BY William Pearce Clifton on his Bunbury property which lay along the shores of Leschenault Inlet just east of the town. (Jean Baptiste Leschenault de la Tour was a botanist with Baudin's surveying expedition on the Western Australian coast in 1801.) As on most Australian homesteads, building activities were spread over many years, progressing as prosperity increased. Though Clifton's main residence was commenced about 1854 and completed in 1874 the unity of its design was maintained throughout. It now rests under its large protective roof amid its gardens and lawns, musing over its long memories. It has no wish to compete with the grander residences of other parts of Australia because it was built by a modest man, who was nevertheless a member of the Legislative Council of the Colony and Resident Magistrate at Bunbury for very many years.

Before commencing Leschenault, Clifton built two other residences which are still in existence. The first was Upton House at Australind, built for his father, Marshall Waller Clifton, about 1844. Then he moved directly to his own property nearer Bunbury and built the cottage

This photograph, taken about 1902 by a travelling German photographer, shows the Johnston family admiring their pedigreed Ayrshire cows. The Preston River, shown in the foreground, is now confined to a diversion. This is the photograph that was used to decorate the 'Leschenault' Royal Doulton china (see page 244).

The hanging wisteria on the right and its over-hanging trees allow the old home to nestle into the landscape. Its affinity with the surroundings is emphasized by the weatherboard cladding for the half-timbered walls and, in earlier days, by the roof shingles split from the near-by forest.

The picture on the 'Leschenault' Royal Doulton plate was derived from the photograph at the opening of the chapter.

The wide verandah lent itself to outdoor entertaining where guests could take tea while enjoying the beauty of the lawns and garden.

which can now be seen immediately adjacent behind the main residence. These two houses have seen no occupants other than Pearce Clifton and, later, his nephew, Forster Johnston and his children. It now lies under threat of extensions to the Bunbury Harbour, but will undoubtedly be preserved as an essential part of the heritage of Western Australia.

From the days of Pearce Clifton, Leschenault has been one of the centres of the social life of Bunbury, so wide was the influence of family and friends, all received with the warmest of hospitality. As the large Johnston family grew to adulthood the expansive garden and the newly-established tennis court echoed to the laughter of happy young people at garden parties and dances.

Nothing interefered with church attendance, and at the near-by St Patrick's Anglican Church, Rathmines, two generations of Johnstons and their friends were the teachers of what must have been the happiest Sunday School of its time. One of the most illustrious friends of Leschenault was the artist and architect, Marshall Clifton, who painted the watercolour of the old home in its heyday, for the grand-daughter of Pearce Clifton. Now resident in England she made it possible for that picture to be reproduced in this volume.

The Clifton and Johnston families were closely connected with the administrative structure of the Western Australian Company, which established a settlement on Leschenault Inlet at Australind in 1840, planned on the principles of Edward Gibbon Wakefield. Marshall Waller Clifton, previously Secretary of the Victualling Board of the British Admiralty, was appointed Chief Commissioner in Western Australia. His wife, Elinor, was a daughter of Daniel Bell—uncle of Elizabeth Fry and Wakefield's father. Pearce Clifton was the fourth of the fifteen Clifton children, and the eldest son to accompany his father to Australia. Before being forced out of business by a depression, the Company sent nearly five hundred persons to the Colony at a critical stage of its development. Among these were the parents of John Forrest, Baron Bunbury; a grand-parent of Sir James Mitchell, Governor; as well as a number of other notable colonial families. Clifton, Senior, was proposed (unsuccessfully) as the third governor of the Colony and served with distinction on the Legislative Council from 1852 to 1858 where he had the satisfaction of seeing Pearce take his seat.

One of the early team of Australind Settlement surveyors was Harley Robert Johnston, who married Mary Clifton and hung up his surveying chain to manage Alverstoke, one of the Clifton properties. He died relatively young, leaving four children, of whom the eldest was Forster, who subsequently purchased Leschenault, and the youngest was Harry Frederick who, from 1896 to 1915, was Surveyor General of Western Australia, the position once occupied by John Forrest who was born little more than a mile from Leschenault. The love of the outdoor was transmitted to Harry's fourth child, Frederick Marshall Johnston who commenced his surveying career in 1908 and retired in 1949 as Commonwealth Surveyor General. But Harley Johnston's Gunters chain, of 100 links joined by rings, remained in the possession of Forster and was recently unearthed in the old implement shed at Leschenault.

To the left of a wide entrance hallway are the parlour and dining room containing Rose family furniture brought to Leschenault by the present Mrs Johnston. The double doors were thrown open on special occasions, and for dances the furniture was moved away.

When the Australind Settlement was wound up in 1843, and Marshall Waller Clifton retired on his Admiralty pension, Pearce Clifton was appointed as Agent in Western Australia for the Western Australian Company of London. He was, however, able to devote much time to the initial development of the timber industry which, with the cattle industry, became the twin supports of the economic development of the south-western portion of the Colony. Through his father's Admiralty connections, Pearce attempted to interest the Royal Navy in the use of jarrah in ship construction, but it was rejected as unsuitable.

Pearce Clifton employed sawyers in saw-pits to provide the largest share of the first timber cargo exported from Bunbury. He extended the cutting of jarrah to the Darling Range, east of Bunbury, from whence it was carted to the Collie River at Waterloo then floated down the river and Leschenault Estuary to the Port. Before the introduction of steam in the area, Clifton used saws powered by horse-works, where horses harnessed to a pole walked in a circle around a turntable which rotated the driving shaft. From experience with the small markets in Adelaide and Mauritius, the Colonial timber industry was ready to supply sleepers for India when the railway age commenced in the late fifties.

An examination of the three houses built by Pearce Clifton clearly indicates his conversion from an English style of brick dwelling to an early Australian style using timber. First he built Upton House at Australind for his father. It was a small, two-storey house constructed of building materials imported with Australind Settlement supplies, but roofed with

Australian split shingles. A major concession was made to the Australian climate: an Indian 'verandah' was added to protect the ground floor windows and walls.

On his own property, Clifton erected an Australian timber cottage in 1845. Some of the window spaces were glazed with imported windows, one of which is still in place. The Cottage walls are of much more solid construction than is apparent on first inspection. When the wall studs were in place, wattle lathes, cut to the correct length, were fixed and then covered with carefully prepared mud. The solid half-timbered walls were then protected from the weather by a cladding of over-lapping weather-board. The interior of the Cottage was smoothly trowelled, covered by many thicknesses of newspaper and then whitewashed. In some places the last layer of paper, pages from the *Illustrated London News*, was left exposed to provide a literary wallpaper. The well-founded fear of fire decreed the building of a detached kitchen which contained the original brick oven, where the bread was baked by the retained heat after the charcoal of the fire had been raked out.

Because Pearce Clifton and his first wife had no children they virtually adopted young Forster Johnston. With the growth of the homestead operations it became obvious that more accommodation was required, so craftsmen were engaged to build the first stage of Leschenault. Having proved the feasibility of the half-timbered style, Clifton installed panels of adobe between the new five-inch studs to produce an excellently insulated wall, clad with weather-board and further protected by a wide verandah. In keeping with the times the roof was shingled. The loss of his diaries prevents an accurate statement of dates, but the first part of Leschenault seems to have been constructed during his first wife's life-time, in 1854 or in 1869, and provided her with a comfortable dwelling before her death in 1871. While Clifton was on a timber-business visit to England in 1874 he remarried and ordered the completion of Leschenault. The early detached kitchen was retained to service both residences.

The group of small buildings between the shed and the main house was built in 1845 as 'The Cottage'.

'Leschenault' was painted in water-colour by Marshall Clifton, F.R.A.I.A., for the grand-daughter of Pearce Clifton, Mrs Philip Clark of England, who kindly agreed that a photograph should be made available to the publishers.

Pearce Clifton had vacated his seat on the Legislative Council, but for many years he remained Bunbury's much loved Resident Magistrate. At his death in 1885 the town went into mourning with the closing of shops and the flying of flags at half-mast. His widow soon returned to England with her young children. Forster Johnston then moved from the Cottage into Leschenault, since when it has been the Johnston home until the present day.

Leschenault really came into its own as the home of Forster Johnston and his large family. His first wife, Frances Clifton, bore him three sons. By his second wife, Bessie, daughter of Thomas Hayward, he had eleven sons and daughters. The estate prospered. His proud display of pure-bred Ayrshire cattle was photographed by a travelling German who later sold his photographs to the producers of Doulton china in England. Eventually Leschenault Doulton came on the market in Perth and many items have been retained by the Johnston families. As befitted a patriarch with large social and domestic responsibilities, Forster Johnston was an active member of his church and many public bodies, a conscientious temperance advocate, and a keen supporter of the Bunbury Hunt Club.

Elderslie *Queensland*

Text: Peter Forrest   *Photographs: Richard Stringer*

This grave on the Mitchell Grass Plains near the Western River is a haunting reminder of the stark isolation of the Diamantina country.

This shed was originally designed for storage and to house the blacksmith's shop. These usages have continued largely unchanged. The roof frame and verandah posts are of local bush timber. Note the double slope of the iron roof—the projecting overhang shades the main walls and discharges rain water away from the foundations.

THE 1870s AND 1880s saw the last great rush for land in eastern Australia: a rush that was to take up the last remaining vacant land in Queensland—the country along the river systems draining toward Lake Eyre. Two factors combined to bring about this rush. Firstly, exploration of what was previously a blank on the map was stimulated by the sending of search parties for the lost explorers Burke and Wills, who disappeared in 1861. Secondly, from 1872, boom conditions in the south created a need for investment outlets in the pastoral industry and, in particular, the imagination of Victorian investors was fired by reports of the seemingly endless well-grassed plains of Queensland's far west.

It was against this background that Elderslie Station came to be established along the Diamantina River near the confluence of that stream with the Western River. Elderslie was the first of the far western Queensland stations, and its history may be taken as an excellent exemplification of the vicissitudes the pioneer pastoralists and investors encountered in this hostile region.

The Diamantina country was completely unexplored until John McKinlay was sent from Adelaide in late 1861 to look for Burke and Wills. McKinlay followed the east bank of the river from near the present location of Birdsville, north-easterly to the junction of the Diamantina with Middleton Creek. From this point (twelve years later to become the approximate southern boundary of the Elderslie aggregation) he followed Middleton Creek north-west to the present Middleton town site and from thence he struck out for the Gulf of Carpentaria. Thus, in about April 1862 McKinlay and his party were the first white men to touch upon what was later Elderslie country. This expedition expanded the frontier of geographical knowledge several hundred miles westward from William Landsborough's documentation of the Thomson River headwaters in 1860. Landsborough established the vast Bowen Downs holding along the Thomson River system in 1862 and from there he set out in 1866 to explore 'further out'. On this expedition he followed the Western River to the Diamantina, naming the latter river after the Countess Diamantina Roma, wife of Sir George Ferguson Bowen, the first Governor of Queensland.

Landsborough was possibly the most experienced and effective of all the Australian land explorers and his commentaries on newly-discovered country were highly respected by seekers of new lands. Landsborough reported (accurately) that while the Diamantina country was well grassed in season it would be subject to acute drying out of surface water and that stocking might be hazardous. In view of this cautious report, and the finan-

cial depression which prevailed from 1867 to the wool boom of 1872, it is not surprising that little or no interest was shown in the area until July 1873, when William Forsyth took up leases of some of the Elderslie country.

Some understanding of the legislation relating to Queensland land settlement is necessary for a full appreciation of subsequent events. Historically, Queensland Government policy has been on the one hand to encourage pioneer settlement by offering limited security of tenure over newly-settled lands, while on the other hand encouraging closer settlement by effecting progressive resumptions from the pioneer holdings. Lands in newly opened districts were divided into roughly surveyed 'runs' (of one hundred square miles each in far western districts) and those who sought country could take up any number of runs and obtain fourteen-year leases over them provided that certain stocking and improvement conditions were met.

Invariably the earliest run holders were speculators lacking the financial capacity to meet the stocking and improvement conditions. To overcome this, partners had to be brought in, or alternatively the rights to the runs sold or allowed to lapse. The opening up of the far western Queensland country coincided with a willingness and ability on the part of southern capitalists to support the pioneer run-seekers with liberal infusions of money. Victorian money was to the forefront, and so it was that the early western holdings came to be controlled by the Wilsons, Rileys, Chirnsides, Fairbairns, Caseys, Manifolds and Frasers. Unfortunately for these people, the prospect of bountiful returns on their considerable investment proved as illusory as the mirages to which the district is subject. Few were to overcome the obstacles in the path of early settlement and the enormous losses caused by the prolonged adverse seasons in the district from 1896. Subsequent owners were to acquire the earlier holdings at discounted values and to reap the benefit of huge expenditure on buildings, artesian and other water improvements, and yards and fencing.

An analysis of the history of the taking up and subsequent dealing in the Elderslie leases illustrates the point. On 24 July 1873 William Forsyth applied for and was subsequently granted leases over the runs Doveridge Nos. 1-4 (running from east to west along the Western River from the Pelican Waterhole to the Diamantina River); Diamantina Nos. 1-7 (up and down the Diamantina River); and Middleton Nos. 1 & 2 (toward Middleton Creek). Each of these runs was of 100 square miles (260 square kilometres) and lay five miles on either side of its relevant water course. 'Back country' away from the water frontage was ignored. In September and

This view under the verandah of the blacksmith's shop and storage shed shows the construction technique of rough coursed sandstone blocks laid straight on the ground. The soft mortar made from a mixture of sand and clay can easily be patched and can accommodate the movement of the foundation soil, which is highly responsive to variations of moisture content and temperature.

A 'willy willy' has unroofed this shed to reveal the bush timber rafters and sawn battens. Destructive local wind storms caused by thermal currents are frequent.

October 1875 Donald Smith Wallace applied for and was later granted leases over the runs Diamantina Nos. 8-11 (down the Diamantina) and Donald, Cathedral and Cadell Nos. 1 & 2 (all being situated along Cadell and Middleton Creeks to the north and west of Forsyth's country). It is likely that the leases granted to Wallace were over country occupied a year or so earlier by him or on his behalf in association with Forsyth. There must have been some close link between Forsyth and Wallace, for the 1875 *Postal Directory* indicates a mail run to 'Elderslie (Wallaces)' situated near Pelican Waterhole. This was otherwise known as 'Wallace's Camp', and was situated on Doveridge No. 4 run, officially the property of William Forsyth, at least until some time later in 1875 when all of Forsyth's runs were transferred to Samuel Wilson of 'Oakleigh Hall', East St Kilda, Melbourne. Wallace's holdings were transferred to Wilson in 1879, and it is fair to infer from the whole course of events that there were three stages of ownership and development from 1873 to 1879. Firstly, Forsyth in 1873 took up the closer in and more favoured country along the Western and Diamantina Rivers. Forsyth sought and found a monied partner in the

Disciplined coursing of rough hewn stone and the flat window arch on the blacksmith's shop indicate well-considered craftsmanship.

The bedroom wing was an early addition developing the original rectangular plan into an 'L' shape. The addition maintains the original integrity of materials and style.

Victorian pastoralist Wallace who, in the second stage, assumed de facto control of Forsyth's holdings and added to them. As soon as this was accomplished in 1875 Wallace brought in his Victorian colleague Samuel Wilson, who took a formal transfer of Forsyth's runs. Wallace and Wilson conducted the aggregation in partnership until 1879 when, in a third and final stage of consolidation, Wilson became sole lessee by acquiring Wallace's interests. Support for this inference can be found in a study of the careers of both Wallace and Wilson.

Wallace was born in 1844 in the Victorian Wimmera where he acquired pastoral holdings at an early age. He moved into Queensland when the Peak Downs area was opened in the early 1860s, and diversified from there into various pastoral ventures throughout the State. One wonders whether these ventures were as successful as his acquisition of the wonderful race horse Carbine for 3,000 guineas in the horse's four-year-old year. Carbine was to race with fantastic success for Wallace, and had almost equal success at the stud, before Wallace sold the horse for 13,000 guineas to the Duke of Portland for stud duties in England. Carbine's most illustrious Australian son was named simply and appropriately Wallace. Donald Wallace sold out his Queensland interests from 1878 and returned to represent his home South West Province in the Victorian Legislative Council. He died in 1900.

Samuel Wilson was born in Ireland in 1832 and came to Victoria in 1852 in search of gold. After working on the Victorian gold-fields he gained experience in pastoral pursuits through the management of his brother's sheep station. He sold his Irish interests to acquire the noted Wimmera property Longerenong, and later bought interests in other Victorian and Murrumbidgee stations. Like Wallace he moved early into Queensland's Peak Downs area and from there invested in newly-opened areas of the colony wherever opportunity offered. He represented the Wimmera district in the Victorian Legislative Assembly and later in the Legislative Council. Wilson was knighted in 1875, the year in which he first acquired an interest in Elderslie. He held Elderslie until his death in 1895.

Little is known of Forsyth but it is noted that he pioneered Malvern Downs in the Peak Downs area, and no doubt he came to know Wallace at that time. Quite possibly he was sent into the far west by Wallace as agent. His name is perpetuated in the Forsyth Range, the low plateau which forms the watershed between the Thomson and Diamantina Rivers.

Wilson's acquisitions from Forsyth and Wallace had given him a total of twenty-one runs by 1879. At some time prior to 1890 Wilson took up an additional nine runs, comprising previously unoccupied country contiguous with his other runs. Some of these runs must have been smaller than the conventional 100 square miles, for the first Lands Department reference to the Elderslie consolidation appearing in 1890 gives the total area of 2,489 square miles (6,475 square kilometres). Departmental records of about the same time contain the first references to station improvements, including the old and new homesteads.

'Wallace's Camp' on Doveridge No. 4 run has been referred to. This camp was situated near the Pelican Waterhole at the extreme eastern edge of the aggregation, and was near the common boundary point of Elderslie,

Vindex, Bladensburg and Oondooroo Stations. It is said that a permanent pisé homestead and yards were built at Wallace's Camp, and it is here that Elderslie's first manager John Haines lies buried. No traces of this settlement remain today. The old homestead was listed in 1875 as being on the mail route from Aramac, 181 miles to the south-east. In that year the pioneers at the old homestead were joined at the Pelican Waterhole by one Robert Allan who established a shanty and store to take advantage of the passing trade along the mail route. Allan had been the Sergeant of Police at Aramac, and no doubt he was inspired to make his move by information concerning pastoral development given to him by the mailman. Apparently Allan's shanty was a resort for the worst characters in the West, and to its existence many crimes were traceable. In 1876 Allan was forced by a high flood in the Western River to spend a week on the roof of his hotel. During this time he observed an area about a mile away which remained above water, and as soon as the flood receded he relocated his establishment to this higher ground. During this move he was joined by the teamsters Corfield and Fitzmaurice, who had journeyed south-westerly from Charters Towers in search of a suitable site for the establishment of a store. Their intended destination was the Conn Waterhole, where Government surveyors planned the establishment of a town to be known as 'Collingwood'. This site was near a camp on Doveridge No. 4 run established by Isaac Hopkins and William Bucknell, who had applied for a lease of the area. Their application was refused in view of Forsyth's prior claim. Their camp was to become the approximate site of the new Elderslie Homestead. Hopkins and Bucknell moved further on down the Diamantina to establish Brighton Downs.

Corfield saw that the Conn Waterhole site was unsuitable for the development of a town and he chose to join Allan and another teamster, Lynett, in building near Elderslie Homestead and the Pelican Waterhole.

253

A prefabricated steel shearing shed recently replaced the original thirty-two stand shed which was located on a portion of the original run now resumed.

This was the genesis of the town of Winton, which was named by Allan after his birth place, a suburb of Bournemouth, England. In 1883 areas were resumed from the Elderslie and Vindex leases to create reserves for township and police paddock purposes.

Perhaps it was a combination of circumstances which prompted Wilson to order the abandonment of Wallace's Camp and the establishment of a new homestead some forty miles (sixty kilometres) to the west, beneath Mount Booka-Booka and near the confluence of Wokingham Creek and the Diamantina and Western Rivers. Certainly the new site was far more strategically placed near the centre of the aggregation, while the floods of 1876 and the development of the town of Winton would have been seen as disadvantages attaching to the old site. The date of the move cannot be established with any real precision, but the circumstantial evidence points to the years 1881–2 being coincident with Wilson's commencement of a lavish expenditure programme, and with the first indication that the township of Winton would achieve permanency through official recognition and sponsorship.

More conclusive evidence can perhaps be seen in the description by James Dickson of the building of Oondooroo Homestead in January 1883. Oondooroo is situated some thirty kilometres to the north of Winton, and the almost identical plan lay-out and construction techniques used at both Oondooroo and Elderslie Homesteads support local belief that the two complexes were constructed by the one builder. The same local belief holds that Elderslie was the first of the two homesteads, and if this is so then Elderslie can date no later than December 1882, when Oondooroo was commenced.

Dickson (later to become Premier of Queensland as Sir James Dickson) and Samuel Griffith (later Sir Samuel and Premier of Queensland, and Chief Justice of the Queensland Supreme Court and Australian High Court), were in western Queensland for electioneering purposes during the summer of 1882–3. Dickson described the construction of Oondooroo Homestead as follows: 'a new stone residence is in the course of erection, and approaching completion, and other buildings of stone, including manager's quarters, quarters for single men and a store, will shortly be commenced. The stone used is a kind of limestone, and the mortar a mixture of clay and sand obtained in the neighbourhood. The same mixture forms an excellent cement, but requires to be worked very carefully, and in a manner different from that adopted with the ordinary cement, or it will peel off rapidly.' Elderslie was built in identical fashion, except that the sandstone readily available at Mount Booka-Booka was used instead of the limestone which outcrops at Oondooroo.

On 29 July 1891 an inspector of the Department of Public Lands described the improvements of Doveridge No. 4 run as comprising the old Elderslie head station (value £50) twenty miles of fencing and 'several paddocks, dams and dairies belonging to the people of Winton and several Chinese gardens'. On Doveridge No. 1 run, the site of the new homestead, stone and iron buildings were described as including the homestead house (value £900), laundry and servants' rooms (£900), kitchen (£350), butcher's shop, store, office, men's room, stables, blacksmith's shop (£400), men's hut, store and cottage (£300), cottage (£150), carpenters, wheel-wright's and saddler's shop (£60), gardener's cottage and garden (£60). During the same inspection four earth dams having a total capacity of 39,000 cubic yards, an overshot, and sixty-two miles of fencing were listed. The total value of all improvements was given as £9,670.

Significantly no woolshed improvements were listed, and it would there-fore appear that Wilson worked Elderslie as a cattle station only, despite the fact that his best country would have been more suited to sheep. The absence of any mention of artesian bores is also surprising. Wilson had pioneered the building of earth tanks in Victoria and had made his fortune by thus opening up vast tracts of formerly waterless pasture. Apparently he was not so quick to exploit the possibilities of artesian water, which had been first tapped in the West in 1887. Wilson was at this time mainly resident in England at Hughenden Manor, the former home of Lord Beaconsfield, and was unsuccessfully endeavouring to gain election to the House of Commons. No doubt these diversions distracted him from the latest innovations in the Australian pastoral industry.

An older style wool press contrasts with new, wire mesh wool bins.

The fact that Wilson spent little or no time at Elderslie during its development also explains in part the unadorned plainness of the home-stead buildings. The Queensland homestead tradition is one of straight-forward, functional and honest buildings, reflecting a concern of their owners and builders with practical matters rather than with art for art's sake. Elderslie homestead does not pretend to be anything more than a group of working buildings providing space and shelter in an isolated and climatically harsh environment. The position may have been different had Wilson built the homestead for his own occupation.

In 1892 Elderslie holding was divided into two parts—one of 1,678 square miles (4,400 square kilometres) over which a lease was granted to Wilson, and the other of 843 square miles intended for closer settlement, but over which Wilson was granted a licence to occupy. Both sections were transferred by Wilson's executors in 1896 to the Ramsay family of Harrow on the Darling Downs. The Ramsays embarked on a further improvement programme and between 1896 and 1912 stocked the property with sheep, established thoroughbred and draught horse studs of considerable note, and sank three artesian bores with flows of up to one million gallons of water per day each. It was probably during this period that the main house at the homestead was extended by the addition of two bedrooms and was decorated with Wunderlich pressed metal wall and ceiling sheeting. On completion of this work the house attained its present form.

That the Ramsays managed to achieve these improvements is a remark-able thing. The period of their ownership coincided with resumptions which reduced the area of the station to under 1,000 square miles (2,500 square kilometres), and with unprecedented drought years. The annual rainfall for the period 1896–1906 averaged under seven inches (175 millimetres) and sheep losses were: 1897—27,000; 1898—43,000; 1900—47,000; 1901—10,000; 1902—20,000; 1905—14,000; 1906—9,000. In addition, 25,000 cattle and 565 horses were lost over the same period. The Bank of Australasia was in possession as mortgagee for a number of years, but the Ramsays discharged all debts in 1911. Undaunted by their adversi-

ties the Ramsays, in 1910, were the first to introduce motor vehicles into the West, and they established many time records on expeditions as far afield as Longreach and Hughenden.

In 1912 the property was purchased by the Queensland Stock Breeding Company Limited and the management was taken over by Mr C. H. Brabazon, a director of that company. Elderslie's area then totalled about 900 square miles (2,330 square kilometres), and the country was described by the Lands Department as 'a large area of open to well shaded Mitchell Grass Downs, with a considerable area in the western section being low stoney ranges and clay pans of very light or nil carrying capacity. A considerable amount of money has been spent in providing water on the holding both in the way of bores and dams including three artesian bores with an aggregate depth of 11,649 feet and twelve sub-artesian bores of an aggregate depth of 11,140 feet. The sheep cut clean weighty fleeces of wool.' The department foreshadowed further resumptions for closer settlement, but these were not completed until after the First World War.

As the Ramsay brothers were instrumental in the introduction of motor cars in an effort to conquer the vast distances of western Queensland, Charles Brabazon was among Australia's first sponsors of civil aviation. On 16 November 1920 the airline Qantas was formed in Winton, and Brabazon sat at the company's first Directors' Meeting held in the Winton Club early in 1922. In November 1922 Qantas flew the first airmail in eastern Australia from Charleville to Longreach and Cloncurry. The advantages of the new mode of transport found a ready acceptance in western Queensland, and it was the liberal patronage from these districts that, in the early days of aviation, developed the industry from the gimmickry of barnstorming and joy flights to commercial viability and permanence.

In June 1924 Elderslie again changed hands, this time in favour of the Australian Estates and Mortgage Company Limited. The price paid was £82,229/15/-. Australian Estates bought the property subject to certain proposed resumptions, but in 1932 the company applied for partial deferment of the resumptions for ten years, on the grounds that between 1924 and 1930 it had incurred cash losses totalling £102,450 in the process of operating the holding. This application was granted after certain adjustments were made leaving a balance area of 481 square miles (1,240 square kilometres). The lease of this area terminated in 1943, but the company was granted an occupation licence until 1950 when the holding was resumed in its entirety. The holding was divided into several grazing homestead leases which were opened for selection by ballot.

In 1954 the homestead block was purchased by the present owners, Mr and Mrs Keith Watts, who found that the buildings had been allowed to fall into serious disrepair. Cattle were grazing in the garden enclosure and horses sought shade on the house verandah. The Watts almost decided to demolish and rebuild, but bravely resolved to repair. Today only 20,000 hectares surround the buildings which were once the centre of a vast holding, but the principal structures remain as built evidence of the dramatic changes in fortune to which the Queensland pastoral industry has always been subject.

While the main house and outbuildings are built of stone, the meat house is executed in timber and galvanized iron to achieve cooler night-time conditions, allowing freshly killed meat to 'set'.

Corrugated galvanized iron is a great traditional building material of western Queensland—and for good reason. It is cheap, light, compact and durable. Iron buildings are hot—but so are all others in this environment, and at least iron cools very rapidly in the evening.

Mount Booka-Booka is the scenic backdrop to the homestead. It is a residual sandstone outcrop which has been protected from weathering down to the level of the surrounding plain by a capping of laterized material. A quarry on this mountain provided most of the building materials used in the homestead complex.

Larra *Victoria*

Text: Mary Turner Shaw   Photographs: Brian J. Lloyd

The chimney of the first squatter's hut, built of stones once scattered from Mount Elephant's volcano, was built into a memorial cairn to mark John Lang Currie's occupation of the run.
An inscription on the far side reads
1883
JLC & TA
SITE OF FIRST HUT
AP 24 1844
The one on the front, 'JLC AP 24 1894', was added for his jubilee. Larra was held by the Currie family until 1947.

MOUNT ELEPHANT IS CONSPICUOUS among the steep volcanic cones that rise from the smooth skyline of western Victoria's basalt plains. In 1836 Major Mitchell, exploring his homeward way across 'Australia Felix', saw the hill from a distance and named it Mount Clarke, after a military colleague. The following year a party of pioneer settlers making an amateur exploratory sweep from Geelong climbed to its 400-metre summit, and impressed by either its size or its shape, called it Mount Elephant, and as this it has been known ever since. To the Aborigines it was Gerinyelam, as they also called the terns or sea-swallows that flocked on a lake near its foot, a more romantic name which lingers today in that of the local township, Derrinallum.

It was in 1844 that John Lang Currie, a twenty-five-year-old farmer's son from the Scottish Border country, heard that James Kinross was selling his new run on Mount Elephant's southern flank. Three years before this Currie had joined his cousins, the Lang brothers, who were already settled at Port Phillip, and they had been followed by another schoolfellow Thomas Anderson, a son of the Selkirk doctor. Currie had some savings, Anderson a little capital; they agreed on a partnership and Currie set out on a journey of more than two days to make an offer on the spot. He reached there to find that an option, due to expire at noon next day, had been given to Duncan Hoyle, then expected from Geelong.

By noon Hoyle had still not appeared, nor did he after another three hours' grace, and at last Kinross accepted Currie's offer. 'We had scarcely struck hands over the bargain,' Currie was to recall, when Hoyle 'came in with his face skinned and generally in a sorry way. Poor fellow, his horse had come down with him and he was delayed two or three hours with doctoring operations . . . We were very sorry for him, but he was too late.' Those last few minutes gave the young John Lang Currie his start on what he was to develop into one of the outstanding wool-producing properties of that expansive area.

For their pooled resources of £750 Currie and Anderson received the 'right of run' over 32,000 acres (12,800 hectares) of leasehold and the possession of 1,500 ewes and lambs, four working bullocks, a dray and the 'improvements'—three primitive slab huts (one for the owners, one for the men and one for a woolshed), a shepherd's watch box, about a hundred hurdles, a pot, a frying pan and a kettle. Many years later, as proprietor of a fine homestead and a sizeable area of the countryside, Currie was to have the rough rocks of the hut's chimney built into a memorial cairn on its original site.

A view of Larra homestead from the north-east. The house was saved from the fires of 1944 largely by the rich green growth around the springs behind it. During the later twenty-four years that Mr and Mrs Laidlaw lived there the garden was regenerated and developed.

To the severe gabled rectangle designed by George Henderson in the 1870s the projecting bay in the foreground was added early in the twentieth century. A verandah, added at the same time, was removed in the 1930s.

A steeple crowns the centre gable of the stables, the first of Larra's major buildings, and makes a decorative virtue of that workaday necessity, the station bell.

Resemblances Currie saw from the start between the Scottish Border country (ABOVE RIGHT) and Larra's plains (BELOW) have increased with the years.
Dry walls of field stone were built by hands skilled in a common tradition, pastures have become richer and smoother and Mount Elephant's once scrub-covered contours are now as bare as the Eildon Hills of Currie's boyhood, seen today beyond the valley of the Tweed.

When Currie made his purchase the run's most obvious shortcoming was a lack of surface water. The huts were supplied from a shallow well in a depression between the rock-strewn rises where tea-tree grew thickly, and where water could be found anywhere a metre or so below the surface. In a drought year these plains must surely have looked very different from the green misty slopes of the distant Tweed valley, yet Currie recognized a likeness, and two years later, with a timing which a less prosaic people might consider miraculous, and which even Currie found 'extraordinary, and difficult to account for', water suddenly appeared on the surface, increased in volume and has continued to flow lavishly ever since, in fair imitation of a Scottish 'burn'.

The greater part of the Western District's fine grazing country was settled by Scottish farmers, and around Mount Elephant these were mostly from the Border country. In 1840 John Brown of Galashiels, pushing westwards from Geelong in search of new land, broke an axle of his bullock dray at a small creek on the approach to Mount Elephant. With enforced

260

leisure to look about them, he and his brothers decided to stay where they were, calling the runs they spread around the mountain Mount Elephant No. 1 and No. 2.

A year or two later James Kinross, bound further westwards with a flock of sheep, was crossing the southern part of Mount Elephant No. 1, then unstocked, when his ewes began to lamb, and the Browns gave him leave to linger there. By 1844 Crown Lands Commissioner Foster Fyans had officially allocated this portion to him, but he had gathered only the basic elements of a sheep station around him when he decided—or perhaps in that poor season was forced—to sell. The new owners first chose as the name of the run Geelengla, the Aboriginal name for one of several emerging springs, but it was later changed to Larra, a name adapted from that of another, which the Aborigines called Lawur or Larrach. A tribe of Aborigines, 'some very fine young men among them', would appear in great numbers when the marsh birds were breeding and swans' eggs were plentiful. There is no record in Currie's time of the brutal conflicts that marked earlier days, but before many years had passed the black men, like the native trees and herbs, the dingo, the emu and the kangaroo, had thinned and vanished before the advance of the merino sheep.

At first, before stone walls and fences webbed the grasslands, flocks were shepherded by day and at night enclosed by hurdles for protection against the dingoes. Bullock drays could take weeks to cart the wool over the rutted tracks to Geelong, and bring stores back again. Station hands, always scarce, were mostly convicts and often untrustworthy, and Larra's partners had their share of weary rides and long night watches. In a gold rush year, when hands became scarcer still, Currie heard of an immigrant ship on the way to Melbourne. Another of his epic rides hurried him on board before anyone had time to go ashore, and he was able to persuade 'six good, honest Scotchmen' to enter his service. Some of these were still among the employees of twenty to forty years' standing who, at a jubilee celebration, which he opened in 1894 with a prayer beside the memorial cairn, presented him with an illuminated address to record 'the kindness and care' that made them respect him as master and honour him as a man.

The diaries and letters of early neighbours speak of the shared exasperations of sorting intermingled flocks, finding lost horses or straying cattle and, more happily, of borrowing a horse, a gig or a bullock team. As sisters and wives began to civilize the male domain there are notes of woolshed dances and lakeside picnics.

By 1850 Larra was prospering. Anderson left to marry one of the still rare young ladies in the Colony; Currie bought out his share and also a further western slice of Mount Elephant No. 1, thus beginning the steady process of extending Larra's boundaries that he was to continue throughout his life.

In 1852 Currie married Louise Johnston and installed his bride in a new homestead set between two springs about half a mile from the old huts. This simple house, built of roughly-squared bluestone quarried near by, in which they were to raise eleven children, became the nucleus of a typically scattered station complex.

The fine workmanship of an unknown stonemason is seen in this corbel and coping on a gable end in the stables.

An arch-headed pair of windows in the stable block shows the unusually accurate cutting and shaping of the tough bluestone and the long narrow slabs used in sill and mullion.

261

The homestead additions of the early twentieth century included this romantic tower which in fact contains two water-closets, back to back. The castellations, like those of the bathroom extension beyond, usefully conceal the necessary water-tanks on the roof.

Looking along the wall of the old kitchen, towards the gable end of the 1870s dining-room, the variations in the stone-work are hidden in a screen of creepers.

In 1857 the painter Eugène von Guérard recorded it in a panorama showing, on the far right, a cluster of homestead roofs among tall young poplars; in the centre a large spread of stone woolshed, with stable roofs beyond it; and, stretching away to the left, a store, a boundary rider's cottage, the men's hut (the cook feeding the fowls in front) and then a distant, small church building with a bell tower. In the green foreground cattle are grazing, a horseman canters towards the woolshed and ibis stand among the reeds of a shallow stream; Mount Elephant broods serenely on the northern horizon.

It is no accident that the woolshed takes place of honour. Although Larra always carried a few Shorthorn cattle it was on merino fleeces that its fortunes were founded. Currie's first stud was based on Saxon sheep from Van Diemen's Land but soon, like many neighbours, he began to breed from survivors of the original Camden Park flock. They were small, light, but sturdy sheep that thrived on the dry plains; their wool, though short in the staple, was dense, lustrous and extremely fine, and it became highly valued in the European markets. Through the 1860s the annual district show at Skipton drew pastoralists from far beyond Victoria, and Currie was always a leader among those winning top prizes and high prices. In time demand swung to a stronger fibre, and breeders to a more heavily-framed sheep. By the end of the century Larra's merinos were giving place to Lincolns and then to Corriedales, while the Shorthorn cattle increased in numbers and importance.

The pastures began to change even before Currie himself first dropped handfuls of English grass-seed in bare earth patches among the tufts of native grasses; they altered again, and for the worse, after the devastating rabbit plagues of the 1880s, and were to change still further with the innovations of the twentieth century. Meanwhile grass had replaced the thickets of banksias, lightwoods and acacias around the foot of the mountain where at one time Currie used to lose his cattle. In compensation he and his neighbour Buchanan led the district in sowing the plantations of tall blue gums which were to spread their shady grid lines across all the open plains. Today these once handsome trees, now at the end of their century's life span are, alas, thinning and splintering under the westerly gales.

In the 1860s, in a logical progression of interest, J. L. Currie became foundation shareholder and chairman of Victoria's first woollen mill at Geelong, where the first piece of cloth to come from the looms was woven of Larra Lustre fleece. In 1879 he was also a director of the first company formed to export frozen meat to England. In district affairs he was a member of the first Roads Board, then a shire councillor and president, and an elder and a generous supporter of the Presbyterian church—but he cannily resisted all persuasion to stand for parliament. A man of weight and substance, his home life remained unostentatious; he collected books and Australiana and he travelled widely.

Although selectors made inroads on Currie's holdings in the land sales of the 1860s he soon acquired more freehold. One such purchase, the 14,000-acre (5,600 hectare) Poligolet on the west, he gave in 1870 to his manager John Dodds, who had shared early hardships and later responsibilities.

The kitchen block of the 1850s and some small rooms beyond it, the oldest of Larra's surviving buildings, are linked by a wall to the newer parts of the house.

The northern neighbour, John Brown, left Gala in 1853, and after passing through the hands of six more of his countrymen it was divided in 1871 as freehold, Alexander Buchanan taking the western section and calling it Titanga. In 1886 Currie bought Titanga's 17,000 acres (6,800 hectares) and three years later the 20,000-acre (8,000-hectare) Gala, his sway now extending even beyond the Browns' original domain. Leaving his sons to follow almost literally in his footsteps he moved his own home to Melbourne, to a house in St Kilda he called Eildon. He died, a rich man, in 1898.

With the new century came the wane of the great pastoral empires, fragmented as they were by inheritors, whittled away by closer settlement and invaded by crops and dairying. Nevertheless the descendants of Selkirk farmers were to have a place in the pattern of pastures around Mount Elephant for many years to come. Currie's second son, another John Lang Currie, became the owner of Larra. The eldest child and daughter Henrietta, who had married a Lang kinsman from Selkirk, inherited Titanga. (It was said that she shared equally with his sons

The drawing-room, now modernized, was once dominated by an elaborate Victorian mantelpiece that towered from floor to ceiling. Banished earlier this century, it found refuge under another Currie roof at Gala.
Today's beautiful furniture came with the present owners, Dr and Mrs A. G. McKinnon, from another old family homestead, Boisdale, in Gippsland.

because, travelling with him on one of the two occasions he was shipwrecked, although women and children were ordered to the boats, she refused to leave his side.) Of the younger sons, Edwin, after experience on a station of his father's in Queensland, took over Gala; Sibbald was apportioned an eastern part of Larra, renamed Ettrick; and Alan a westerly section of Titanga that he called Mount Elephant. Today, on acreages much reduced over the past seventy-odd years, a Currie still lives at Gala, and at Titanga there are grandchildren and great-grandchildren of the first John Lang Currie.

The history of Larra's buildings must be pieced together from what Currie's descendants can recall and from fragmentary printed sources, for almost all the station records and documents have been lost. In 1944 one of the great grass fires that periodically devastate wide tracts of the Western District swept down past Mount Elephant and wiped out Larra's fine woolshed, the men's huts, seven cottages and all the other scattered buildings except the stables and the house itself. It also licked into the

264

family's first homestead, by then used as the office, leaving nothing but the blackened walls and cinders of all the plans, accounts, letters or station diaries that might have given precision to Larra's story. (At that time Currie's granddaughter, living there alone, saved her life by driving her car straight into one of Larra's springs, while the willow leaves shrivelled and dropped from overhead.)

Major building changes seem to have occurred about every thirty years, beginning with the stables in 1873. When Alexander Buchanan built his elegant new homestead at Titanga (illustrated in Volume One of *Historic Homesteads of Australia*, p. 250), he had engaged a young Scottish architect, George Henderson, to design it, and it was not long before Currie sought his talents for Larra. In the new stables, on a rocky rise near the house, Henderson planned stalls for the homestead horses, a carriage house, harness room, feed room, forge and groom's quarters around high walled courts. Under his supervision the intractable bluestone was

The dining-room, with a view northwards across Larra's grazing paddocks, is still graced by the table and chairs, which suit it so well, introduced by the previous owners, Mr and Mrs Ralph Laidlaw.

The forge, after long years of disuse, has some of its equipment still in place. At one time all the many station horses would be brought here to be shod.

quarried and worked with a finish that contrasts with the earlier rugged stonework; perhaps some day the name of this skilled stonemason will come to light. If, as relatives believe, the northern wing of loose-boxes was a later addition, to house John Currie junior's stud of thoroughbred race-horses, the junction of old work and new is imperceptible. Today, happily, the thoroughbreds, quarter horses and ponies of the present owners bring back the clatter of life to the old stones.

Henderson's next brief, probably about 1875, was to add a separate living and bedroom block to the east of the detached kitchen. The living quarters of the 1850s then stood about where their stones have now been rebuilt into garage and stores, a little to the west of the kitchen and its attendant buildings. These can be discerned in the Guérard painting of 1857, and are still in use. Henderson's long rectangle, with a gabled roof across each end, its severity broken on the north by a small central gable flanked by battlemented bay windows, had at first the Scottish look that Currie is said to have demanded.

This service passage runs along inside the back wall of the stables. The door on the right leads to the feed store in a projecting wing, and on the left the sliding shutters open directly over the feeding troughs of the stalls and loose-boxes.

Early in the twentieth century John Currie junior took a hand. His extension of a bay from the drawing-room on the north-east, with a verandah around it carried across the north facade, added an Australian flavour. At the southern end another verandah between square turrets and a separate small turretted building housed bathroom and water-closets to keep pace with the demands of modern hygiene and service. Pantries and store-rooms were also added along the north wall—built then or earlier—that links dining-room to kitchen and extends past old stone rooms flanking the kitchen courtyard to end with a flourish in a small octagonal tower —also containing a water-closet.

In the 1930s J. L. Currie's granddaughter, in quest of sunshine, removed the north verandah and banished the ironwork of the south one. Further changes have included minor internal remodelling and decoration, and the conversion of the kitchen to the family living patterns of today. Throughout them all Larra still retains its sturdy individuality, showing the strength of an old tradition imposed upon a raw, primeval land.

In 1947 the Closer Settlement Board resumed Larra from its third and last Currie owner, Mrs Frank Thornthwaite. Under the Soldier Settlement Act the homestead block, then of 1,375 acres (548 hectares) was sold to T. C. McKellar; in 1951 by him to Ralph H. C. Laidlaw; and in 1975 was bought by Dr and Mrs A. G. McKinnon—all names, the sentimental may note, maintaining an unbroken link with the Scotland of their origin.

The bluestone stables were designed for John Lang Currie in 1873 by the Scottish architect George Henderson. The austere form and the precision of the masonry contrast with the traditional rambling walls of field stone, and the roughly squared rubble of earlier buildings.

A final detail of the precise tailoring of the stonework in the stable block.

Poltalloch *South Australia*

Text: Stewart Game   *Photographs: Marcus B. Brownrigg*

It was on the undulating country bordering Lake Alexandrina and extending down to the northern shore of Lake Albert that, in 1843, John Malcolm took up 24,000 acres (9,600 hectares) on which to run cattle and a dairy herd. He named the property Poltalloch Estate, after his home at Poltalloch in the County of Argyle, Scotland, and proceeded to build himself a modest home with a large dairy located at the rear. The house has a commanding view over Lake Alexandrina as well as to landward and remained the homestead until the present Poltalloch homestead was built some thirty-three years later. Point Malcolm, named after John Malcolm, is a dominating land feature at the junction of Lake Albert with Lake Alexandrina, and it was on this prominence that the Mundoo Light was erected in 1878 as a navigational aid to the very busy paddle-boats and other craft using the Lakes. Many river boats passed this light on their way from Goolwa or Meningie en route for the distant waterways of the Murray, Darling and Murrumbidgee Rivers, trading with distant stations as well as the gold diggings in the eastern States.

Across the narrow neck of water is the small township of Narrung, and it was to this place that anyone wishing to proceed to Adelaide from Poltalloch or the surrounding area would have to be rowed across from Point Malcolm, in order to take the river boat *Jupiter*, which used to ply between Meningie and Milang, from whence passengers then proceeded by road to Adelaide. Today, Point Malcolm and Narrung are served by a ferry and the Mundoo Light no longer plays its part in the romance of the Murray river boats.

Paddle steamers with their barges were the main means of transporting all manner of goods, and a property with a water frontage was in a most fortunate position: it could load its wool on to the barges or river boats from its own jetty to go to Goolwa or Murray Bridge. Sometimes the seemingly

Poltalloch homestead OPPOSITE *faces north across Lake Alexandrina. The grand two-storey Victorian house sits well in its walled garden setting; the wide verandahs, with the curved iron roofs and superb cast-iron lace work, providing a welcome shade to the ground floor walls. The garden wall and some of the shrubs and trees date back to the early days of the property.*
The front door ABOVE, *with its heavy, cedar panelled door and sidelights, is offset by the rusticated and carved stone surround brought from Swan Court by river boat.*

The spacious verandah, with its gently sweeping iron roof, reflects the light from the trees and lawns to emphasize the pattern of some of the finest cast-iron lace work of this period in South Australia. The effect is one of lightness as well as welcoming shade.
The original gateway in the garden wall is viewed through the columns.

The battlemented parapet ABOVE of unusual design, acts as a foil to the cornice brackets of the eaves; the stone dressings to the quoins and window have chisel drafted margins and pick worked faces; the surround to the window has stop chamfers. The stone was worked off the site and transported from Swan Court to Poltalloch by river boat. Dressed stone was brought by bullock wagon for the 1911 additions.

placid lake could suddenly become very rough and the winds strong; and barge loads of wool would finish up in the water, with horse teams needed to salvage the load. These river boats were the work horses all along the Murray and one, the *Aida and Clara*, was named after two cousins of the Bowman family. What a sight it must have been, looking out of an evening across the lake, to see these river boats floating past.

When John Bowman set out from England in the early 1840s it was his intention to go to South Australia, one branch of the family already having reached the new Colony from Tasmania in 1836. However, his ship did not visit South Australia, but proceeded to Tasmania, where John Bowman landed. He took up residence in Hobart, where he married his wife Jane.

It would appear that John Bowman had come to South Australia prior to 1873 and was a land holder in Crystal Brook as the Deed of Conveyance for the purchase of Poltalloch states:

'This Indenture made the Fourth day of November in the year of our Lord one thousand eight hundred and seventy three Between John Malcolm of Poltalloch in the County of Argyle in North Britain and of Great Stanhope Street Abayfan of Middlesex in England Esquire on the one hand and John Bowman of Crystal Brook in the Province of South Australia Stock and Station Holder William Charles Bowman of Mount Vernon in Tasmania Stock and Station Holder and Thomas Richard Bowman of Crystal Brook as aforesaid Stock and Station Holder of the other part Witnesseth . . .'

The document lists the eighty-four sections of 'The Poltalloch Estate' totalling 7,673 acres (3,069 hectares) and the twenty-three sections of 'The

Viewed from the stair landing the archway gives a glimpse of the spacious hall and one of the beautifully carved hall seats. The thickness of the wall and the elegance of the mouldings of the archway show the quality of the work of the builders and tradesmen. The timber stairs and skirtings are in cedar. All mouldings are in balance with the proportions of the interior.

The entrance hall is large and well proportioned, with all its architectural elements in balance. The mouldings of the cornice are strong, as are the mouldings to the large archway leading to a fine cedar staircase. Substantial and well-moulded cedar skirtings and architraves are enhanced by the carefully-selected decor and the carved antique furniture.

Campbell House Estate' totalling 9,088 acres (3,635 hectares) in the Hundred of Barker; the Deed was duly executed on 17 September 1875.

At one time Thomas Richard Bowman owned Martindale Hall in the Mintaro area as well as other properties in the north of the State; also the properties of Narrung and Tatiara.

It was John Bowman who ran the Poltalloch property. He introduced sheep in place of cattle, and the property has continued as a sheep station up to the present time, although a few cattle are still to be found in the paddocks.

When John Bowman died the property was passed on to his son, Keith Dudley Bowman, but as he was under twenty-one at the time the property was managed by his elder brother Albert until he was of age. How time must have dragged; one newspaper reported K. D. Bowman to be a 'young man in a hurry', for as soon as he reached adulthood in 1902 he immediately did two things—took control of Poltalloch, and married Margaret Hepburn Gale on 16 April 1902; they had two sons and three daughters, the sons unfortunately did not reach adulthood.

The young owner kept 'moving', and bought Lake Albert Station, an area of some 7,000 to 8,000 acres (3,000 hectares) which bounded on to Poltalloch. This brought the holdings to about the original size of Poltalloch when John Malcolm took it up in 1843; the large woolshed built by his father proved to be adequate, handling up to 30,000 sheep per year. Some years the numbers would be well down, as in the drought year of 1914, when the sheoaks on the property were cut down to feed the sheep. The area has an average rainfall of 430 millimetres and used to rely on the lake water remaining fresh: if the river level dropped the lakes would become salt, before the barrage was built, and water for domestic use would come from catchment storage, usually in large underground tanks like the one under the courtyard at Poltalloch. Lake Albert Station was sold in 1913.

The dining-room, like the other main rooms, is well proportioned and provides an excellent setting for the large, heavily-carved Welsh sideboard. This antique, along with the chairs, was bought when the house was refurnished in 1911. The large circular table can be extended to seat sixteen, and the room is large enough to accommodate that number with ease.

W. P. Hart came to live at Poltalloch with his wife and family when the young K. D. Bowman was married. The Harts ran the store on the property, which was open on Saturday afternoons for the men who would come in from the out station for supplies and for the Aborigines employed on the property as shearers or on other jobs. Jean Hart was bookkeeper for the property until her retirement some few years ago. Others who, over the years, have become a part of the Poltalloch family include Jack Cameron, a part-Aborigine, who married 'princess' Sara Karpany and lived on the property until his retirement. In the early days he drove the mail cart to Narrung and later looked after the cars; he died in the Murray Bridge Hospital early in 1976 at the age of ninety-one. In its heyday there would be up to twenty men in the men's quarters and six families living on the property. Electricity was provided by a generator and great glass jars, all housed in the pumphouse; the same engine driving the pump and the generator. In 1911 a larger battery plant was installed which provided 110 volt power.

Mary Rosamund Bowman, eldest of K. D. Bowman's three daughters, married Trafford Cowan of Lucindale, a property in the south-east of the State. Their son James and daughter Margaret were born in the early 1930s. Keith Dudley Bowman died in 1933 and Trafford Cowan managed the property until he enlisted in World War Two. He was taken prisoner by the Japanese in Malaya where he died in a P.O.W. camp. Mary Cowan carried on the management of the property until her son James was able to take over and manage Poltalloch for the family.

In 1947 Poltalloch was divided between the three daughters of K. D. Bowman. The portion known as Poltalloch Plains went to Daphne Bowman; the portion now known as Poltalloch to Mary Cowan; and the third portion known as Poltalloch Bluff to Nancy. (She had married Norman Jude, later Sir Norman, who had other property interests in the south-east as well as being a very energetic parliamentarian.)

In 1876 John Bowman built the present homestead. From 1875 onwards the large woolshed and other buildings, which comprise a most interesting complex, were built resembling a small English village, with the village green extending down to the waters of Lake Alexandrina. The new homestead is some six kilometres west of the original house built by Malcolm and is closer to the water's edge. It is a fine, two-storey Victorian house with large sweeping verandahs on three sides of the ground floor and a first floor balcony to the front elevation. The courtyard at the rear, which contains a large underground tank, is flanked by the two-storey wings with their balconies, and off the courtyard is the large billiard room. The big cedar front door opens into a spacious hall with the drawing-room off to the right and the dining-room to the left, then, through the splendid archway, to a living-room to the right. On the left is a fine cedar staircase leading to the bedrooms above; a full glass door with a semicircular fanlight leads out into the courtyard.

Although no records exist as to who the architect and builder were it is known that a John Oldfield and his son worked on the building as stone masons. The work commenced on the homestead in 1876, one year after the building of the woolshed. The limestone for the walls came from the

The unique chimneys at Poltalloch have a character all their own, with a swept moulded octagonal cap, supported not only on the chimney stack, but also on four pilasters set into niches. The eaves cornice brackets are strongly moulded.

The simple lines of the mouldings to the niches flanking the archway in the entrance hall provide a beautiful setting for the two fine matching antiques.

The two houses OPPOSITE were built for
the manager and the overseer and their
families. The same care went into the
building of these houses as into the homestead. There is evidence of a feeling for
design in the verandah details; as well as in
the finish around openings and at the
quoins. They are important elements of the
complex of buildings forming the 'Village'.

*The coachhouse, stables and barn build-
ings are an interesting group situated at
the western end of the 'Village' and near
the entrance to the homestead. The
groom's room was in the section with the
window and the cast-iron capping to the
wall. The cut out barges to the barn gable
cast an interesting shadow pattern on the
limestone walls. The stable yard and horse
stalls are behind the stone wall and barn.*

property and the lime for mortar was burnt on the site; other materials
would have been transported to the site by boat and wagon. The dressed
stones for the quoins and surrounds to openings were brought from Swan
Court by boat, commanded by Captain Cremer, a well-known identity in
the area. The external walls are of squared, random-coursed limestone,
with lined joints, which act as an excellent foil to the dressed stonework
with drafted margins and carving, as at the front door, or the pick face
work to other areas.

Everywhere there is a feeling of solidity; this is exemplified in the beautiful cedar timber that was used so tastefully throughout the interior. The
ceilings to the major rooms are finished with beautifully-moulded coved
cornices, the cornices to the entrance hall being exceptionally fine, its
decorative brackets leading to and supporting the strong moulding extending out on to the ceiling. The mouldings are echoed in the moulds to the
archway and springing, with recessed panels in the soffit of the arch and
the decorative keystone. The semicircular leaded niches with their simple
mouldings add to the elegance of the hall, which is most tastefully
decorated and furnished as is the whole of Poltalloch homestead.

In 1911 additions were made at the rear and the house was completely
redecorated and refurnished; only a few pieces of the original furniture
remaining. The new furniture, which is still in use today, is in the style of
the early eighteenth century designers and shows a continental influence
very much in the vein of Johann Schübler or Daniel Marot, who used deep
carving to great effect in their work. One seat in the entrance hall has the
date 1713 carved into the back. In the dining-room the circular table
extends to seat sixteen; and the chairs and the beautiful Welsh side-board
are in a similar style to the furniture in the hall.

The outbuildings are particularly interesting in many respects. They
were all built about the same time and in the main with the same
materials as were used in the homestead. Throughout the years some
alterations and additions have taken place, but in no way has the charm of
their setting been upset, and the buildings form a gentle arc to the east of
the homestead; beginning with the woolshed on the eastern tip with the
men's quarters, store, carpenter shop and blacksmith leading around to
the houses occupied by the managers of the day and the overseers; finishing at the western end with the stables, coach house and barns. The woolshed was built in 1875 with limestone rubble walls and dressed stone
arches and surrounds to openings. The roof is unsupported, curved,
corrugated galvanized iron, shaped on the property in rollers which are
still in use today. The gauge is heavy and the malleable iron is still in good
condition after 100 years of exposure to the elements.

The manager's and overseer's houses have obviously been designed, and
are vastly superior to the secondary buildings one sometimes finds on
properties. The same can be said for the other buildings, but the stables,
coachhouse and barns deserve a special mention as a delightful building
group, and for the decorative barges to the barn gable and the cast-iron
detail to the wall capping. The gable has a semi-circular arched opening
over the doorway. Door and window openings have cambered arches with
keystones and plain surrounds that offset the random limestone walls.

The woolshed, built in 1875, with its un-supported curved iron roof, would have been a busy place when up to 30,000 sheep a year were sheared at Poltalloch. The limestone walls show dressed stone sur-rounds to openings similar to those of the homestead.

Behind the barns and the stone wall with the cast-iron capping are the stables, which have been constructed with solid tree trunk posts support-ing a rough hewn cap. They form two sides of the exercise yard, sur-rounded by a stone wall; attached to, and to the south of, the stable area is the yard and stalls for the race horses.

All the buildings which form the 'village' have a back drop of gum trees, some of which would have been in existence when the buildings were erected. One of these old trees has suffered the fate of time and termites and was blown down during a recent storm.

The small community on Poltalloch in its early days had to look to itself for the needs of day to day living because of the distance from the larger towns; also because of the means of transport available which, until the introduction of the motor car to the area, was confined to the horse-drawn vehicle or the river boat. Entertainment would have been self-generated and, because of this, enjoyed to the full. Occasions such as Christmas would be enjoyed by all on the property, usually in the court-yard of the homestead, which would have been decorated for the occasion with tree boughs and other festive decorations. For the young Bowmans the problem of school was taken care of by the services of a governess until they reached the stage when it was necessary to go to finishing schools in Adelaide. The days would drag between holidays when they could return with a feeling of freedom to follow their own pursuits, or to become once more a part of the work force on the property. Entertain-ments included tennis parties on the court immediately south of the billiard-room wing, and the visiting of other neighbouring properties.

Poltalloch homestead today carries its 100 years gracefully without any obvious scars of change. Other houses were erected amongst the trees to the west of the homestead, one of which is now occupied by Mary Cowan. Poltalloch is now occupied by James Cowan and his family. It was in 1957 that he married Cecily Hayward and took her to Poltalloch, where they lived in one of the houses on the property, later moving into the homestead from whence he manages the property. Recently some areas of the homestead have been altered internally and brought into line with present day needs. The kitchen is now nearer to the dining-room and designed to provide a flexibility to suit today's way of life, in which rising costs and the scarcity of domestic help make it essential that such areas must function efficiently with the minimum of effort. Cecily Cowan has created a relaxing atmosphere in the decor and furnishing of all the rooms, and her taste and interest in paintings by Australian artists is displayed to advantage on the walls.

Mary Cowan's daughter Margaret, who married James Bullock in 1958, and now lives in Adelaide along with their five children, uses one of the houses on the property, while her mother occupies one of the adjoining houses.

The property now has a much smaller acreage than when it was originally bought and turned over to sheep (which were mainly cross-breeds, with, later, the addition of some Corriedales). The number of families and men employed on the property has decreased, but the feeling of the past lingers among the trees and the buildings of Poltalloch.

The road to Point Malcolm ferry now runs past the homestead, connecting the Narrung and Point McLeay areas, now focal centres for the Aboriginal population. Here they manage their own affairs under the guidance and assistance of both State and Federal Departments. In recent years areas of the Coorong have been declared conservation reserves and, in some instances, access to them is totally prohibited. This is designed to encourage the rehabitation of rare and endangered species of bird life as well as other flora and fauna necessary for the preservation of the environment.

The story of Poltalloch is that of a family, a house, and the people that came to work and live in what must be some of the most subtle landscape in South Australia. May the story continue through the years to come.

The 'Village', with the village green going down to the water's edge; the men's quarters on the left; the store, carpenter shop and blacksmith in the centre; and the overseer's and manager's houses on the right. The old gum tree in the centre has been blown down since this photograph was taken.

Gracemere *Queensland*

Text: Ian T. McDonald   Photographs: Richard Stringer

The homestead was designed and built in 1858 under the supervision of Colin Archer, who later attained world fame as designer and builder of the Polar vessel Fram. *He also invented features of boat design which added greatly to their safety.* OPPOSITE: *Wood from the narrow leaf iron bark was used to shingle the roof, which is now covered with corrugated iron.*

GRACEMERE, THE MUCH-LOVED HOME established and still owned by the Archer family, is set upon a sweeping natural peninsula within a lagoon or 'mere' situated about eleven kilometres west of Rockhampton, Central Queensland. A visitor to Gracemere is impressed by the beauty of the close relationship between the home and the garden: an affinity with the environment that inspires people, who are fascinated by its unique charm and character.

My most memorable impression was on a pleasant autumn evening, looking across the broad expanse of the mere to the setting sun with all its reflections of failing light, with clouds shot with the brilliant colours of orange and red that are part of this warm northern sky. The short twilight preceded a full moon rising through branches of century-old trees, and across the still waters came the soft sounds of varied wildlife. I passed along one of the many paths winding past sweeping, falling plant life, across the front lawn to the homestead. Under a soft mellow glow of light was caught the strength and character of old woods with deep shadows across wall and floor; with here and there on table, shelf and wall the traditions that are part of this great pastoral family. Not dead—not past— but alive with incredible reality, with an overpowering peace and stillness, an indescribable sense of closeness with nature.

Around the walls hang family portraits. William and Julia Archer, the parents of the nine sons who moved out through many parts of the globe; partly led by Charles, the eldest, who, with William, discovered and named the land and waters of the Fitzroy in 1853. Then there is Thomas, whose charming wife Grace gave her name to the property by popular choice; Alexander, who opened the first Bank of New South Wales in Rockhampton and became General Manager for Queensland; Archibald,

Gracemere homestead is picturesquely set on a peninsula encircled by the lagoon or 'mere'. The garden presents delightful vistas in almost every direction. A group of spoonbills parade the water's edge, and a darter dries its wings.

The stone wall surrounding the raised front lawn and other walls throughout the garden were constructed by destitute miners after the failure of the Canoona Gold Rush in 1858.

The pathway from this rear angle of the building leads to the kitchen and servants' quarters. The spring flowers of the Beaumontia creeper cover this northerly wall.

member for Rockhampton and Treasurer in the Queensland Parliament; Colin, the naval architect who designed the Polar vessel *Fram* which carried Nansen to the North and Amundsen to the South Pole; John, who was the first to arrive in Australia back in 1833 and later lost his life at sea; James, the youngest; and David, the third brother.

The long and costly war with Napoleon and the resulting depression almost ruined the Scottish firm of Charles Archer and Son. The family traded as timber merchants with their own ships out of Newberg on the Firth of Tay. French privateers had sunk many of their small vessels and there was no money to replace them. In 1825 William migrated with his wife, Julia, to South Norway and settled in the beautiful little town of Larvic where they reared nine sons and four daughters. Charles Archer, a grandson, wrote of them '. . . here they brought up their large family in plain living and straight thinking; and from there they sent out many tall sons to seek their fortunes in the world, chiefly in Australia, where several members of the mother's clan (the Walkers) were already, in the eighteen thirties, prosperously established . . .'

John Archer, the second son, was the first to reach Australia, in February 1833, as an apprentice seaman. He was most impressed and his letters were the strong influence that brought David to Australia in 1834, at the age of eighteen, to work on his uncle's property Wallerowang, near Lithgow. William and Thomas followed in 1837.

David handed the management of Wallerowang to William in 1840 and, with his two brothers, John and Thomas, entered into partnership to drive 5,000 sheep north to select land in what is now Queensland. On the Castlereagh River the disease scab (caused by a mite which burrowed into the skin of the sheep) infected the flock and, though repeated dipping in arsenic eventually overcame the complaint, lambing and shearing had to follow. The party was twelve months behind schedule and did not reach the Condamine River until August 1841. The delay proved disastrous as most of the rich open Darling Downs had been occupied. Moving on, they crossed the Dividing Range near Eaton Vale to Lake Claredon, from whence they proceeded north and, in October 1841, the Archers settled just off the Stanley River near the present town of Woodford. The Aborigines had already named the place for themselves—'Durundur'.

Emu Creek and Cooyar were taken up in 1845, and Eidsvold and Coonambula in 1848. Cooyar and Emu Creek were then sold, the latter for £250 stocked. The years from 1843 to 1852 saw changes among the brothers. John went back to sea but was replaced by the eldest brother Charles. In 1849 Thomas startled his brothers by becoming a Californian 'forty-niner'. While Queensland Agent-General in London many years later, he recollects being questioned by the Minister for the Colonies.

'I suppose the original settlers in Queensland were a very rough and uncultured set of people.'

'Yes,' replied Thomas with a laugh, 'and I was one of them.'

'Oh, indeed. I beg pardon,' was the reply.

The conversation turned later to California and the Minister tried again:

'Well at any rate,' he offered. 'I am sure that the original settlers in California were an unmitigated lot of ruffians.'

'You are quite right,' Thomas agreed smiling, 'and I was one of them also.'

'Well, well, I never made two such bad shots in my life.'

David Archer returned to Norway and England in 1852, after guiding the family business in the Colony for nearly twenty years. Colin, the eighth son, replaced him. In 1853, Charles, William and Colin were living at Eidsvold and Coonambula. Restlessly, they probed north from the Burnett on to the Dawson, in search of Leichhardt's river: the mighty river that, the explorer had told them, must carry to the sea the combined waters of the Dawson, Mackenzie, Comet and Nogoa.

In April 1853, Charles and William Archer rode to Rannes. On previous expeditions they had headed north-west or north. Now they turned their horses north-east for the first time. On 4 May 1853, after four days tough riding, they ascended a range. Jubilantly Charles Archer writes, 'Upon topping the range, a most astonishing view lay beneath us. Through a large and apparently open valley, bounded by table topped pyramidal and Domite Mountains with here and there fantastic sandstone peaks, a large

river wound its way towards the sea. We supposed the river to be the Dawson and Mackenzie joined, and the sea before us to be Kepple Bay. Returned to our noon camp . . .' They named the river the Fitzroy and discovered a pleasant site for a homestead on a beautiful lake, about eleven kilometres from the river.

The Archer brothers had found good, well-watered grazing land and cheap water transport for their wool and supplies. In Maryborough, Colin Archer bought the *Ellida*, a 13-ton ketch, in which he was to find the mouth of the Fitzroy and navigate the river for the first time with the extra supplies.

In August 1855 the Archers occupied Gracemere with 8,000 sheep. The cavalcade that escorted the sheep from 'Coonambula' mustered Charles and William Archer, seventeen other Europeans including eight German shepherds, two native policemen, four Aborigines and their women, ten horses and twenty-four working oxen.

The landing point on the river developed as a small settlement with a handful of buildings, until the discovery of gold at Canoona just to the north in 1858, sparked off one of the most disastrous 'rushes' in Australian history. Up to 15,000 diggers were stranded, subsequently founding the town of Rockhampton, which was named by Land Commissioner Wiseman and Charles Archer. Following the early failure of the field the town prospered; stores, banks and hotels sprang up in support of the port to service the spreading hinterland now called Central Queensland.

1858 also saw the construction of the present Gracemere homestead, designed by Colin Archer with the front of the L-shaped building facing the lagoon. This consists of the living-room with the fireplace panelled in carved reliefs; the main bedroom and an attached gauzed room with roll down blinds; the rear wing, of vertical, pit-sawn Burdekin Plum planks, which joins with a narrow pantry; then the dining-room, with a bedroom at the end; the old cellar is sited below this section.

Accommodation is also found in a two-bedroom guest cottage in the garden equidistant from the kitchen and servants' quarters. Extending back along the entrance road are the office and bookkeeper's quarters, the carpenter and blacksmith's shop which, with a stallion box attached, stood in front of the existing vehicle shed; and further up, the stables, still standing, and the cattle yards. Opposite stood the workers' cottages, stretching up to the site of the woolshed.

The rolling country near the lagoon was a popular Aboriginal camp site, where a number of artifacts, including axes, cutting implements and rubbing stones, are currently being found. As was the custom with early white settlements, the chief of this tribe (Bikalbura) received a breast plate with 'King Mickey of Gracemere' engraved upon it. On a nearby rise, up from the kilometre-long entrance avenue of tamarind trees, is the site of the station cemetery, containing many graves of people who lived there.

Following the occupation of Gracemere Run in August 1855, improvements were constructed for man and beast with the establishment of a sheep station. On marine plain country, twenty-four kilometres to the south, Archer Cattle Station was formed, together with a Heifer Station at Nankeen across the Fitzroy River. The country proved ideally suited for

The length of trees suitable for splitting slabs was predominant in the choice of angle at which they were laid. In this case Colin Archer achieved the maximum use of split lengths by employing a lower wall plate, which acts in turn for the head to doors and windows and sill for the ventilation openings above. An extremely practical use of materials obtaining a maximum flow of air.

Work on the house began by May 1858 and was completed on Monday 19 July 1858. Colin Archer wrote in his diary: 'Having finished bricking the chimney of the new house we have taken possession and find it very comfortable and roomy after the old place, which is now 'Bachelor's Hall'. OPPOSITE: The walls of Iron Bark Slabs are arranged in matched sections with the joining studs meeting tie beams noticeable along the top wall plate. Each panel contains ventilation opening, window and door. The table in the foreground and other practical pieces were made by Mr Smalley, the station carpenter.

Panelling around the fireplace and the fire screen (ABOVE) were carved this century by Mrs Robert Stubbs Archer and Mrs Alister Archer. The original floor is Oregon pine, which has white-ant-resisting properties.

OPPOSITE: The angle formed from the junction of the rear wing presents a pleasant atmosphere adjacent to the living-room with the main bedroom on the right. Below a ventilation opening and window stands a tea table carved by Mrs R. S. Archer. The small shelf on the window sill held a large earthenware flask (water monkey) of cool water, positioned to catch the slightest breeze.

The dramatic line of portraits BELOW on the inner wall of the living room (17 feet by 32 feet) depicts William and Julia Archer with all of their nine sons. Two original dining chairs stand against the far wall below a portrait of Charles Archer. The carved chair in the foreground was carved by Mrs Alister Archer to a Norwegian peasant design.

cattle, and numbers steadily increased from 4,000 in 1859 to 11,000 in 1868. The highest recording of sheep on Gracemere was over 48,000 in 1866.

The sheep quickly over-grazed the softer Blue and Kangaroo grasses, leaving the less edible 'seedy' species which began to dominate the pastures. The most severe of these grasses was the 'bunch spear', which had the ability to penetrate the flesh of the sheep. Consequently the sheep lost condition and wool yields suffered. In 1874 the sheep were moved to Minnie Downs following the purchase of this western property.

Cattle continued to thrive on Gracemere. Selective breeding was commenced in 1856 with the establishment of a Shorthorn stud, but a comparison of breeds soon proved Herefords to be superior. Consequently, in 1862, a Hereford stud was formed and from 1866 Shorthorns were gradually phased out.

An outstanding period of management followed, especially under the direction of Robert Stubbs Archer who managed Gracemere for forty-six years, 1880 to 1926. Son of David Archer, he was President of the Rockhampton Agricultural Society for thirty years, Chairman of the Rockhampton Harbour Board, a local Director of Mount Morgan Gold Mining Company and also Manager for a short period in 1912.

The love of a beautiful garden has been one of the foremost family pleasures. Plant stock brought in the 1850s from the Sydney Botanical Gardens began the Gracemere garden, from whence many magnificent trees and shrubs in Central Queensland trace their origin. The soil and climate is especially suited to bougainvillea, of which no less than sixteen different colours abound within some following varieties: Mrs Butt (scarlet), Soldier's Jacket (red), Alton Downs (pinkish red), Tomasei (deep pink), Mr Kenna (deep pink), Louise Waltham (apricot pink), Bois de Rose (pinkish purple), Trailei (royal purple), Common Purple, and Alba (white). The Beaumontia creeper with white, bell-shaped flowers, and the beautiful pink bracts of *Colvillia rasimosia* are favourites of Mrs Alister Archer, who has lived at Gracemere most of her life. Dominant in the garden are the many frangipani, the towering royal palms, and the Leichhardt trees which are native to the Fitzroy.

The almost endless array of plants and trees extends right to the edge of the lagoon, which is a fauna sanctuary; the first declared in Queensland. The waters abound in all major species of bird life: black swans, pelicans, brolga and jabiru. Of the many ducks the black, wood and whistlers are the most common. The rare magpie and pygmy geese, water hen and stilts, egrets, herons, white ibis, and spoonbills, cormorants, darters and the lotus bird are also found.

The lagoon is on old water course country which now fills from the overflow from nearby Scrubby Creek. It is not permanent and has been dry six times. On one such occasion, in 1856, a race meeting was conducted around its dry bed.

Following these dry periods the warm summer rains again sweep the surrounding countryside, overflowing the lagoon and returning its abundant life; for Gracemere will live on in time—as timeless as the soft call of the black swan, or the low sweep of native duck.

Padthaway *South Australia*

Text: Elaine Lawson   *Photographs: Marcus B. Brownrigg*

The first house at Padthaway was built of local stone. Its unpretentious style is typical of the early dwellings of Australia's pioneers—long and low with a touch of Georgian detail. The rough timbers of the verandah are of great interest to students of early constructions.

THE HOMESTEAD AT PADTHAWAY achieves an ideal too often forgotten in the buildings of today, for not only is its appearance pleasing to the beholder, but it is also comfortable and manageable for those who live in it. The house was completed in 1882, and the generations of Lawsons dwelling there have been able to watch the surrounding countryside change from dense forests to cleared grazing lands, and finally to an intensively-cultivated farming area. These changes would surely have pleased rather than surprised Robert Lawson, who pioneered this country, proving as they do that his faith in his own judgement was well justified.

Having set sail from Newton-on-Ayr, Scotland, aboard the *Superb*, Robert Lawson arrived in South Australia in 1839, the settlement being then only three years old. He lost no time in establishing himself at Mount Barker, some fifty kilometres from Adelaide. As South Australia was at no time a convict colony, settlers were encouraged to acquire some type of trade or skill before emigrating, and although Lawson had inherited valuable real estate in Ayr, he had been apprenticed as a cabinet maker. However, it was sheep farming which attracted him, and statistical returns of 1841 show him to have had a flock of 550 sheep, and improvements consisting of a dwelling place, yards, and a seven-foot well. He is credited with being one of the discoverers of copper at Callington at this time, which resulted in an influx of miners to a previously peaceful spot. This, perhaps prompted him to seek land further afield.

For some time there had been rumours of good country to the South, and Lawson joined one of the expeditions in search of it. He accompanied Messrs Scott, Binnie and McLeod, and they were fortunate in having a reliable native guide named 'One Toe Charlie'. Their venture proved successful, and on 9 December 1845 this report appeared in *The South Australian*: 'We have pleasure in announcing the return of several parties from the Tatiara; all report most favourably. In addition to Messrs McDougall, Scott, Lawson, L. McLeod, Disher and Harriott, several others have taken or are about to take out runs for sheep.' In fact, Lawson's name does not appear on an application for a run until 1847, and it must have been at this time that he set out for Padthaway which was recorded as being an area of 53,760 acres (21,500 hectares).

Unlike many other settlers, who preferred to leave their families in safe and familiar surroundings, Robert Lawson was accompanied on this long and arduous journey by his intrepid young wife. Eliza Lawson was born Eliza Bell of Craig Brae, Dalmaney, Scotland, and she arrived in South Australia on the ship *Bessorah Merchant* in November 1845. She was a

The second homestead at Padthaway stands less than twenty metres from its forerunner. It is built of similar stone but in a more imposing style. The cast-iron lace work on the verandah and balcony probably came from the South Australian Foundries at Gawler.

member of a family well known in Mount Barker, her brother Allan having made a name for himself as an agriculturalist by winning prizes for wheat in Europe and America. It is said that Eliza Bell followed her brother to Australia in order to recover some money which she had lent him. If other stories of her determination can be taken as a guide, this great journey for such a reason is quite credible.

Robert and Eliza Lawson set out on the 320-kilometre journey in bullock wagons; travelling to Lake Alexandrina, then across the Murray to Meningie, and then through the Coorong. At this time the lake districts and the Coorong were hunting grounds for the Aborigines, who naturally resented the intrusion of the white man into their domains, and the Lawsons' camp sites were frequently disturbed by angry natives. On arrival at Padthaway, however, the couple were quick to establish a working relationship with the tribe living there. The name 'Padthaway' is a corruption of an Aboriginal word meaning literally 'good water', and the name of the tribe was the Potaruwutj. Eliza Lawson found the native women willing and helpful. They especially liked washdays, as the bubbling of the soap suds fascinated them. Some enjoyed inside work and came to rely on Eliza for protection. One lubra, terrified of thunder, would come running to the house from wherever she might be, to crouch under the nearest table, apron pulled tightly over her head, until the storm had passed.

The building of a house must have been a matter of prime importance for Lawson, and the simple Georgian cottage which became their home for thirty years is still standing and in good repair. It is built of local free-stone, the external walls being over two feet thick, while the interior walls are wattle and daub. The six rooms comprised a 'parlour' and bedrooms. The kitchen and dining-room were separate buildings erected close to the house. The roofs of the buildings were all originally of wooden shingles,

The texture of the stone in the walls of this old kitchen can only be achieved after many years of weathering. The flat iron and rolls of the roof covering is very early, but beneath it lies an even older roof of wooden shakes.

The plan of this house is arranged about a hallway along its main axis—simple archways open into the stairhall at its centre.

and in several places these are still visible beneath the iron which was later nailed on top. The cottage, store rooms, stable, woolshed and shearers' quarters share a basic simplicity, but the stone of which they are built has weathered to a soft, pinkish hue which offsets the severity of design.

The clearing of the land which Lawson had acquired was a tremendous task, and when he added 'Campion's Run' to the original 'Moschito Plains' lease, the total area amounted to 131 square miles (340 square kilometres). At the present time 5,000 acres (2,000 hectares) remain of the original holding. By 1860 a great deal of the country had been cleared, and on it he ran 27,000 sheep and 250 head of cattle. He was also breeding horses for the Indian trade with considerable success. He had a good eye

for sheep and the wool sold well. It had to be carted overland by bullocks to Guichen Bay—a trying journey through swamps, sandhills and thick scrub—and thence to Geelong.

Of Robert Lawson himself little is known other than that he lived quietly taking no part in public affairs. When one considers how isolated Padthaway was at the time this is not surprising. Lawson's one outside interest was the Presbyterian Church, and he was a member of its first committee in Naracoorte. He was particularly interested in birds, and took pride in stuffing and mounting one of each variety he saw on his land. He died suddenly in Adelaide at the Glen Osmond home of Mr James Brown, survived by his wife, two sons and four daughters.

After Lawson's death the family was compelled to engage in lengthy litigation because of the dishonesty of one of the trustees of his will, a former friend, and a man well known and respected in Naracoorte and Bordertown. He is alleged to have misappropriated a considerable sum of money from the estate, and the outcome of the case was that judgement was given in favour of the Lawsons. It was reported in the press of the day, and the Adelaide *Lantern* published a cartoon depicting a camp oven and some of the identities in the case, the title being: 'As nasty a stew as ever was cooked in a colonial oven.'

Robert Lawson did not live to see the present homestead. It was completed in 1882 under instructions from the trustees of his estate. As were the earlier buildings, the homestead was built of freestone quarried on the property, with the result that all the buildings blend well together. In contrast with the first house, the homestead displays the Victorian love of ornamentation, but fortunately in this case it was never carried to excess. The cast-iron detailing of the balconies is delicate, and the verandah posts slender and elegant. The entrance hall is well proportioned and spacious, with a particularly beautiful staircase rising from it. The newell posts and balusters are finely but simply carved. This staircase is thought to have been made in England and reconstructed at Padthaway. A full-length window on the halfway landing affords a restful view over the wisteria, prunus and acacias close to the house, and then across the orchard to the stately bluegums in the paddocks beyond.

As Eliza Lawson was of a sombre outlook, no hint of frivolity or lightness crept into the household furnishings in her lifetime. As was often the way in those days the accent was upon dark colours, and upon preventing the sunlight from entering the house.

The gardens in the front of the house consisted of small, symmetrically-arranged flower beds, all edged with box hedges, while on the northern side there were orchards and vegetable gardens. Eliza Lawson's elder son, Robert, was particularly fond of gardening, and his diaries of the 1880s contain almost daily references to his activities in this sphere. An entry for 10 March 1887 begins thus: 'In the forenoon pruned some of the shrubs in the new garden and tied up the chrysanthemums', and on the 14 May, 'Weather showery. Heavy fall of rain early this morning. Grafted 5 Royal Georges and 4 Red Peach up at the orange bed today, 2 at the old peach tree at the front of the house and 1 at the tree opposite the dining room. All scions of Royal George peach.'

The Victorian formality of the design of the house is softened by the rambling garden, more than a hectare in area, which surrounds it. OPPOSITE

This staircase has painted balusters and polished handrails.

The marble mantelpiece of this drawing-room was a standard requirement in South Australia's large houses of the period.

Young Robert Lawson took over the management of Padthaway from his uncle John Bell, who had run the property for his sister for some years after her husband's death. Her younger son, Allan (who married Lucy, a daughter of Senior Inspector B. P. Hunt), went to live first at Riversdale near Wellington, and later to Lake Roy which was adjoining Padthaway. They had three children: Bessie, Keith and Ernest. Robert Lawson never married, and continued to remain at Padthaway with his mother and sisters until his early death at the age of forty-eight. Jessie was the only one of her daughters to marry. On 6 July 1887 she became Mrs William Smith and went to live with her husband at Hynam, near Naracoorte. There is an account of the event in Robert Lawson's diary: 'Weather fine. About 10 o'clock Mr W. Smith and Jessie were married. We then adjourned to the breakfast room when after partaking of refreshments the Bride and Bridegroom left for Hynam amidst the congratulations of their friends.'

Eliza Lawson lived until 1913, when she died at the age of ninety-one. Her unmarried daughters went to Naracoorte for their remaining years. The property was then managed by William Hutchison until Allan Lawson's elder son, Keith, had completed his education. He came to Padthaway in 1919, where he lived until 1936, and then again from 1949 until his death in 1975. He set out with quiet determination to maintain the already high quality of the sheep; to improve the pastures; to repair the fences which had fallen into disrepair after his grandfather's death; and to deal with the rabbit problem, which by this time had reached almost nightmarish proportions. Like his father and uncle, he was an excellent all round sportsman: a good cricketer, a champion shot, a skilled horseman, and a successful owner and breeder of racehorses. He took a keen interest in local affairs, and was also one of the earliest civil aeroplane pilots in South Australia.

England has provided much of the mahogany and cedar furniture used in this style of country dining-room, helping to create a warm and inviting atmosphere.

The 1903 shearers' quarters are in keeping with the other station buildings and constructed of similar stone.

This stable building dates from the earliest times of the settlement at Padthaway. Its sturdy timbers are straight from the forest, untouched by saw or adze.

In 1948 extensive renovations to the homestead were begun, and it is to Mrs Keith Lawson and her husband that credit must be given for the charm of the house and gardens as they now stand. The major structural work undertaken at the time included the addition of a sunroom, whose windows overlook the orchard, and the addition of a new kitchen complex to replace the original one, which was not attached to the house, and was therefore extraordinarily inconvenient. Repainting of both the exterior and interior of the house revealed its full beauty.

At the time when the house was restored, the character of the garden was changed radically; restful sweeping lawns and an informal park replacing the small beds. The trees planted at this time are now attaining maturity, while many of the trees planted in the early days of the garden still remain. Amongst them are large almond, walnut, pear and loquat trees. A magnificent Kurrajong tree, which formed an arch over the entrance to the main garden, fell down without warning two days after Mr Keith Lawson died in 1975.

Nestling under the rambling roses which cover their roofs, are several stone buildings, originally store rooms, one of which houses many items of interest collected over the years by Mrs Keith Lawson. This little museum contains a wide range of cooking and domestic equipment, including long-handled pots and pans, a dozen different types of smoothing irons, apple corers and peelers, mangles, mincers and many different types of bottles. There are several Aboriginal weapons, implements, and baskets, all of which were made on the property, and a variety of early firearms, including the long-barrelled pistol which Eliza Lawson kept for her own protection. Agricultural tools have not been forgotten. The collection includes wooden rakes and spades, adzes, scythes, sickles, broad axes and roofing tools. The family are always looking for relevant items to add to this collection. Some years ago Mrs Lawson acquired one of a pair of cannon which came from the ship *The Buffalo*. This ship arrived in 1836 bringing Captain John Hindmarsh who was the first Governor of South Australia.

At the present time Padthaway is managed by Mr Richard Lawson, a great-grandson of the founder, who lives in the homestead with his mother, wife and children. Although the family has been able to retain only a small portion of the original acreage, it is nevertheless pleasing that they have been able to share in the developments which have recently taken place in this extremely fertile area. Thousands of hectares of a variety of crops cover land which was originally thickly-wooded scrub country. Vines, vegetables, cereal crops and oil seeds are all thriving, while the country still provides excellent grazing land for sheep and cattle. The present occupants hope that their descendants will derive as much enjoyment from living at Padthaway as previous generations have done, and that they will continue to regard the upkeep of the homestead and the surrounding buildings as a responsibility to be proudly accepted for posterity.

St Aubins *New South Wales*

Text: Michel Reymond Photographs: Douglass Baglin

ST AUBINS, THE HOME OF Sir Alister and Lady McMullin, is situated on a sloping eminence about one mile on the south-western side of the town of Scone in the Hunter Valley of New South Wales, and from its position commands the southern approaches to the town.

The house itself stands on part of the land originally granted to William Dumaresq, who arrived in Sydney in 1825 and became for a short time, under Governor Darling's patronage, Civil Engineer and Inspector of Roads and Bridges. After his retirement in 1829 from these positions and his marriage in 1830 to Christiana Susan, second daughter of the former Colonial Secretary, Alexander Macleay of Elizabeth Bay House, Dumaresq devoted his time to acquiring and developing his estates near Scone, which within a few years totalled over 13,000 acres (5,200 hectares). He named these estates St Aubins after the house of his forebears in Jersey, and in about 1832 he erected the old St Aubins homestead, which originally stood about one mile south of the present house. It was a wooden structure built in the colonial style containing smallish rooms with a flagged verandah and porch and had extensive outbuildings, a feature of which was the carved Dumaresq crest on the mangers and saddle-brackets. Dumaresq's property, which became a showpiece, was described by J. D. Lang as 'one of the best-regulated estates in the colony . . .', and with his brother Henry's neighbouring estate St Heliers embraced over 26,000 acres (10,500 hectares) of rich grazing country on which sheep, cattle and some horses were bred and grazed extensively.

However, William Dumaresq did not remain at St Aubins for very long. After 1840 he lived mainly at Tivoli, Rose Bay, returning only occasionally to St Aubins; then, following his wife's death, he moved to Queensland where he lived at Cleveland, near Brisbane, with his daughter Susan Frances Sophia, the wife of the Honourable Louis Hope, a brother of the fifth Earl of Hopetoun. There he died on 9 November 1868. For a time his son William Alexander Dumaresq lived at St Aubins and exercised a general superintendence over the management of the estates. However, he soon left the care of the estates in the hands of a manager, and not long afterwards died, in May 1880. His executors then began negotiations to sell the St Aubins estates. After numerous delays and offers they subsequently received an offer from William, John and Tom Bakewell to buy the estates for £34,500, which they accepted, the sale to the Bakewell brothers being completed in July 1885.

John, Tom and William Bakewell were three of four brothers, the sons of Christopher and Ann Bakewell (née Gretton) and were all born in Nottingham, England. Their father was a builder and they, like him, were to

The earliest known photograph of the house, taken in about 1900. It shows the original colour scheme with the principal features high-lighted in dark colours, the original cast-iron verandah between the side wings, and the Bakewell garden pots. The Elizabethan gables above the bay windows, or what the Victorians may have called Scottish, are a feature of the house, as are the Minton pictorial tiles set below each of the bay windows. The original east verandah, which collapsed when the house was acquired in 1936, was rebuilt under the supervision of the Architect, D. Forsyth Evans, in about 1940. The walls are enriched by run plaster mouldings, and above each of the bay windows can be seen both the name and the date of the house. Around the house is a path of Bakewell terra cotta tiles set in a diamond pattern. TOP The only known surviving photograph of William Bakewell, taken at 'The Manor', his Sydney home, shortly before his death.

Through the moon-gate is a view of the rose garden and part of the southern side wing of the house, beyond which is the courtyard. The entire garden was re-constructed in 1940 to a design by, and under the supervision of, Jocelyn Brown.

The Minton pictorial tiles in brown and white are set below each of the bay windows at the front of the house and show the Victorian love of idyllic scenery and romanticism.

OPPOSITE: *Situated in the middle of the courtyard at the rear of the main house and framed within the delicately designed courtyard gates is the Italian style terracotta fountain made at the Bakewell Potteries. Of exceptional quality and graceful design the fountain illustrates the superb design and workmanship produced at these potteries. Beyond the fountain is the rear verandah of the main house which still retains its original cast-iron columns. In the foreground may be seen two very fine Bakewell terra-cotta urns at the top of the two courtyard gate supports.*

become builders. In their youth the three brothers came first to New Zealand and then to Sydney, between about 1867 and 1872, where they lived at first in Redfern. Little is known of their early activities except that they were bricklayers, contractors and builders of numerous terrace houses and shops in the area between Paddington and Newtown. They established a brick factory and later a pottery factory at Macdonaldtown, which was to be greatly enlarged during the 1890s. By July 1885, they had accumulated sufficient assets and capital to enable them to purchase the St Aubins estates.

At first the Bakewell brothers, when they stayed at St Aubins, lived in the old homestead, but following a heavy flood in about 1887 William Bakewell decided to erect a new house on higher ground about a mile to the north. The house he built is the present one. Although the precise date of its construction is not known it is thought William Bakewell commenced building it some time after his brother John's death in September 1887, finishing the main part of the house in the following year, with the side wings and outbuildings being completed over the next two or three years.

When his brother John died St Aubins comprised more than 14,000 acres (5,600 hectares) with 14,000 sheep, 480 cattle and 160 horses, and was improved considerably by William Bakewell in the next decade. Having inherited half of his brother John's real estate William purchased the remaining half and also purchased his brother Tom's interests. By December 1890, he controlled the St Aubins estates as well as both the brick and pottery works. No long afterwards, in September 1892, his brother Tom died. It was during the 1890s and the following decades that the brick and pottery works of 'Messrs Bakewell Bros of Macdonald Town', as they were so often described, reached their zenith.

In July 1893 the firm received congratulations from the editor of the *Building & Engineering Journal* for 'their perseverance and ultimate success of their indomitable efforts to turn out first class Terra Cotta of local manufacture'. Harder, stronger, and with a better sheen and purity of colour the terra cotta products of the firm were much sought after. The

Above is the extremely fine and detailed Italian style fountain, which was made by Bakewell Bros, and which is situated in the centre of the courtyard at the rear of the house between the two side wings. Below is a decorative cast-iron motif in the shape of a foot scraper with a galah in the centre of the ring, possibly made by, or to a design of, William Bakewell. At the right is a close up of the detail from one of the Bakewell urns in the garden, showing the neo-classical mask in the style of Pan.

process by which the firm produced terra cotta was described in the *Journal* at length: 'The clay, after being dug from the beds, is broken and weathered, and afterwards mixed with various substances necessary to give it a good texture. This is a matter which requires extreme judgment and care, and is indeed the trade secret of the art . . . Before it is in a fit condition to be placed in the moulds, it is kneaded on benches by men in the same manner as bakers knead their dough . . . The clay is now soft and tempered to a great degree of plasticity, ready to be moulded into any required design. Of course it is in the designing of these moulds that much of the artistic taste and power of adaptability comes into play. The pattern suitable for the purpose in view, having been selected, the mould is fashioned from Plaster of Paris, brought to the required degree of moisture, and afterwards baked. Just as in the casting of metals, the product will, of course, be the exact counterpart of the mould, raised in parts where it is sunken and sunken where the mould is in relief. In the case of cylindrical ornaments, such as vases or small pillars, a double mould has to be made, with right and left hand portions corresponding with great exactness . . . When withdrawn from the mould the still plastic terra cotta is submitted to the finisher, who, with his delicate instruments, removes from it all blurs and imperfections. It is then placed to dry in a room especially fitted up for the purpose. The next operation is that of burning, and to secure that rich, elegant buff, which is so sought after by architects, and so happily attained by Messrs. Bakewell Bros., long burning is required, as well as a highly experimental knowledge of firing, and a thorough acquaintance with the effect produced upon the particular clay in use under the influence of the different degrees of heat.'

They also produced 'perhaps the best double pressed dark red brick to be found in Sydney, which harmonises splendidly with terra cotta . . .'

William Bakewell retained the bulk of the St Aubins estates until he died in 1917. He was described then as 'a man of untiring industry and great business capacity, free in his gifts to the town [Scone] . . . the more meritorious because they were made unostentatiously . . .' He gave the land there for the old Good Templars Hall as well as portion of the land for the old hospital, the land for the Presbyterian Church and the land for the Catholic Cemetery. He permitted the Polo Club and many other clubs the free use of the area then known as the 'town paddock' adjacent to St Aubins for sporting and recreation purposes until it was later sold, and then promptly set aside another area for the use of those organizations.

St Aubins was designed by William Bakewell and it is typically eclectic Victorian, its main features being inspired by Elizabethan models. The building is very extensive, being built of brick and rendered in imitation of ashlar. It contains the main house, which is rectangular in shape and off which extend two wings at the rear to form a courtyard, the longer and southernmost wing being itself L-shaped. At the front of the house is a tiled verandah ten feet wide paved in black and white marble tiles leading to a spacious hall. Off the hall there are a sitting-room, two bedrooms and two anterooms. The sitting-room leads to a large reception room which has folding doors leading into the dining-room, off which was originally the breakfast room and pantry and which is now the kitchen servery.

In the main house all the rooms have fourteen-foot high ceilings, with tiled fireplaces and marble mantelpieces. The chimney pieces are marble, two being exceptionally fine in the Louis XV style which reflect the Victorian taste for the French eighteenth-century manner. Most of the interior woodwork is cedar and there are four-panelled doors and splendid plaster centrepieces and cornices. The interior four-panelled doors show the Victorian love of different materials, having panels of oak and styles and rails of cedar. The skirtings which are moulded plaster reflect the technical achievement of the Victorian age.

Following William Bakewell's death the St Aubins estates were sub-divided and sold in 1922, the homestead then being reduced to an area of 327 acres (130 hectares). In 1936 a family company controlled by Mr W. J. Smith, a relation of one of the present owners, acquired the homestead and about 3,000 acres (1,200 hectares) of the original estates. The house was then in a dilapidated state and a careful restoration programme was undertaken to restore it as near as possible to its original state. The front verandah had collapsed and the garden was very neglected.

In 1940 the present beautiful gardens were designed by Jocelyn Brown, who relocated the numerous original fine Victorian pottery ornaments manufactured at the Bakewell Potteries. Many of these are impressed 'Bakewell' or 'Bakewell Bros'.

In 1958 Mr W. J. Smith's family company transferred the house and over 1,000 acres (400 hectares) to the present owners. During his lifetime Mr W. J. Smith made St Aubins the centre of a highly successful horse stud which had its Sydney stables at 'Newmarket', Randwick.

The house, which has long been the centre of an important sheep, cattle and horse breeding area, is today still the centre of an important horse stud, dairy and cattle-breeding property. The grounds of the house today are immaculately maintained by the present owners and are in excellent state of preservation.

A view of the walled rose garden and the moon-gate, which was re-constructed of old bricks found in the Scone area, and which was built to a design by, and under the supervision of, Joycelyn Brown, in 1940. In the centre of the garden is a sun-dial made at the Bakewell Potteries, while in the far corner is a bust of Captain Cook, also made at the Bakewell Potteries. These Bakewell pottery pieces illustrate the excellence and quality of the work produced at their potteries which equalled, if not excelled, the work produced by any other contemporary Australian pottery.

The courtyard, which is at the rear of the house, was originally a garden court to the main house and had many Bakewell urns in it. Today it is typically more relaxed and Australian in feeling.

A view of the rear of the house from beneath the valances of the original carriage canopy, within which is framed the back of the house, with its balancing gables which carry on the Elizabethan style of design, but in a plainer manner, to the front of the house.

Wylarah *Queensland*

Text: Bessie Wilshire   Photographs: Richard Stringer

The south side or back entrance to the house, showing the entry, above which are the gable ends of the great hall. On the extreme right is the meathouse and next to it the windmill, which pumps water from the underground tank to the rain water tank topping the two ripple iron bath rooms. This water is reticulated to the house.

The interior of the great hall from the entry or southern end: this shows the roof treatment, the table of Tasmanian blackwood, the 'Henty' book case on the left, and the 'Salisbury' book case at the far end.
On the right is the cedar 'slab' where the children ate their bread and milk, and the harmonium. The wire bell-pull connected with the bell on the roof, is at the top end of the hall.

THE GREENUP FAMILY and their descendants have occupied Wylarah continuously since it was selected in 1890 by Alfred S. Greenup, Manager of Maryland, near Stanthorpe. The present owners are John O'Shanesy and his three sisters; children of Frances, second daughter of Harold Greenup, and great-grandchildren of Alfred Greenup.

The family came originally from the Lake District of England, in the vicinity of Keswick. They lived for many generations at a place called Condbeck near Carlisle, 'respectable but not wealthy'. They were known as 'Cumberland Statesmen', farmers owning their own farms or estates. The Greenup property was called 'Darcey Hey'. Alfred Greenup visited this property when on a trip to England in 1874.

About the time of Charles I, an ancestor, Antony Greenup, went to London, where he became a lawyer and a 'gentleman' (lawyers were proclaimed 'gentlemen' about that time by act of Parliament!). Antony was probably a Roundhead during the Civil War, as he had a friend, Job Hartopp, who was a Captain in Cromwell's Ironsides. Job gave Antony his New Testament, in Latin and dated 1699; this is still in the family.

In 1800, William Greenup of Halifax, Yorkshire, son of another William, was granted a Coat of Arms (shown to the writer at Maryland by her cousin Victor Greenup, who now owns that property). William's son George, who died in 1832, was the father of Dr Richard Greenup. As Medical Superintendent of the immigrant ship *John Knox*, Dr Greenup sailed for Australia with his wife and large family, arriving in Sydney on 29 April 1850. Their first home was in Fort Street, Sydney.

Richard Greenup thought he would like to become a pastoralist, and inspected properties in the Riverina District of New South Wales, but did not buy. He also visited his cousins, Matthew-Henry and Charles Marsh, in New England, but eventually decided against life on the land. He practised medicine in Parramatta and was Superintendent of the Lunatic Asylum there from 1852. He owned a farm of 600 acres where he grew citrus fruits, and a home, 'Darcey Hey', at Castle Hill, now a boys' home run by the Government. His two sons, Alfred and Edgar, attended the new Kings School as day boys.

A southern view of the house from beside the old dray shed, harness room and blacksmith shop.

A Master of Arts (Cambridge) as well as a Doctor of Medicine, he was intensely interested in Sydney University, then in its infancy. He became the first Registrar and Secretary, a lecturer and examiner, and retained his interest in the University until his death in 1866.

In 1857 Alfred Greenup left school at the age of fifteen and engaged in pastoral pursuits, at first on the Marsh's property, Salisbury Court, at Uralla; then as manager of Maryland from 1868 until 1905, the Marsh Brothers having taken up this property in 1844.

In 1876 he married his cousin Marion Marsh. Their children were: Richard (1877–1953), Edith (1879–1953), Mary (1880–1915), Alfred (1881–1882), Margaret (1883–1962), Harold (1884–1957), Jane (1886–1957), Victor (1887–1918), and Bessie (1890–1891).

Early in 1890, Alfred Greenup selected a grazing lease of 9,000 acres (3,600 hectares) and an agricultural farm of 1,267 (506 hectares), part of the first resumption of Burrandowan Station, owned at that time by the Borton family. He named the place Wylarah, the New England Aborigine's name for black cockatoo. The agricultural block was separated from the leasehold land by another property, and so was several miles away.

In the mid-winter of 1890, Alfred and his eldest son Richard came by train from Stanthorpe to Dalby and rode the fifty miles to Wylarah. His man had built a hut in the gully where the house dam is situated. During this trip the Greenups called on Mr Youngman, recently established at Taabinga Station, Kingaroy.

1891 saw Alfred and Richard again visiting Wylarah, and a slab hut was built on the ridge near where the present homestead now stands. This hut later formed the kitchen portion of the cottage Coolah, which Harold Greenup built when he married Ruby Bassingthwaighte in 1912.

Wylarah was built by a Victorian named Gibbs. Begun in 1891, it took him over a year to complete, being eighty feet square. He built it single-handed, except for assistance from Alfred with some of the framework and the pit-sawing of the verandah floor boards. The bricks for one wall of the kitchen, the four double fireplaces, the set-in copper and Colonial oven, four-foot square sink and long brick drain, were fired on the spot from clay obtained from a gully near by. The timber, iron bark, beech and cyprus pine, was milled at Chinchilla.

The original plan for Wylarah was for the rooms to be built round a U-shaped courtyard with a narrow gallery round the inside and a twelve-foot verandah round the outside of the rooms, except for the south side: the open end of the U. When the building was partly completed it was realized the courtyard would be rather small, so it was floored (as were the rooms) with beech, and roofed with twin gables, lined instead of ceiled, for greater effect. This centre hall measures fifty feet by thirty-five feet. Bats live above the ceilings of the surrounding rooms and zoom about at night.

The five main bedrooms and maid's room measure fifteen feet by fifteen feet. There are three smaller bedrooms, two store-rooms (one now a bathroom), a pantry (now a bedroom), and an office with one wall consisting of a glass-fronted, built-in bookcase. All the walls are single and panelled in iron bark and cyprus pine as illustrated in the photographs. They are the same on each side.

The eastern view of the house with the old meathouse on the extreme left of picture. From the left can be seen the kitchen bedroom, kitchen verandah, and verandah outside, two bedrooms and the dining-room on the north-east corner.

The view from the living-room through to the hall, which one enters from the entry or south side; showing the 'Henty' book case.

In the dining-room on the north-east corner of the house, the built-in sideboard runs almost the full length of one wall. It has a polished brigalow top. The glass-fronted book case is also built-in, and the mantelpiece is of polished swamp oak and brigalow.

There is a built-in bookcase in the hall known as the 'Henty' bookcase, as it contains all the works of this prolific writer. In the hall also, is the 'Salisbury' bookcase, a glass-fronted piece from Mrs Greenup's old home, 'Salisbury Court'. The long polished table in the centre of the hall, which seats twenty-six comfortably, is of Tasmanian blackwood, sent by a friend from Tasmania and built on the spot by Tom Fortescue of Dalby. He told the writer he wore out five sets of planes on the hard wood.

A table of the same wood graces the dining-room. A third of it was cut off to make a dining table for Harold when he was married. These are very solid tables, requiring four or six men to lift them. The original tables were of cedar.

The french windows which open on to the outside verandah from all rooms, have rounded glass in the top panes, and at the ends of the two gables in the hall on the south side are glass louvres. Gibbs built washstands and dressing tables for each bedroom and large built-in cupboards each side of the fireplace in these rooms.

Wylarah had some quite modern ideas for those days, as, except for the two ripple iron bathrooms downstairs and a little away from the main house, it was built on one level and under one roof, the kitchen being incorporated in the whole instead of, as was the custom, at the end of a long gangway. The bricked-in copper and water laid on for the tubs on the back verandah were also most convenient and unusual for those days. Rain water is stored in a large, underground cement tank roofed with planks. Water is pumped by a small windmill into an iron tank on top of the ripple iron bathrooms and reticulated to the house. Wylarah was first lit by gaslight, and the shed which housed the gas machine adjoined the bathrooms. Weights were wound up each day to the top of a tower alongside the shed.

There is a belfry (shown in the photograph of the northern aspect of the house), topped by a weathercock. This houses a large bell, originally the woolshed bell from Maryland, and anyone venturesome enough to climb up and look, may see through the wooden shutters, the word 'Maryland' on the bell.

The outside features include a high, enclosed tankstand, on top of which is the men's room, and on top of that again the water supply tank for the garden. Water was pumped from the dam, half-a-mile away and latterly, from a well. The bottom portion of this stand is used as a shed or double garage. A building nearby (illustrated) contained four stables, the saddle room, the barn, with a large weighing machine, the coach shed and what was known as 'the old workshop'. The 'new' workshop was later built on to the dray and harness shed and blacksmith shop. A hay shed, calf pen and milking shed join the stockyards.

The endless chain, hook and pulleys now used on a tripod, were suspended from a big box tree alongside the yards with two large wooden blocks for butchering beef killed there. The meat would hang up all night

306

The living-room, which has a fireplace each end. Originally, it comprised the drawing-room and a bedroom, but was converted into a single, long bedroom in Harold Greenup's time, and used by him and his wife as their bedroom. A good example of the panelling may be seen here.

and before sunrise would be cut up and carted to the meathouse in a wheelbarrow, salted and placed in a wooden cask. A certain amount of fresh meat would be hung in the large meat safe which stood on top of the brick Colonial oven.

Alfred Greenup loved trees and planted many varieties at Wylarah. Besides the universal pepper tree, he introduced jacarandas, Portuguese cork wood, bamboo, Chinese elm, Bunya and Stone pine, the Indian deodah, peccan and Queensland nut, chestnut and oleander, olive and carob bean, as well as almost every variety of citrus, stone fruit, mulberry, loquat, persimmon, grapes and bananas.

He fenced a small plot as a family graveyard and planted it with trees and shrubs. He stored timber in the coach shed for his 'box', as he called it. When Alfred died, it was discovered that the ground in the plot was too

The hall, as seen from the east door to the living-room, showing the doorway to one of the perimeter bedrooms. All the doors off the central hall are glazed, which helps to give the building a transparent feeling. The only other light to the hall is from the southern skylight.

stony and he was buried further down the hill by the old orchard. His grand-daughter, Frances, and her husband are buried beside him.

In 1891 the whole Greenup family (Alfred, Marion and their seven surviving children) spent the Christmas holidays at Wylarah. They came by coach from Maryland, some riding, and spent a night with the Bells at Jimbour House on the way.

It was November 1897 before the family came to live at Wylarah permanently, and 1905 when Alfred (who continued to manage Maryland until it was sold), made it his home. Richard attended the Toowoomba Grammar School and Harold and Victor, the Armidale School. In 1902 Harold was brought home from school to help skin dead cattle in the devastating drought of that year. Harold and Victor worked on Wylarah almost continuously. Victor was killed at the end of the First World War in 1918. Alfred and his daughter Mary died in 1915, and in 1920, his wife and unmarried daughters, Meg and Jane, went to live in Toowoomba, where Marion died the following year.

308

Harold took over the old home at Wylarah (where he remained until his death in 1957), at first managing the property for his sisters, whose interest he bought in 1924. The lease was cut in half during that year and Harold took the more rugged portion, Benroy, as it was called.

Wylarah was situated in the Gayndah parish, and visited quarterly by the Bush Brothers. They rode the hundred miles from Gayndah, leading a pack horse. Later they came in a buggy and then by car. All denominations came to these services, which were held in the morning with lunch provided by the Greenup family, and cricket and tennis was played in the afternoon.

About 1927, Wylarah became part of the Kingaroy parish, services still being held there for many years. Private dances, public balls (to raise money for the Kingaroy Hospital, run by subscription in those days) and family weddings were held in the hall. The writer, her younger sister, Katharine and their aunts, Edith and Jane, were all married there.

In the Church of England in Kumbia hang two large prints of pictures by Doré, presented in memory of Harold Greenup by his family; two more remain in the hall at Wylarah. These pictures were bought by Alfred Greenup during a trip to England in 1874.

Occupied first by Alfred and Marion Greenup, succeeded by their son Harold and his wife and family, the house was then left to his second daughter Frances, who died in 1964. Her son, John O'Shanesy and his three sisters now own Wylarah. John and his wife Joan are doing their best to maintain and restore, where necessary, the old house, which is in a reasonably good state of repair.

Their young son Andrew is the fifth generation of the family to live at Wylarah.

This outbuilding housed four stables, saddle room, barn, workshop and a coach and buggy shed. These buildings were in good repair until badly damaged by a severe wind storm about 1965.

Bimbah *Queensland*

Text: Peter Forrest   *Photographs: Richard Stringer*

The east (entry) elevation of Bimbah is cloaked by the foliage of drought-resistant pepperina trees. This main wing was built in 1898, while the nursery wing on the right was added in 1904.

BIMBAH HOMESTEAD is situated on the banks of the Thomson River about twenty-two kilometres to the north-east of the town of Longreach in Queensland's Central West. The history of the homestead and of its occupiers, the Edkins family, is intertwined with the larger history of Western Queensland's exploration, settlement and development. Rowland Rule Edkins, the present occupier and part owner of Bimbah, is the grandson of Edward Rowland Edkins, one of the first pioneers of the great pastoral areas of central and north Queensland. One of the vast holdings developed by Mr E. R. Edkins was Mount Cornish, which in 1872 was severed from its parent station Bowen Downs. It was from Mount Cornish that Bimbah was resumed in 1889 and taken up by Edward Rowland Huey Edkins, son of E. R. Edkins and father of R. R. Edkins. Each of these three generations of men made outstanding contributions to the pastoral industry and community life of Queensland. The homestead at Bimbah is a reflection of the history and character of this notable family and the buildings are dramatic proof of the truism that historic structures are the best evidence we have of the influences which have shaped our civilisation.

E. R. Edkins was born in 1840 at Bridgnorth, Shropshire, England. He came to Victoria in 1852 with his newly widowed mother and other family members. Apparently the young man adapted quickly and well to colonial life, for it is recorded that he began droving in the late 1850s and in 1862 was the first to take cattle across the Burdekin River in north Queensland. On his return to Victoria from that trip Edkins learned how to inoculate cattle against pleuropneumonia. In 1864 he was engaged to employ this skill on cattle runs near Rockhampton and he spent the next two years mixing this work with the overlanding of cattle to newly formed stations on the Flinders and Saxby Rivers in north-west Queensland. Much of this work was undertaken for a syndicate comprising Messrs Glen Walker, Robert Morehead and Matthew Young, and this association was to have a decisive impact upon Edkins' later life.

Walker, Morehead and Young were at this time involved in the settlement and development of 'Bowen Downs' — an enormous pastoral holding which straddled the Thomson River and its tributaries and which stretched for 240 kilometres from above the present towns of Aramac and

On the west side wooden lattice blinds shield the verandah, which in turn protects the main rooms. The blinds are adjustable for ventilation and light. The verandah balustrading features 'Union Jack' bracing with a central boss, while pre-cut timber mouldings are used to form a capital on the chamfered verandah columns.

In arid inland areas care and water is lavished upon feature garden plants rather than on extensive planting, and garden maintenance is minimised by the spreading of gravel. The verandah roof is a 'lean-to' off the central building core while the main roof is capped by decorated ventilators.

Muttaburra to a point about 48 kilometres below the present town of Longreach. This country had been discovered by William Landsborough and Nathanial Buchanan in 1860, and on his return from this exploration Landsborough applied to take up the land in his own name. Although a superb bushman Landsborough had recently failed in establishing runs on the Kolan River west of Bundaberg, and consequently he was bereft of the capital needed to stock his new lands within one year of the application for lease as was then required by Queensland law. Landsborough therefore sought partners who could provide financial backing, and in June 1861 a Sydney solicitor, William Walker, agreed to buy a half share in the various runs. Landsborough then set off to look for Burke and Wills and in this search became the first man to cross Australia from north to south. During this absence William Walker had second thoughts about his investment in Landsborough's remote and risky venture and he approached Robert Morehead, the manager of the Scottish Australian Company, with a view to selling his interest in the Landsborough runs to that company. The Company had been established in Aberdeen in 1840 to provide an outlet in Australia for Scottish capital. Morehead came to Australia in 1841 as manager, and at first found no difficulty in placing money on loan to pastoralists, and to merchants who were seeking to expand to take advantage of rapidly developing opportunities. However, by the late 1850s the gold rushes had transformed the Australian economy and it became much

The verandahs around Bimbah are unusually wide and ideally adapted for sleeping out in summer.

more difficult for financiers to place money on loan. This change had caused Morehead to consider direct investment of company funds on its own account, preferably in the pastoral industry which was then booming and expanding into western Queensland. Morehead was therefore receptive to William Walker's proposal and he sought the opinion of an experienced adviser, Edward Cornish, on the quality of Landsborough's lands. Cornish reported: 'it is the finest and most splendid pastoral country I have ever seen'. Morehead then committed the Scottish Australian Company to the venture.

The 'Landsborough Runs Operation', as Morehead called it, was launched on the basis that the Company would take a half share in the enterprise in return for the provision of most of the capital, the engagement of required labour, and the furnishing of the numbers of stock required to obtain leases. Landsborough took a quarter interest, while Edward Cornish and Nathanial Buchanan took an eighth share each. Cornish was appointed General Superintendent and Buchanan the Resident Manager. It was decided to stock the runs with cattle in the first instance because they could be moved more quickly to the runs and would require less labour. By May 1862 Buchanan had marked the route from Port Denison (later Bowen) across the Great Dividing Range to the runs, and in October 1862 the first draft of 5,000 cattle arrived at Bowen Downs. Unfortunately it was found that the route from the station lay through a belt of country in which poisonous shrubs were prevalent, and the hazard of heavy stock losses on this route ruled out the possibility of exporting cattle by driving them across to Port Denison for slaughter or live shipment. This problem led the Bowen Downs syndicate to turn to the Gulf of Carpentaria as an outlet, and in developing this outlet a strong and long standing association with Edward Rowland Edkins was to commence.

William Landsborough had reported on the Gulf Country in glowing terms, describing it as the 'Plains of Promise'. Morehead and Cornish saw that their syndicate had more than a head start in any race for the Gulf lands, for others moving into the new country would have to pass through Bowen Downs. A strip of strategically-placed Gulf land between the Albert and Nicholson Rivers was applied for, and in February 1865 Buchanan raced to it with 1,500 cattle to forestall the challenge of a competing syndicate headed by Sir John Robertson, then Premier of New South Wales. The new country was called 'Beamesbrook' and was intended by Cornish to be a depot for Bowen Downs cattle before slaughter and boiling down for tallow at a works established by Cornish at the Gulf port of Burketown.

Edward Rowland Edkins with his brother Henry contracted to run the boiling-down works, and the brothers arrived in Burketown in April, 1866. Within a year they had initiated new techniques for curing beef and had established markets in Batavia, Singapore, Brisbane and Sydney. The industry and success of the Edkins brothers was the one redeeming feature

A verandah section was screened and lined to create the dining-room. Silky oak doors lead to a sitting-room.

of the Gulf Country operations for the Bowen Downs syndicate. In October and November 1866 first Cornish and then his wife succumbed to 'gulf fever', leaving eight children in the care of Robert Morehead. The 'promise' seen by Landsborough in the pastures of the Gulf was not fulfilled, while the depredations of hostile Aborigines, the lack of ready markets and paucity of shipping facilities all combined to make the operations indescribably difficult and unprofitable. Edward Rowland Edkins was appointed manager of Beamesbrook and other stations held by the syndicate, and under him prospects brightened temporarily.

In October 1867 Edward Rowland Edkins married Edwina Marion Huey, the daughter of a Launceston doctor. The first home of the couple was at Beamesbrook where the first two of their eight children were to die of gulf fever and where Mrs Edkins' brother, an army captain on leave from India, was to be fatally speared in 1871. Edward Edkins himself caught gulf fever in 1871. Although he survived, the narrow escape was one of the factors leading to the decision taken by Morehead to close down the Gulf of Carpentaria enterprises, and to transfer the cattle to the lower half of the Bowen Downs country, which was to be run as a separate entity known as 'Mount Cornish'. Certain other factors influential in that decision should also be described.

By 1871 it had been proved that the management of the lower part of the Landsborough runs from the Bowen Downs head station was an impossible task, and who better to undertake the management of Mount Cornish than Edkins, who had proved himself against adversity in the Gulf? The discovery of a route around the 'poison country' to the new seaport of Townsville meant that the Gulf outlets were no longer needed. The need for separate and closer management of the lower part of Bowen Downs was dramatically demonstrated by two events occurring in 1870: firstly, the loss of 2,000 cattle in severe floods, and then the loss of another 1,000 head in the most daring and famous cattle theft in Australia's history. The circumstances of this theft were to be embellished and passed into Australian folk lore through Rolf Boldrewood's novel *Robbery Under Arms*, and the basis for Boldrewood's story of 'Starlight' was in part the exploits of one Henry Redford.

Redford was a remittance man who, in 1869, squatted on country near present-day Windorah, and then gained employment as a teamster with William James Forrester. Forrester held country on the southern boundary of Bowen Downs and it seems that he and others took regular advantage of the absence of close management to gather small mobs of cattle for sale in Blackall, Tambo or Roma. Redford became familiar with the locality while working for Forrester and became known to Bowen Downs' employees as a remittance man of good background and a religious frame of mind. The theft of small mobs of cattle was not for Redford who, early in 1870, embarked upon a much grander design. On country later to become Bimbah, near the future site of Longreach, Redford commenced to muster Bowen Downs' cattle and, at the end of March 1870, Redford with two associates and about 1,000 cattle commenced the trek toward Adelaide across 1,200 kilometres of unoccupied country. Included in the mob was a distinctive white bull which had earlier been imported from

This standard door and fan light links a bedroom with the western verandah. Note the light-weight construction technique — a single wall lining of chamfer boards inside studs placed eighteen inches apart. The wall is painted ox-blood red and the verandah ceiling mid-green.

The built-in furniture in this bedroom is original. 'Built-ins' did not become common for two decades after the construction of Bimbah in 1898. Other early innovations at the homestead were reticulated water and electricity.

England by the Archers of Gracemere, near Rockhampton. By June 1870 Redford had reached the settled parts of South Australia where he exchanged the white bull and two cows for provisions. Shortly after, the balance of the mob was sold for £5,000 to the owner of Blanchewater Station. The thieves promptly left the colony of South Australia.

In May 1870 the Bowen Downs head stockman, William Butler, noticed the absence of the white bull from the Bowen Downs herds, and he also noticed Redford's tracks and improvised stock yards. Butler pursued the thieves to South Australia obtaining further evidence as he went, including the white bull, which was thought to be conclusive proof of the theft and Redford's guilt. Redford was apprehended in January 1872 but was acquitted by a jury at Roma in February 1873. There can be little doubt that the acquittal was a reflection of the admiration won by Redford for the skill and daring of his feat three years earlier.

This was the background to the arrival of Mr and Mrs E. R. Edkins at Bowen Downs in 1872. Their first abode was the 'Mud Hut' outstation about six kilometres from the present town of Muttaburra, but before long Mr Edkins had a new homestead built by two German stonemasons and this was to serve as the head station for the new 'Mount Cornish'. A photograph taken in 1880 shows a handsome house set in a formal garden and nearly a score of well-dressed ladies and gentlemen (some with tennis rackets) — a far cry from the first party of settlers to arrive on the western downs less than two decades before. This was the setting for the childhood of Edward Rowland Huey Edkins, who was born in January 1871 and who, after an education at the Church of England Grammar School, Launceston, and some experience in the pastoral industry as a jackeroo, was to take up Bimbah in 1889 when that country was resumed from Mount Cornish for closer settlement.

E. R. Edkins had, while managing Mount Cornish, acquired and developed extensive private pastoral interests, and his son's concern was to use Bimbah as a base and depot for similar expansion. In partnership with Francis Campbell extensive areas of first-class country were acquired, most of which continues to be held today by the firm Edkins Campbell under the management of Mr R. R. Edkins.

The first homestead building at Bimbah seems to have been built very soon after the station was acquired by Mr E. R. H. Edkins. The first structure was of two rooms built of flagstones bonded with sand and lime mortar, and served until the present timber homestead was built in 1898. Mr E. R. H. Edkins married Miss Lucy Elizabeth Rule in 1894, the new bride being a daughter of John Rule, one of the pioneers of Aramac Station in 1863. It is likely that the couple lived for a few years in the new town of Longreach while the new station was being fully developed. During this period E. R. H. Edkins was actively engaged in the life of the burgeoning Western community, being responsible for the foundation

Galvanized iron cladding is conspicuous on the jackeroos' quarters and staff bedrooms seen from the office verandah. Oxblood red paintwork with white trim is used throughout the complex and achieves pleasing unity.

The meat house is designed to achieve cool conditions and security from insects and predators.

of the Longreach Club and the Longreach Jockey Club which he served as President for forty years. When, in 1903, the Longreach Shire Council was carved out of the Aramac Divisional Board area Mr Edkins was the first Shire Chairman, continuing a tradition set by his father, who had headed the Aramac Divisional Board six times, and to be followed by his son R. R. Edkins, who was to serve as Longreach Shire Council Chairman for several terms. At Bimbah merino sheep and thoroughbred and draught horse studs were established to enable the stocking of their Edkins Campbell holdings with first class progenitors. Animals bred at Bimbah won distinction on showgrounds and race courses throughout Australia and the family 'All Brown' racing silks are still pre-eminent. The wool scouring firm Edkins Marsh and Company was established, and the softening effect of the local artesian water resulted in scoured wools which were strongly sought after on the specialist wool market in London.

Despite the wide range and intensity of these activities Mr and Mrs Edkins found time to develop at Bimbah a gracious and comfortable homestead which is an outstanding example of traditional North Australian architecture. The homestead is situated on the high Eastern bank of the Thomson River, dammed at this point by a stone pitched over-shot, which is in itself an outstanding example of combined workmanship and artistry. The waterhole created by the over-shot provides a water supply for domestic purposes and irrigates an extensive citrus and vegetable garden. To ensure that each room in the main house obtains the optimum benefit from every cooling breeze, the homestead complex is laid out in a linear formation. The house was originally one room wide, extending from north to south with a wide verandah on the east (front) and west (rear) elevations. The addition of a nursery wing at the north end in 1904 formed an 'L' shape but did not destroy the essentially low linear pattern. Outbuildings including men's quarters, meat house, office and the stables at the southern end of the house, round off the homestead complex and strikingly demonstrate that a western Queensland homestead is not merely comprised of a dwelling house, but is a group of buildings facilitating self-sufficiency in an isolated situation.

Despite the range of functions of the homestead buildings, they all share the common characteristic of light-weight timber frame construction with a separation from the ground achieved by low stumps. Cladding is of the ubiquitous galvanized iron or wooden chamfer boards while roofs are of iron. These materials are all light-weight, portable and durable, and thus ideally situated for use in a remote area. Although the relatively insubstantial building fabric of timber and iron absorbs heat quickly during the day, that heat is dissipated just as quickly at night, providing relatively comfortable sleeping conditions.

Mr E. R. H. Edkins died at Longreach in 1939 and was succeeded in the occupation of Bimbah by his son Rowland Rule Edkins who, with his late wife, moulded the homestead to reflect the personality of new occupiers, while maintaining the built evidence of family traditions which the homestead exemplifies. Today the whole homestead complex creates a feeling of cohesion and 'place' achieved by a unity of scale, materials and colour.

From the south the harmonious grouping of the kitchen, laundry and other buildings is seen.

ACKNOWLEDGEMENTS

The Australian Council of National Trusts, the authors, photographers and the publishers, Cassell Australia Limited, would like here to acknowledge the help afforded by many people in the compilation of this book; in particular the owners of the houses who not only gave permission for their houses to be included but gave so generously of their time and knowledge.

In addition, the authors extend their special thanks to the people and organizations named below. Where appropriate, these acknowledgements are followed by a list of the sources referred to by authors in compiling their texts:

VALLEYFIELD: Mr Frank Bolt; QUAMBY: *Examiner* newspaper files, Button *Flotsam and Jetsam*, Baker *The Life and Times of Sir Richard Dry*, Bell and Company Sales Catalogue 1887, *The Tasmanian Cyclopaedia*; GIDLEIGH: Rutledge family papers, quotations from the King papers by courtesy of the Mitchell Library, Griffiths *Some Southern Homes of New South Wales*; GLENROCK: Mr Charles Barbour, the Misses Morrice, Mr and Mrs Peter Muller; Royal Australian Historical Society *Journals*, Roxburgh *Early Colonial Houses of New South Wales*; EMU BOTTOM: Mr and Mrs H. J. Elliott, John and Phyllis Murphy; MARYLAND: Misses E. and A. Thomson; the Mitchell Library, University of Sydney Archives, *The Australian Dictionary of Biography*; DYRAABA: Michael Barnes and Mrs L. A. MacDonald for special assistance; Casino and District Historical Society, Richmond River Historical Society, Bruxner *The Shield Brand*; WOLLOGORANG: Miss Dinah Watson, Mr John Watson; the Mitchell Library, Roxburgh *Early Colonial Houses of New South Wales*; LOWLANDS: Mrs M. A. Richardson for extensive assistance in obtaining historic data and permission to photograph and measure buildings; MADOWLA PARK: Mr and Mrs S. W. Strutt; Madowla Pastoral Company; EYNESBURY: Mr and Mrs A. Ibbotson; Woodhouse Pastoral Company; BANYULE: National Gallery of Victoria for permission to include the property; Mr H. M. Barker, Mrs Irma Woolnough; University of Melbourne Archives; CORRYTON PARK: Mrs David M. Gordon; South Australian Archives; GULF STATION: Mr and Mrs D. Fellows, Dr C. Kellaway, David J. Wilkinson, Peter Watts; WONNERUP HOUSE: Miss K. C. Cammilleri, grand-daughter of George Layman, for historical data; PARA PARA: Mr Frank Cork; LONGERENONG: Mr and Mrs D. M. Gregory, Bruce Lockwood, Myra Orth; THE SPRINGS: Mr T. D. Tourle; family papers and property records; BELTANA: the Board of Directors of the Beltana Pastoral Company Ltd; officers of the Lands Department, for colored transparencies of Cordillo Downs; MT TALBOT: Mr and Mrs D. Officer, Dr Miles Lewis; *Australian Dictionary of Biography*; KOLOR: Mr and Mrs S. Gardiner; LARRA: Dr and Mrs A. G. McKinnon, Mrs Frank Thornthwaite (formerly of Larra); the La Trobe Library, State Library of Victoria; POLTALLOCH: Lady Jude, Mrs Mary Cowan, Mr and Mrs Jim Cowan, Mrs James Bullock; the Executor Trustee and Agency Company of South Australia; GRACEMERE: Mrs Alister Archer, Mr James Archer; 'Land Settlement in the Northern Districts of Port Curtis and Leichhardt' by Lorna L. McDonald (Master's Qualifying Thesis, University of Queensland, 1975); 'Fitzroy Waters—From Sheep to Cattle and Coal' by Archibald Archer (Address to Royal Historical Society of Queensland, 24 August 1972); ST AUBINS: Clive Lucas, for architectural details, K. R. Bernard-Smith, for special assistance, Patricia Hancock, Tom Bakewell, Nancy Grey and other members of the Bakewell family; family papers held by descendants of William Bakewell, the Mitchell Library, documents, deeds and letters—Registrar General's Department, New South Wales and Supreme Court of New South Wales Probate Registry.